IMAGES
of America

RAILROADING IN CONNEAUT OHIO

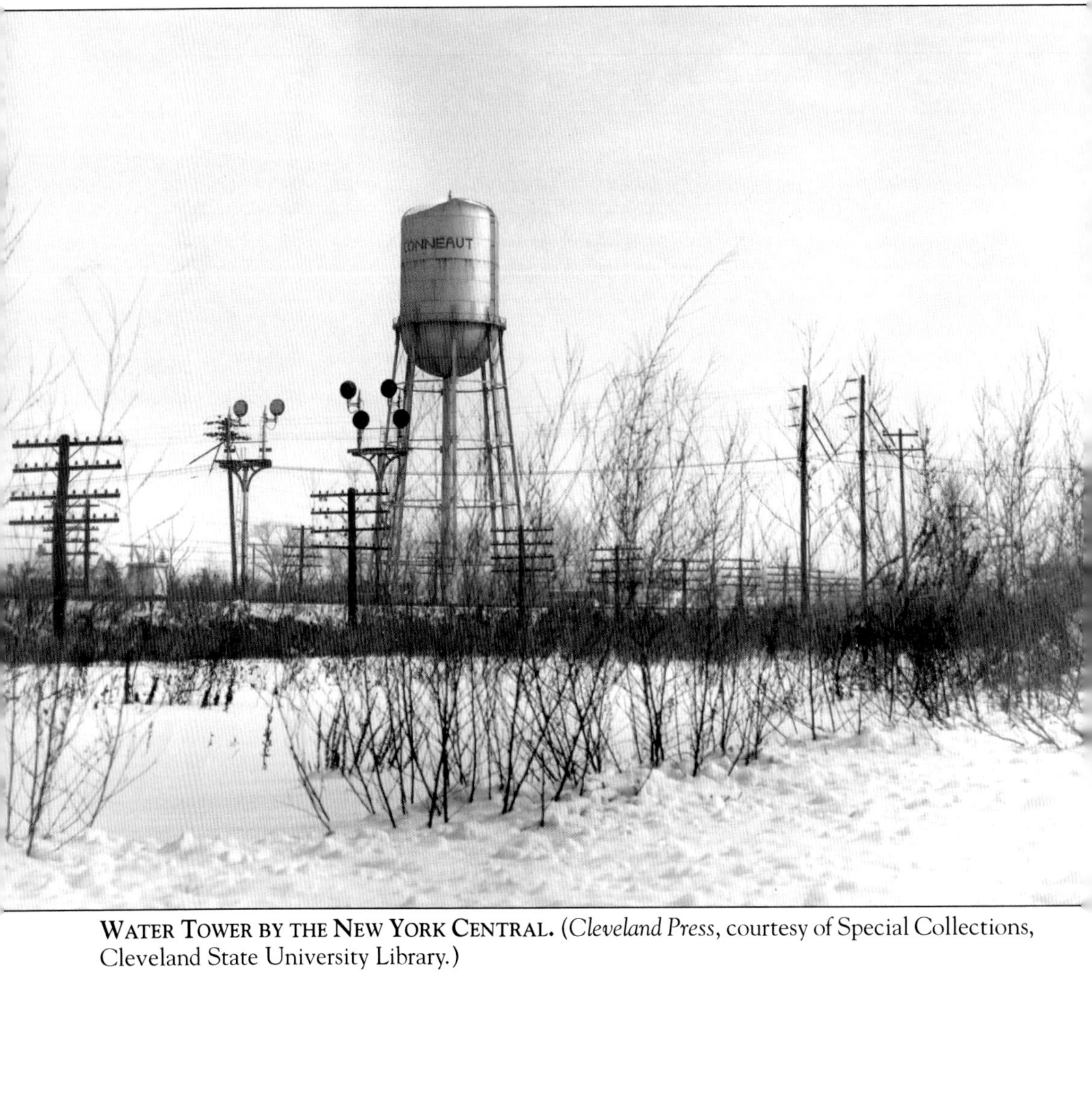

WATER TOWER BY THE NEW YORK CENTRAL. (*Cleveland Press*, courtesy of Special Collections, Cleveland State University Library.)

This book is dedicated to Robert Leach.

IMAGES
of America

RAILROADING IN CONNEAUT OHIO

David Borsvold

ARCADIA
PUBLISHING

ISBN 978-0-7385-2346-0

Published by Arcadia Publishing
Charleston, South Carolina

Printed in the United States of America

Library of Congress Catalog Card Number: 2003105937

For all general information contact Arcadia Publishing at:
Telephone 843-853-2070
Fax 843-853-0044
E-mail sales@arcadiapublishing.com
For customer service and orders:
Toll-Free 1-888-313-2665

Visit us on the Internet at www.arcadiapublishing.com

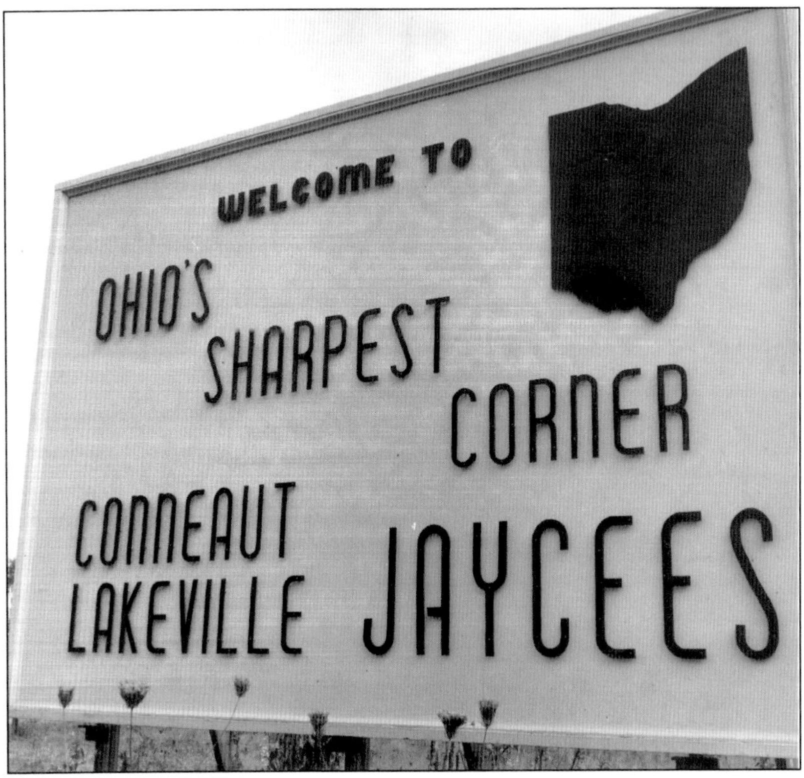

(*Cleveland Press*, courtesy of Special Collections, Cleveland State University Library.)

Contents

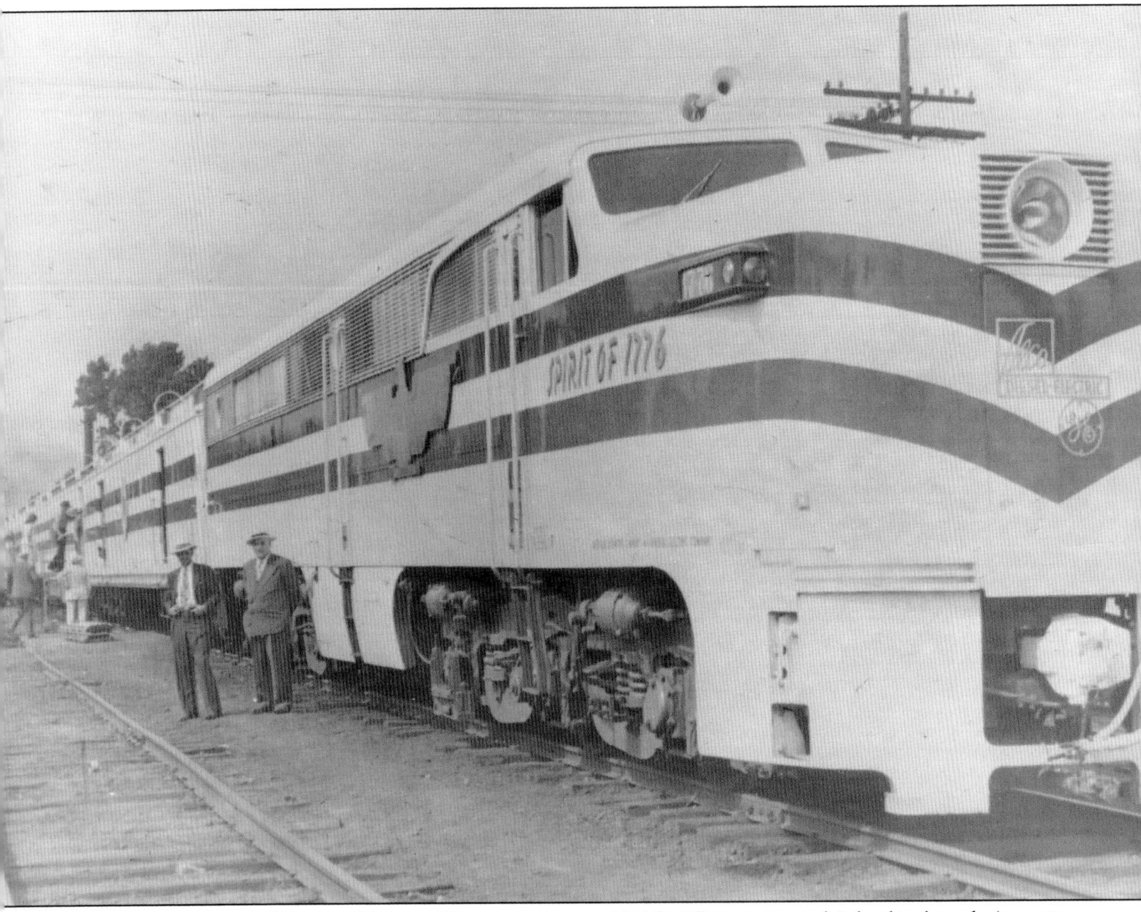

THE FREEDOM TRAIN VISITS CONNEAUT IN 1947. The train, which displayed American historical memorabilia, traveled through Conneaut along the Nickel Plate Road. This brand new PA1 diesel was owned by its manufacturer, the American Locomotive Company. (Courtesy of Conneaut Public Library.)

INTRODUCTION

Conneaut, Ohio has been a fascinating "hot spot" in railroading history. Three of the most renowned railroads of the twentieth century were important parts of life in this small city, located in the extreme northeast corner of Ohio and on the shores of Lake Erie. Conneaut today is a quiet town best known for fishing, boating, and scenic lake views, but decades ago it was full of piercing steam locomotive whistles, the clang and bang of railroad backshops, and the boom of heavy industry.

The Nickel Plate Road, the New York Central, and the Bessemer & Lake Erie each played a distinct and different role in Conneaut's growth, economy, and history. The building of the Nickel Plate's Conneaut roundhouse and yard in 1882, and the opening of the first rail connection from Conneaut Harbor to the steel mills and coal mines of Western Pennsylvania via the Bessemer route a decade later, caused a small town to grow rapidly in population and employment. In the era when dozens of passenger trains per day ran on the New York Central's mainline between New York and Chicago, Conneaut's location directly on the Water Level Route meant that local residents could travel virtually anywhere in America by rail, whenever they chose.

The photographic images collected here represent several decades of mainline railroading at its finest. The aim of this book is to include enough detail to be of interest to hard-core railfans, while not requiring in-depth knowledge for the general reader. Its scope in time has been restricted to approximately 1880-1970 with an emphasis on the mid-twentieth century before the Nickel Plate and the New York Central disappeared in mergers. There would certainly be plenty of interest in the post-merger Conneaut operations of Penn Central, Norfolk & Western, Conrail, CSX, and Norfolk Southern, but focusing on the earlier decades allows for the inclusion of more photographs of steam power, passenger service, depots, traction, and other elements that have vanished from the local railroad scene. Many of the photographs come from the collection of the Conneaut Historical Railroad Museum, a nationally-known institution that occupies the century-old New York Central depot and has preserved a large collection of memorabilia relating to the NKP, the Central, the B&LE, and many other railroads. Visiting the museum on a hot summer day, with cool breezes blowing in from the lake and long high-speed freight trains roaring past the building every few minutes on the CSX main line, is an exhilarating experience regardless of whether or not one is a railroad fanatic.

While most of these images show railroad or harbor scenes, a number of photographs of Conneaut itself have been included as well to give a sense of the town that grew up next to the rails.

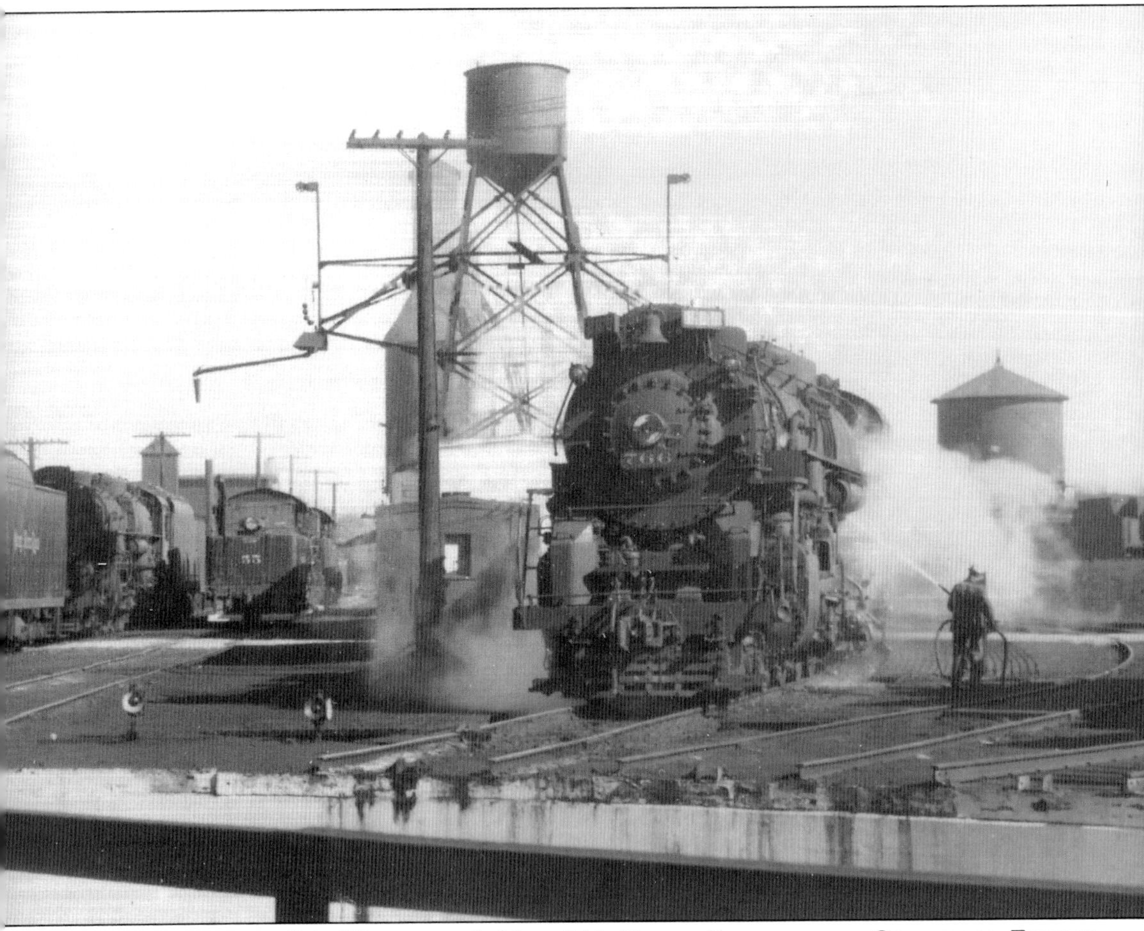

NICKEL PLATE S-2 "BERKSHIRE" NO. 766 BEING SERVICED AT CONNEAUT ENGINE TERMINAL, AUGUST 3, 1948. (Courtesy of Conneaut Historical Railroad Museum.)

One

The Nickel Plate Road

The importance of the Nickel Plate Road in Conneaut's history cannot be overstated. Conneaut yard was the western terminus of the railroad's eastern division and served as a model for other yards in the system; many local residents were employed there.

The New York & Chicago Railway was formed in 1881 by a group of New York investors with plans to construct a mainline stretching from Chicago to Buffalo and with designs on St. Louis as well. The *Norwalk Chronicle* (Ohio) described the New York & Chicago as "the great New York and St. Louis double-track nickel-plated railroad"—giving birth to the moniker Nickel Plate Road, which was embraced by the company. In that same year, the New York & Chicago merged with the Buffalo, Cleveland & Chicago to form the New York, Chicago & St. Louis Railway. The line was extended eastward, and by January 1882, the rails had reached Conneaut. During 1881-82, Conneaut competed vigorously with Ashtabula and Kingsville for the division point yard and eastern division repair shops, offering 70 acres of free land. A party of Nickel Plate VIPs made the first passenger trip over the line's eastern division from Cleveland to Conneaut on February 17, 1882, carrying out a thorough inspection of the physical plant. On March 16, Conneaut was given the nod, to the joy of its citizens. The new roundhouse that was built there had 22 locomotive stalls around its 65-foot turntable, and the yard incorporated 8 miles of track.

By October the NKP's eastern division tracks into Buffalo were complete, as were the new Conneaut facilities. The first two local freights to originate from Conneaut departed simultaneously at 6 a.m. on October 25, 1882, one heading east and the other west. In 1911, a new, larger turntable and roundhouse were built, and the shop facilities were also expanded. Five years later, in accordance with the recently passed Clayton Antitrust Act, the New York Central (which had controlled the NKP since shortly after its inception) was forced to sell the line. Brothers Mantis and Oris Van Sweringen, real estate men from Cleveland, purchased the railroad in order to secure the right-of-way for a planned traction line. In 1922, the NKP took over both the Lake Erie & Western Railroad and the Toledo, St. Louis & Western, becoming a midwestern giant with 1,683 miles of track.

The Nickel Plate's freight hauling was revolutionized in 1934 when the road took delivery of its first fifteen 2-8-4 "Berkshire" locomotives. The NKP leased the Wheeling & Lake Erie Railway in 1949, adding a new stream of revenue, which allowed the Nickel Plate to outperform and outclass its competition in the region with the performance of its mighty fleet of speedy Berkshires. As diesels began to force steam locomotives into retirement in the 1950s, Conneaut roundhouse and shop employees were laid off in large numbers. All fires on NKP steam locomotives in Conneaut were dropped on July 22, 1958. In May and June of 1959, four 0-8-0 switchers returned to service briefly in the Conneaut yard (the last NKP steam power to run in the city), but on August 31, 1960, the few remaining steam locomotives on the system were retired.

In the 1960s, the face of American railroading changed, as many historically important roads disappeared in mergers. Aware of its inability to compete with the sprawling Penn Central that would be the result of the projected New York Central/Pennsylvania union, the Nickel Plate sought to keep alive by joining with another powerful giant. On October 16, 1964, the Nickel Plate and the Wabash (along with the Akron, Canton & Youngstown and the Pittsburgh & West Virginia) disappeared forever into the Norfolk & Western. N&W merged yet again with the Southern Railway in 1982; Norfolk Southern continues to run through Conneaut today on the old Nickel Plate rails.

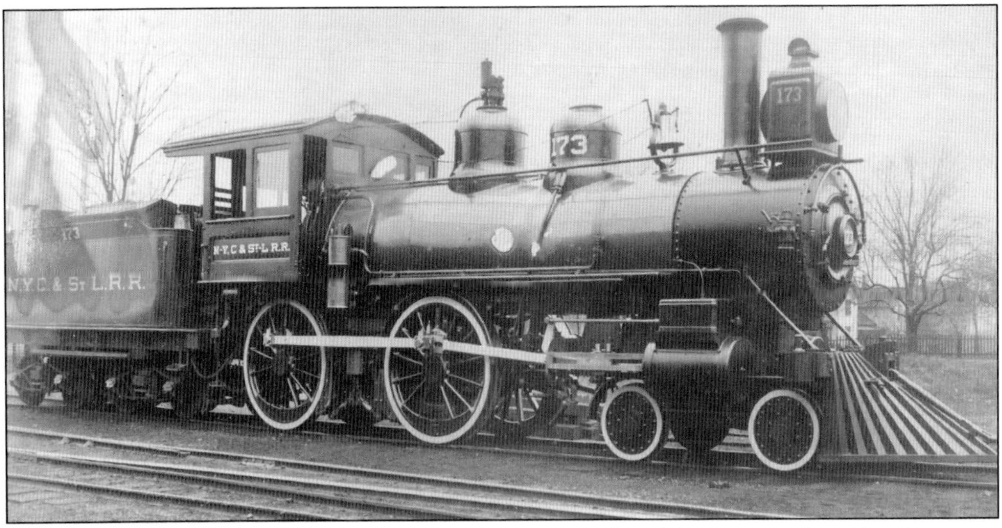

4-4-0 "AMERICAN" NO. 173. An inscription accompanying this photograph at the Conneaut Railroad Museum states that this locomotive pulled the Nickel Plate's first passenger train out of Conneaut. When the road's first passenger trains rolled on October 23, 1882, they were all pulled by this type of locomotive. NKP 4-4-0s were divided into A, B, and C classes: designations for freight service (42 locomotives), express freight (18 locomotives), and passenger trains (8 locomotives) respectively. According to the official 1947 history of the Nickel Plate, Conneaut's first NKP passenger train originated in Bellevue at 6:45 a.m. and was pulled by No. 165, switching to No. 169 at Conneaut before continuing on toward Buffalo. Possibly, No. 173 pulled the first westbound train. (Courtesy of Conneaut Historical Railroad Museum.)

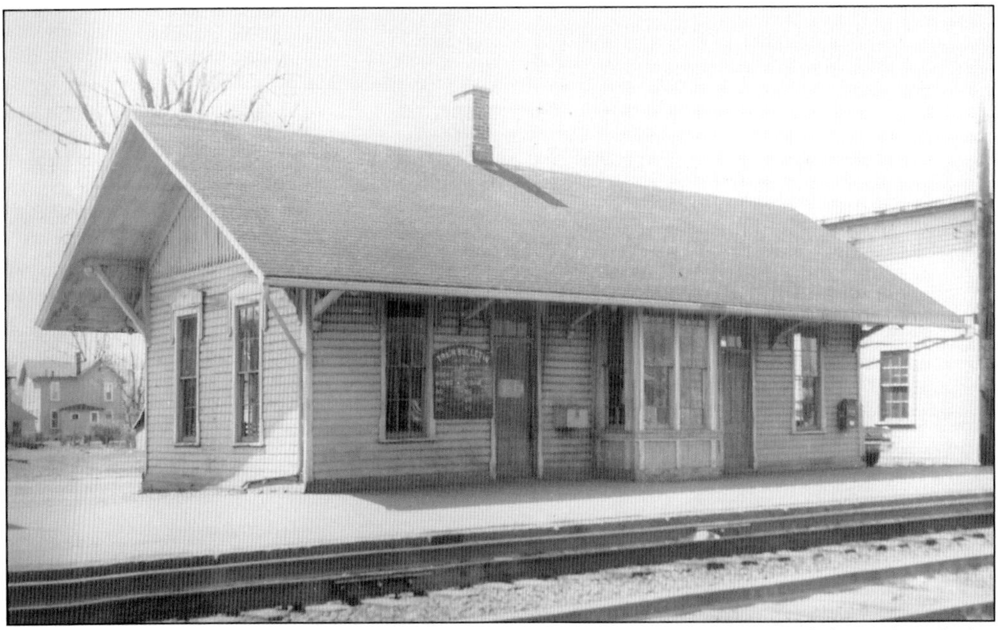

THE NICKEL PLATE'S CONNEAUT DEPOT. Built in 1882 for the opening of the railroad, the wooden structure was torn down long before Conneaut saw its last ex-NKP passenger train (on the Norfolk & Western) in September 1965. Passengers were subsequently accommodated at the two-story division office. (Courtesy of Conneaut Historical Railroad Museum.)

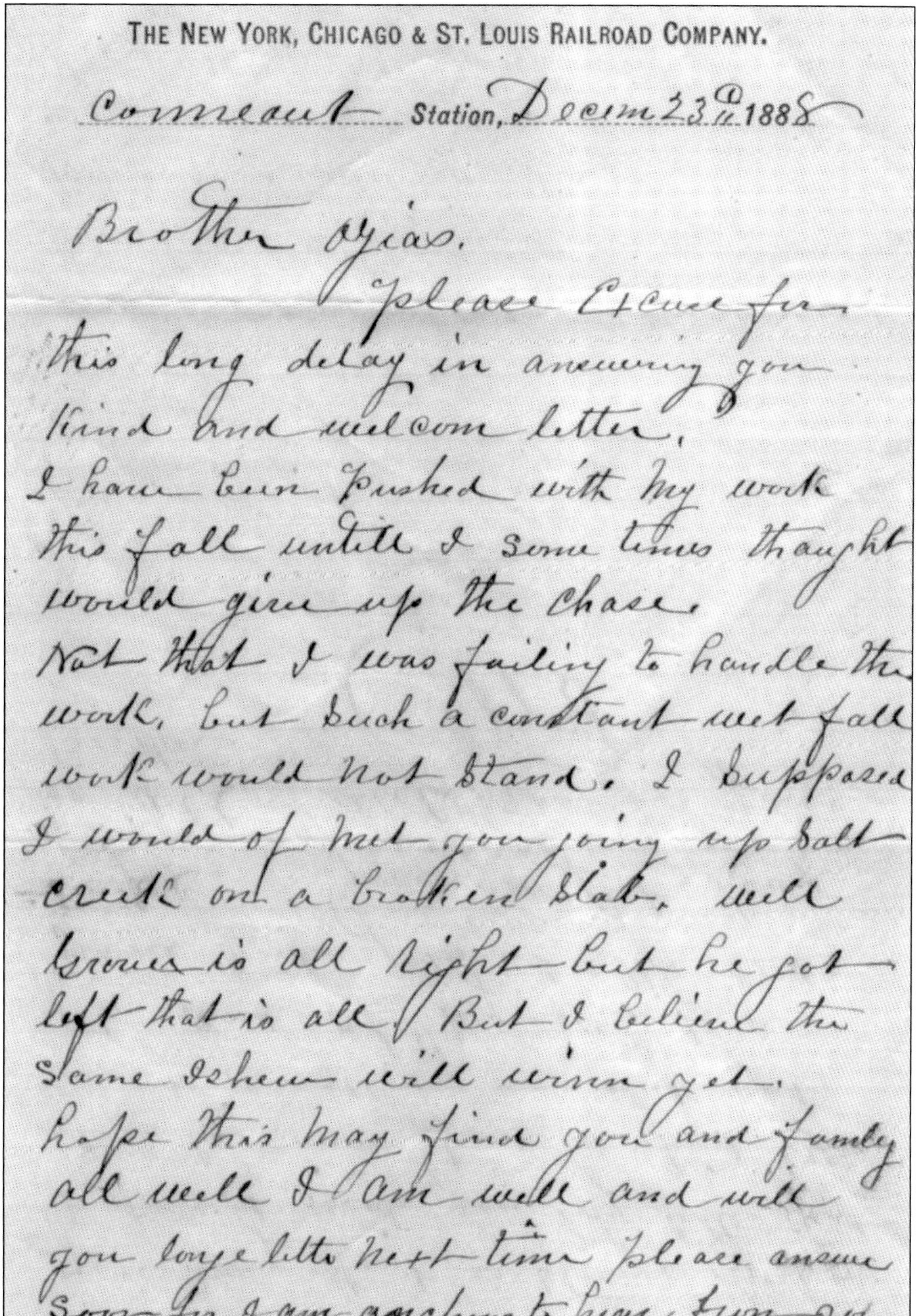

THE NEW YORK, CHICAGO & ST. LOUIS RAILROAD COMPANY.

Conneaut Station, Decem 23rd 1888

Brother Ozias.

Please Excuse for this long delay in answering your kind and welcom letter.
I have been pushed with my work this fall untill I some times thaught would give up the chase.
Not that I was failing to handle the work, but such a constant wet fall work would not stand. I supposed I would of met you going up salt creek on a broken slab. well Grover is all right but he got left that is all / But I believe the same Ishew will win yet.
hope this may find you and family all well I am well and will you longe letter next time please answer soon for I am anchous to hear from you

NICKEL PLATE STATIONERY. In the old days, a depot was in many ways the nerve center of a town; the telegraph office was located here, and mail came in and out on the trains. (Courtesy of Conneaut Historical Railroad Museum.)

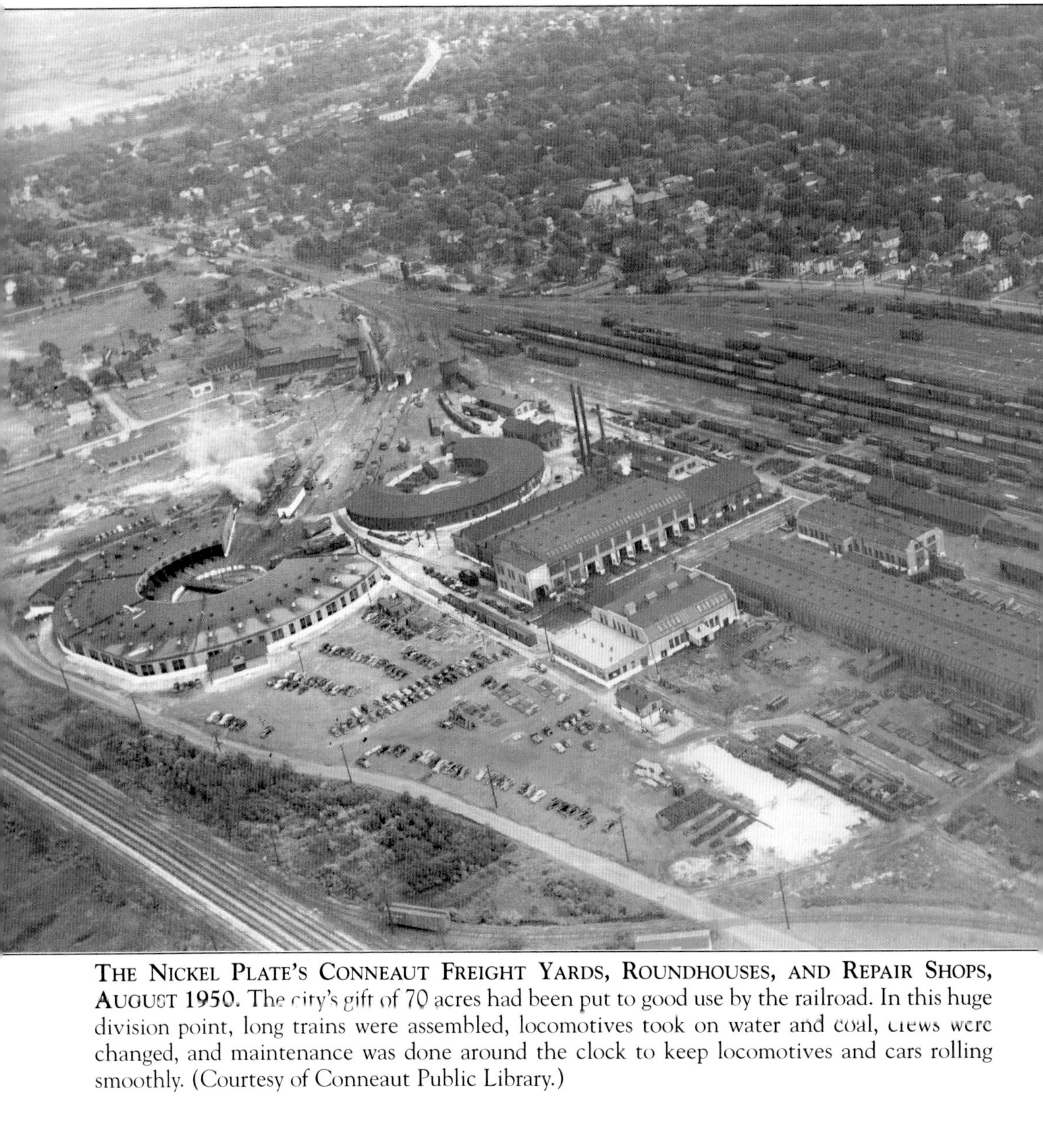

THE NICKEL PLATE'S CONNEAUT FREIGHT YARDS, ROUNDHOUSES, AND REPAIR SHOPS, AUGUST 1950. The city's gift of 70 acres had been put to good use by the railroad. In this huge division point, long trains were assembled, locomotives took on water and coal, crews were changed, and maintenance was done around the clock to keep locomotives and cars rolling smoothly. (Courtesy of Conneaut Public Library.)

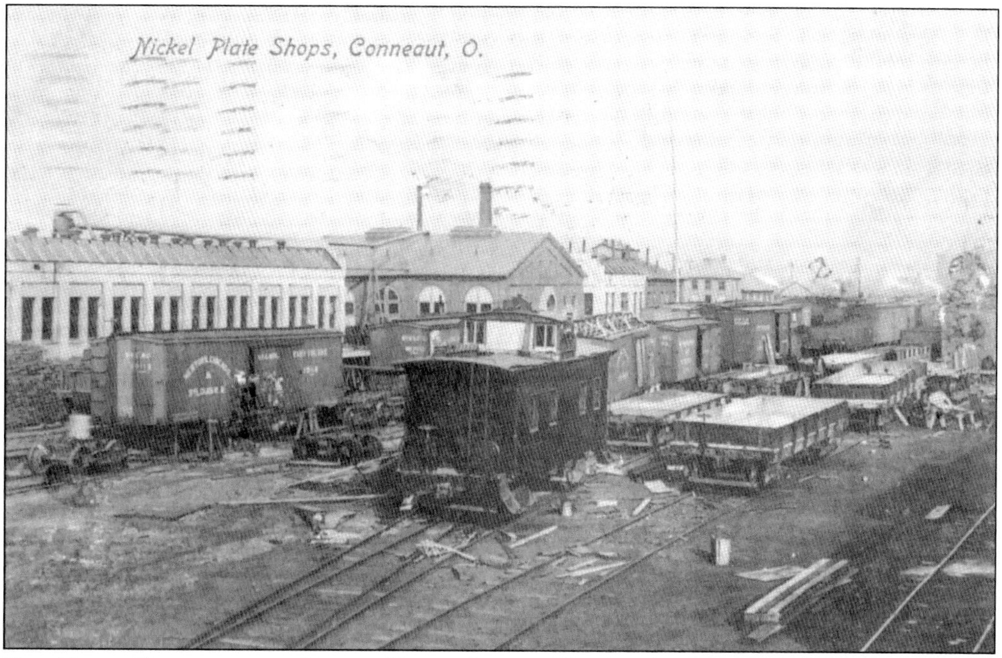

The Early Years of the Nickel Plate Shops. Wooden freight cars and a 1907 postmark date the scene. (Courtesy of Conneaut Area Historical Society.)

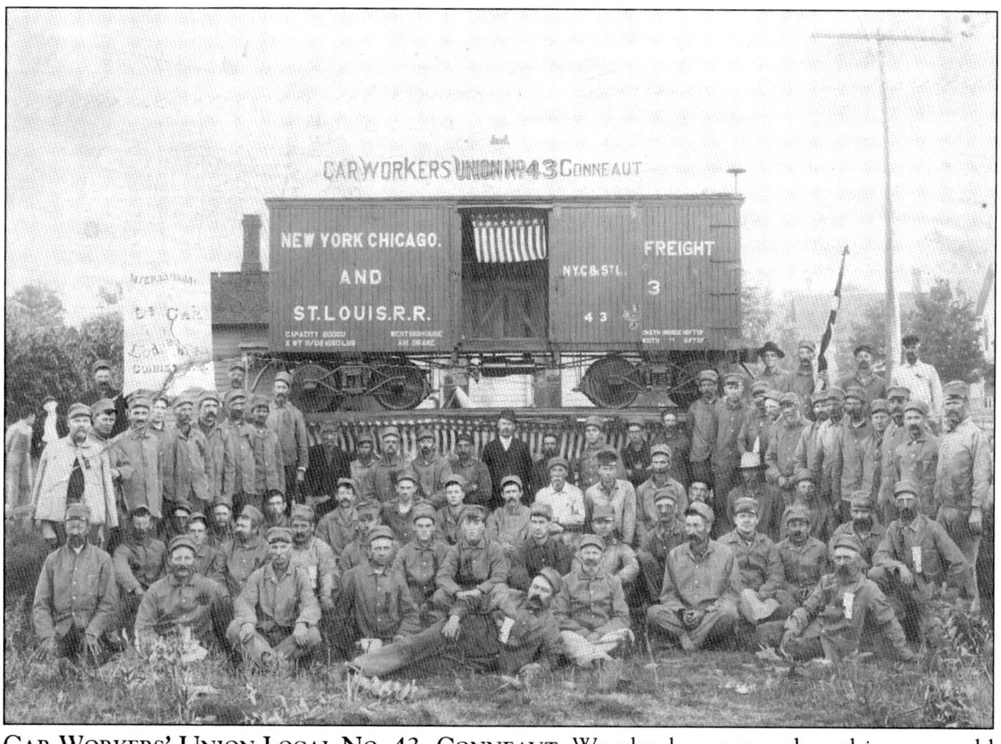

Car Workers' Union Local No. 43, Conneaut. Wooden box cars such as this one would soon fade from the scene, to be replaced by sturdier steel cars. (Courtesy of Conneaut Historical Railroad Museum.)

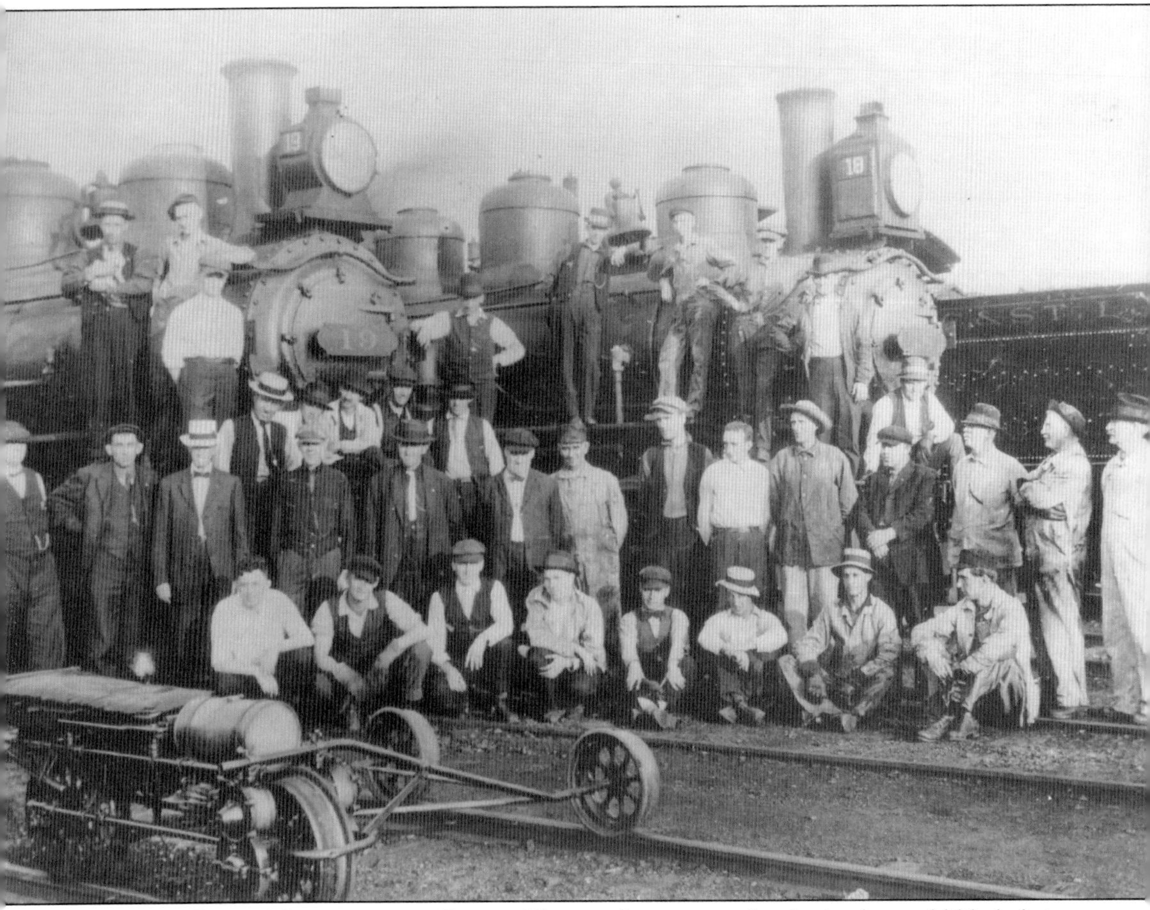

NICKEL PLATE MAINTENANCE CREWS. The gasoline-powered velocipede would likely bring a high price at auction today. (Courtesy of Conneaut Area Historical Society.)

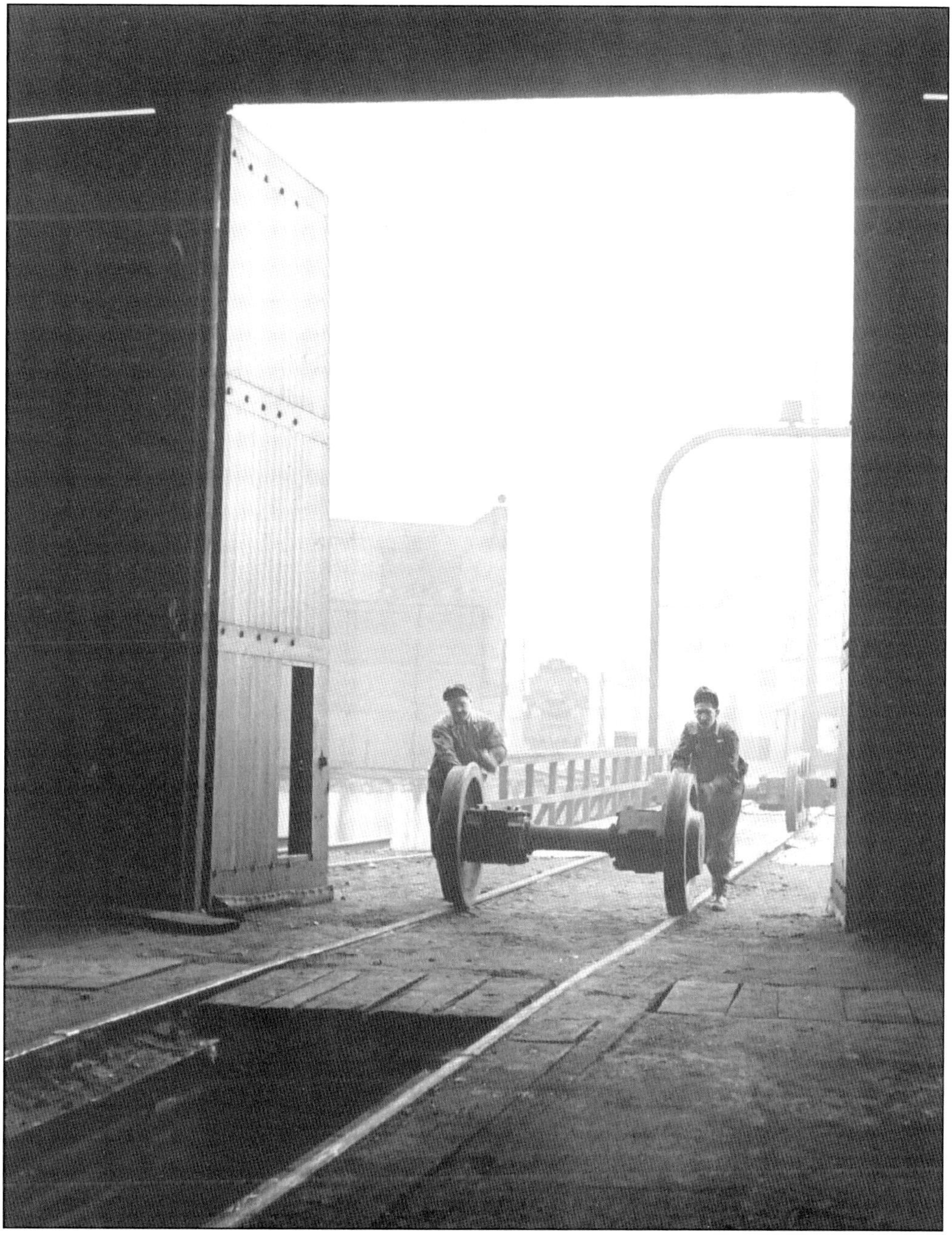

ACTIVITY INSIDE THE CONNEAUT SHOPS. In contrast to diesel repair and maintenance, which often focuses on the replacement of faulty or worn-out engine components, crews that worked on steam locomotives also had to be well versed in the art of repairing and re-using parts. (Courtesy of Conneaut Area Historical Society.)

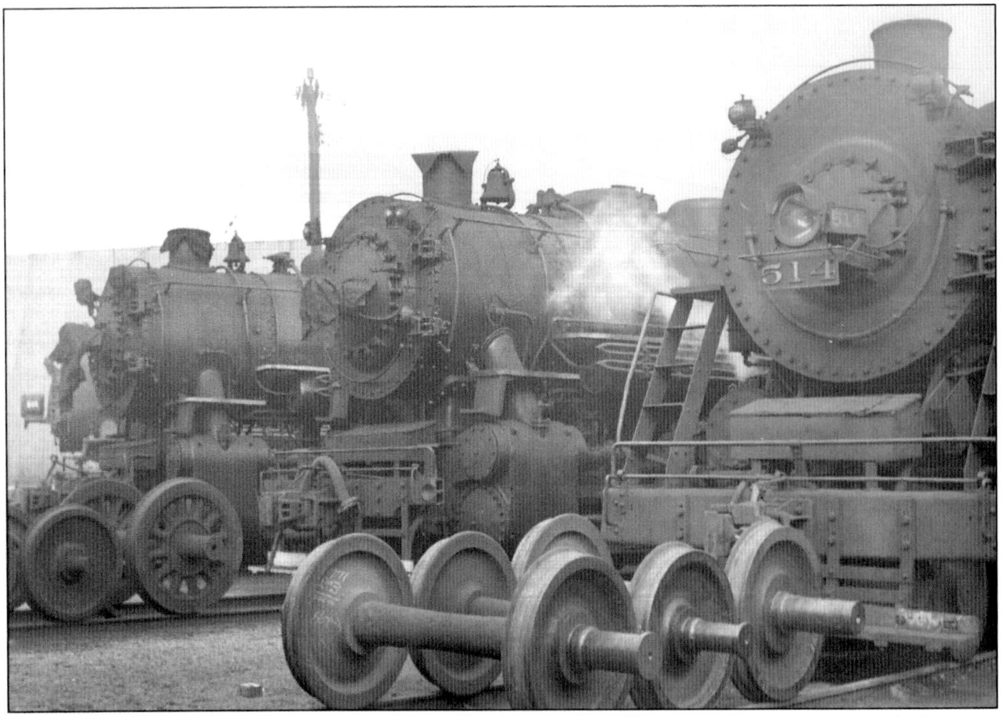

Locomotive Wheelsets. Keeping the wheels "in round" was important, particularly after emergency stops or other heavy braking that could grind flat spots into the rims. (Courtesy of Conneaut Area Historical Society.)

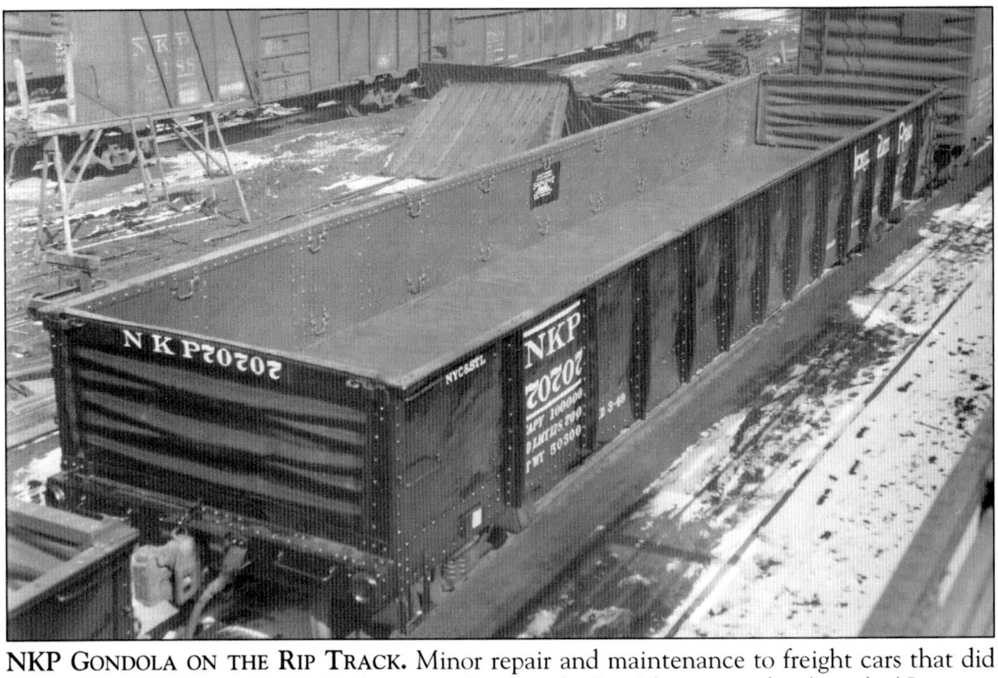

NKP Gondola on the Rip Track. Minor repair and maintenance to freight cars that did not need to be taken apart in the shops was done on the "rip" (repair in place) track. (Courtesy of Conneaut Historical Railroad Museum.)

LOCOMOTIVE MAINTENANCE. Steam locomotives were significantly more expensive to maintain than diesels—one important factor underlying the nationwide extinction of steam in the 1950s. (Courtesy of Conneaut Area Historical Society.)

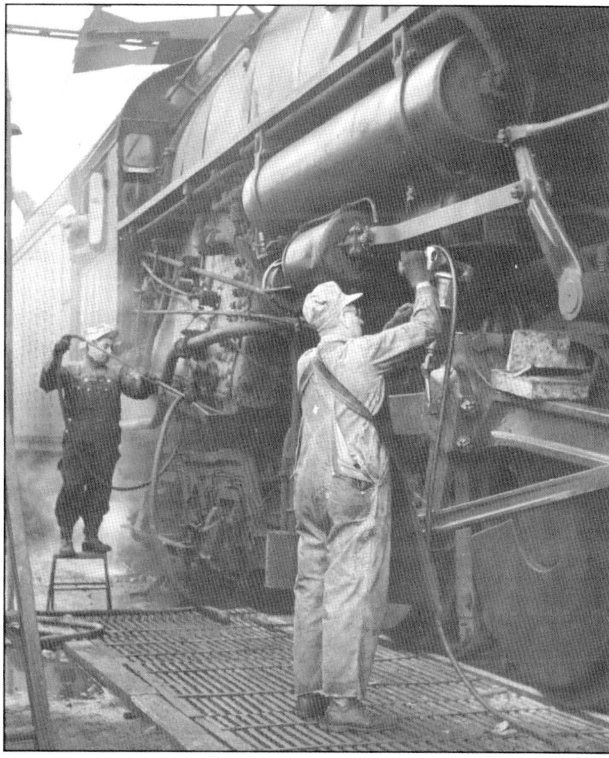

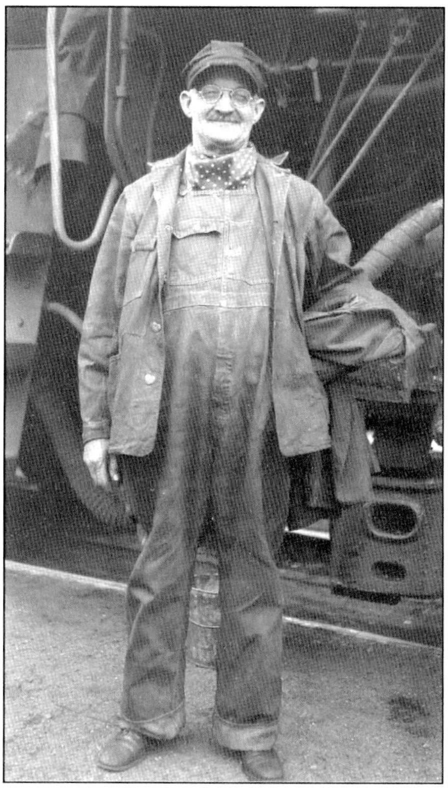

A TRAINMAN SAYS FAREWELL. On August 26, 1937, a photographer captured this image of engineer Charles Thomas after he made his last run from Bellevue, Ohio (another NKP division point) to Conneaut. (Courtesy of Conneaut Historical Railroad Museum.)

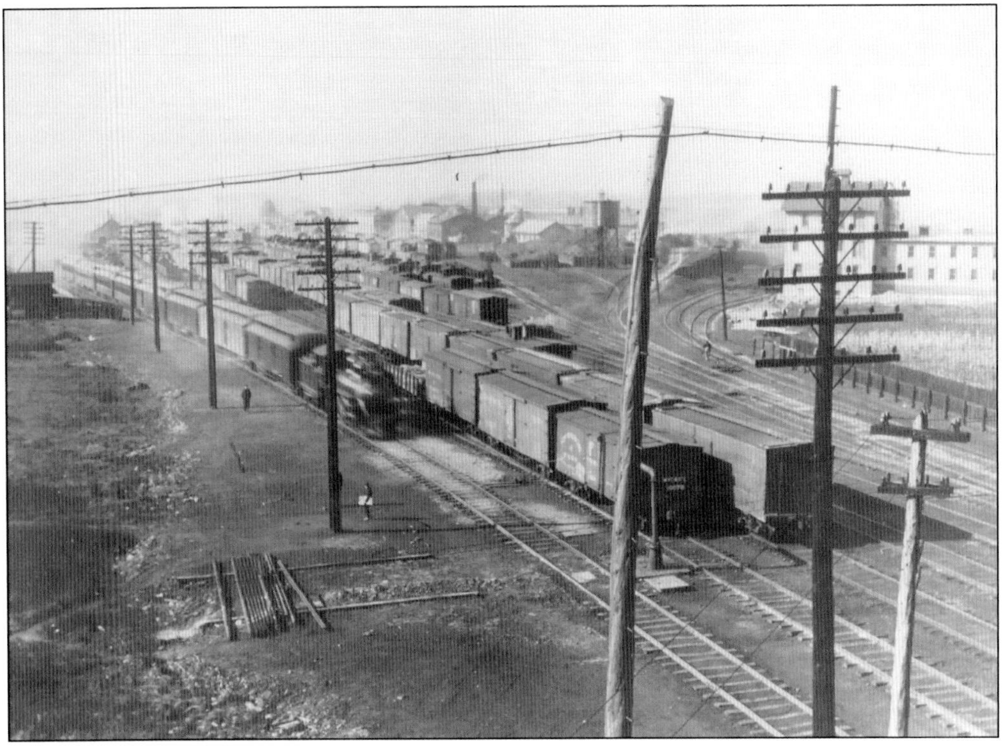

NKP Passenger Train Skirts the Conneaut Yard, c. 1925. The Nickel Plate, unable to compete directly with the numerous passenger trains and multiple tracks of the parallel NYC, concentrated instead on outrunning it in fast freight service and succeeded in doing so most of the time. (Courtesy of Conneaut Public Library.)

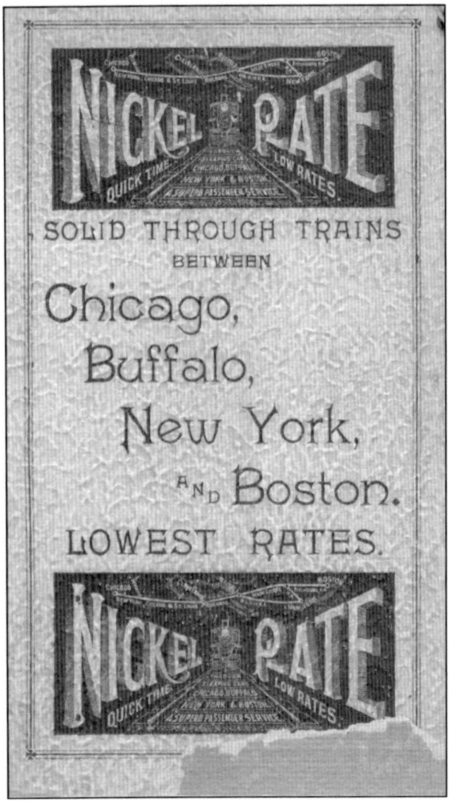

Passenger Advertisement. The Nickel Plate, like the New York Central, was called upon to haul troops in mass quantities during World War II, and it performed this task brilliantly. But a decade of postwar optimism, marked by significant investment in new passenger equipment, was followed by a sharp (and lasting) nationwide slump in rail travel. (Courtesy of Conneaut Area Historical Society.)

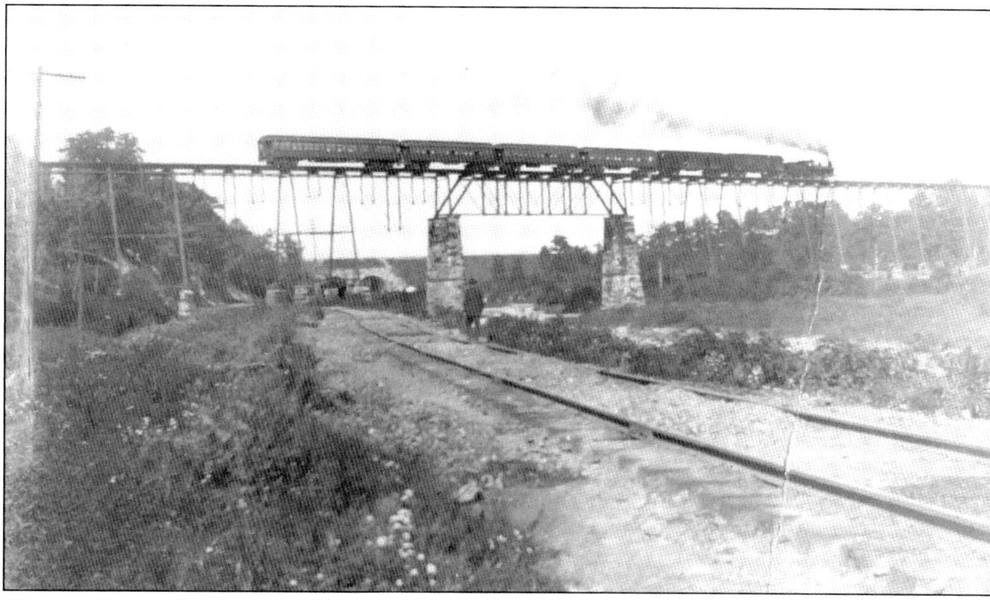

Nickel Plate Passenger Train Over Conneaut Creek, c. 1925. Conneaut's three railroad lines are all in sight in this photograph from the Bessemer & Lake Erie rails. Behind the old NKP bridge is the parallel stone arch bridge of the New York Central. This has long been a favorite spot for rail photographers, who hope to catch trains moving on at least two of the three lines simultaneously. Today, with the valley overgrown with trees, the old Central bridge is difficult to see from this spot. (Courtesy of Conneaut Public Library.)

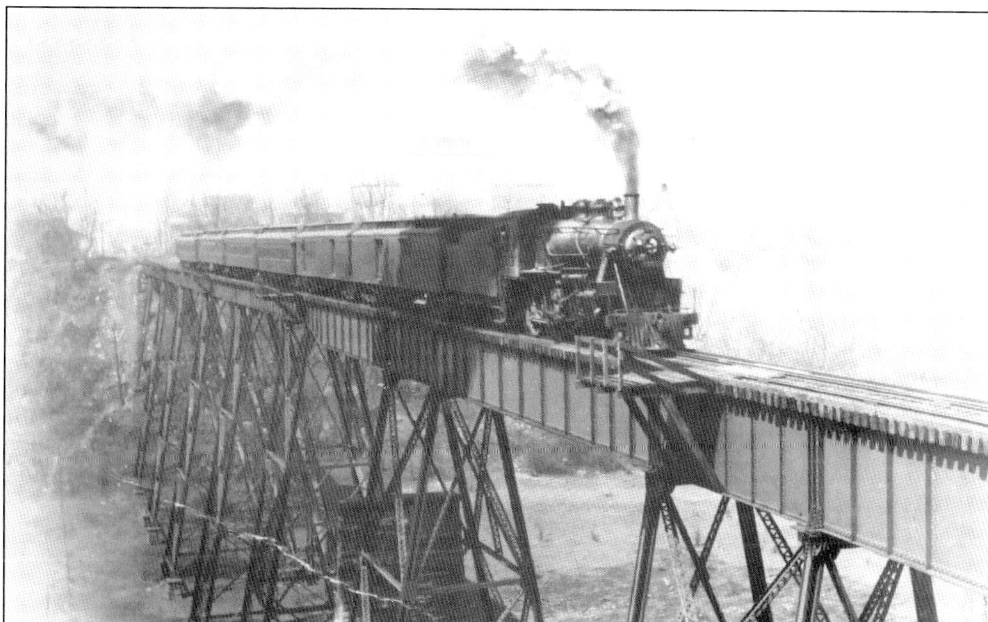

NKP at Conneaut Creek, c. 1930. The bridge in the photograph above has been replaced by this 1320-foot-long plate girder span that still stands today. The Nickel Plate upgraded all of its physical plant to handle the weight of larger and more powerful locomotives. (Courtesy of Conneaut Public Library.)

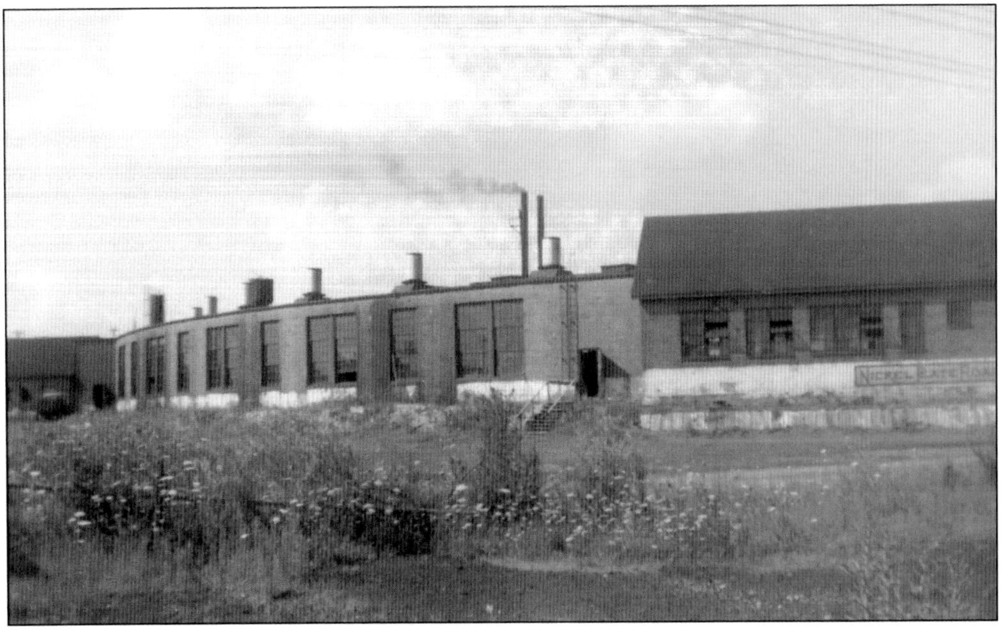

EXTERIOR AND INTERIOR OF NKP ROUNDHOUSE. Day and night, the building resounded with the clatter of hammers and anvils, the hiss of steam valves, and the rumble of idling locomotives. (Both courtesy of Conneaut Public Library.)

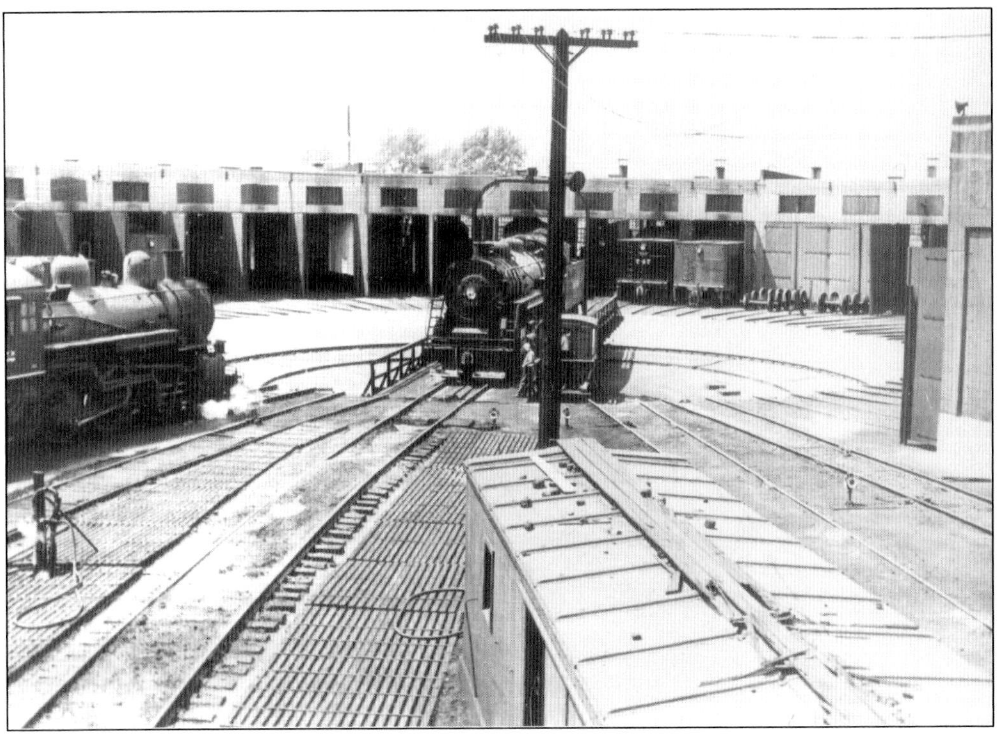

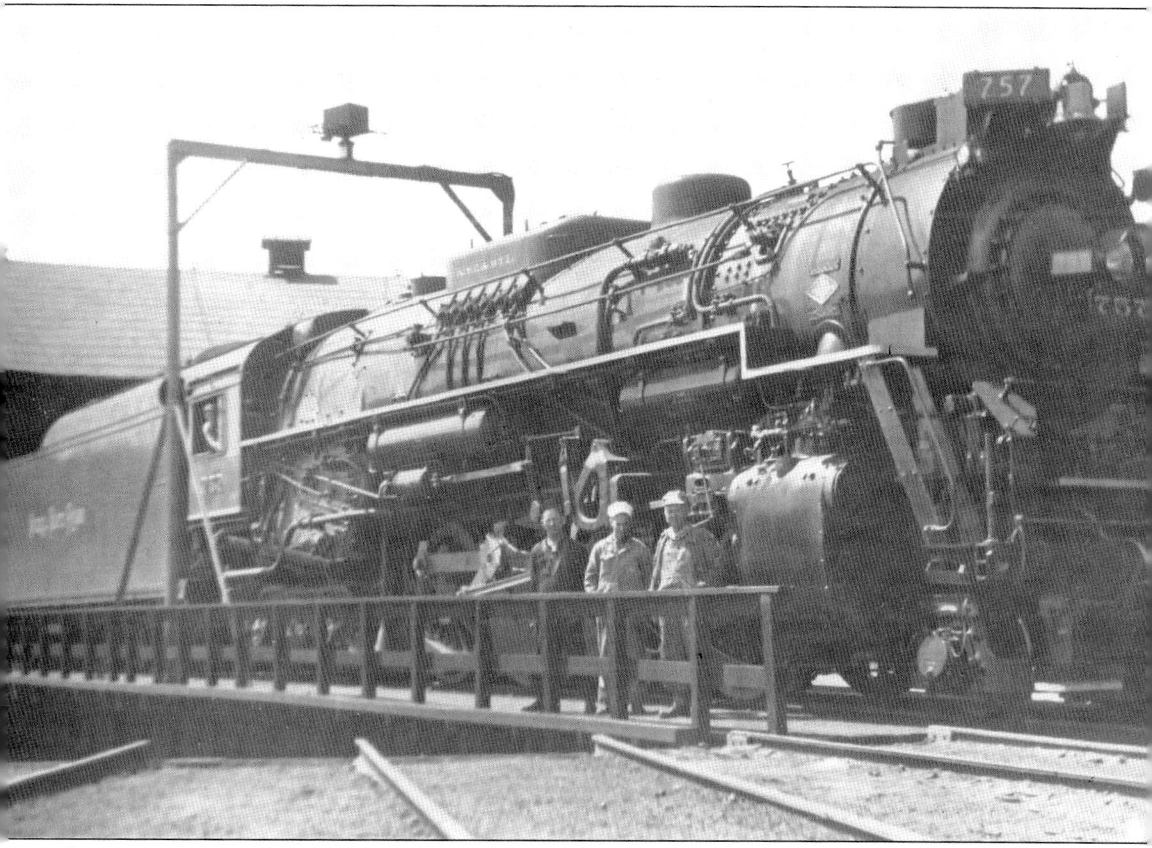

ONE OF THE FAMOUS NKP "BERKSHIRES" AT THE CONNEAUT ROUNDHOUSE. Engineer Hugh Shellito and fireman Merle Cool are seen with maintenance crew members on August 27, 1944, by S-2 class 2-8-4 Berkshire No. 757 (built in 1944 and retired in 1960). The Berkshires, Nos. 700-779, were the often-photographed top-flight steam power of the Nickel Plate. Representing a design improvement upon the World War I era 2-8-2 "Mikados" built by the United States Railroad Administration, they were designed and built at the Lima Locomotive Works and first tested on the Boston & Albany in 1925 with brilliant success. Many other railroads purchased Berkshires as the design was incrementally improved. The NKP bought its first fifteen 2-8-4s from the American Locomotive Company (Alco) with the design modified according to the railroad's specifications and the S-1 class in 1934. Later orders from Lima brought 65 more Berkshires to the road in classes S-2, S-3, and S-4. No. 757 was preserved at the Railroad Museum of Pennsylvania in Strasburg in 1966. (Courtesy of Conneaut Historical Railroad Museum.)

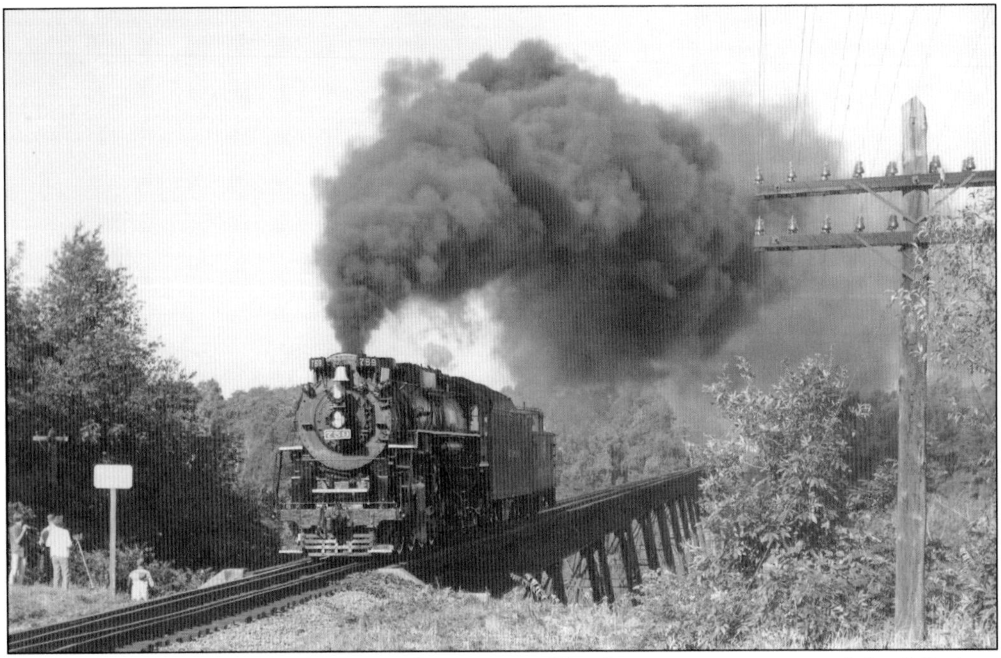

NKP Berkshire No. 759 Leaving Conneaut. This locomotive was part of the S-2 class, the Nickel Plate's third order of Berkshires (from Lima) in June 1943. The NKP overhauled No. 759 at the Conneaut shops in May 1958, and with diesels rapidly pushing steam off the roster, she was in fact the last steam locomotive to be overhauled by the railroad. Happily, she would escape the scrapper's torch along with several other Nickel Plate Berkshires, ending up at a museum instead. (Courtesy of Conneaut Historical Railroad Museum.)

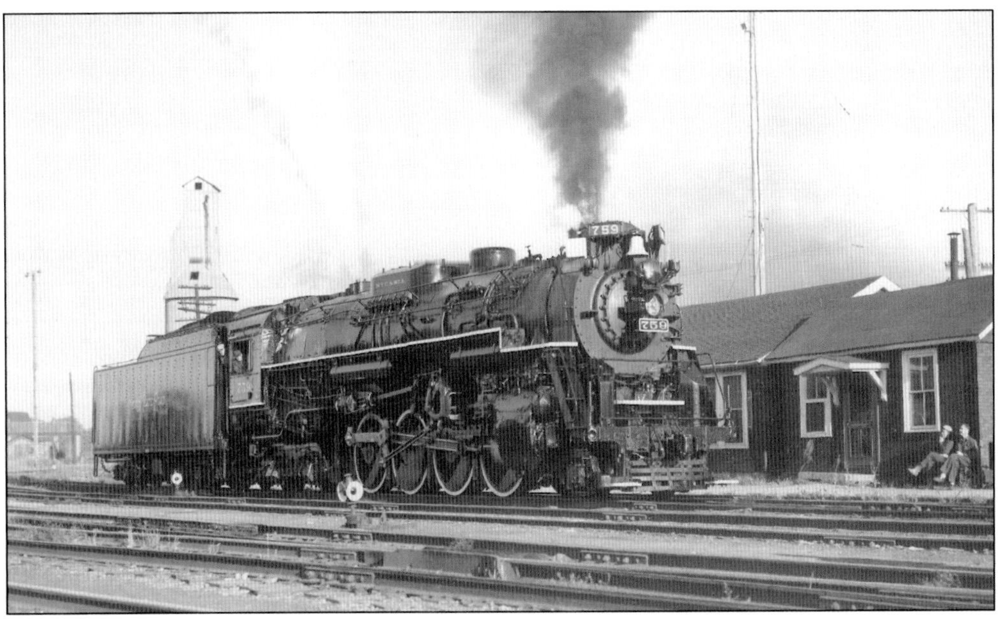

No. 759 in the Conneaut Yard. Behind the locomotive is the yard office, and above the tender is the distinctive NKP coaling tower, which was one of Conneaut's landmarks. (Courtesy of Conneaut Historical Railroad Museum.)

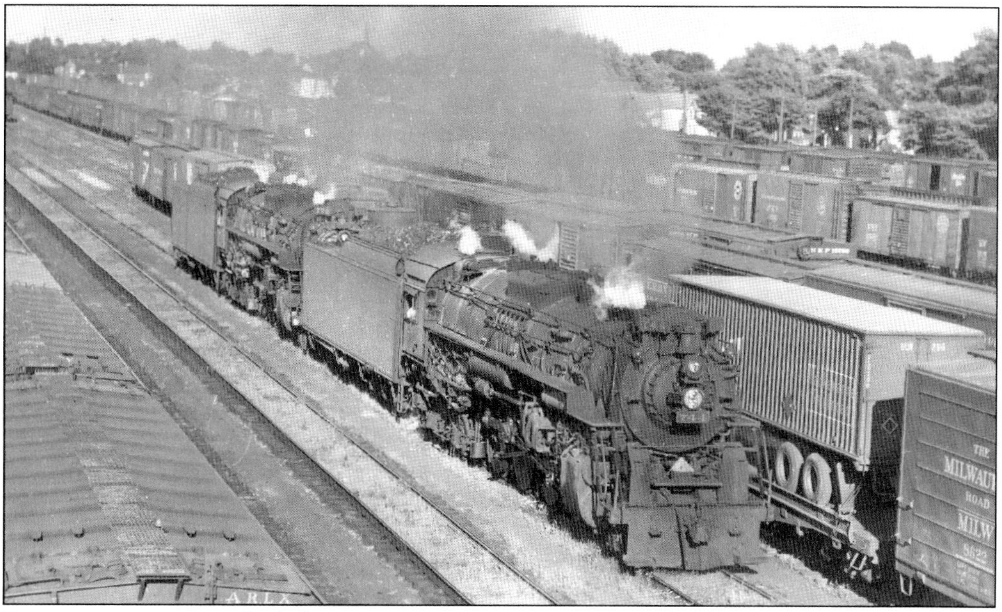

DOUBLEHEADER. Two Berkshires, S-2 class No. 744 (built in 1944) and S-3 No. 776 (dating from 1949) run light to pick up a westbound train at Conneaut Yard on July 28, 1956. Doubleheading was often necessary for getting a heavy train over even moderate grades, but running two steam locomotives in tandem was costly since it required two crews. When diesels came onto the scene, their ability to be run in unlimited combinations by one crew proved to be a cost cutting factor that contributed to steam's demise. After retirement in 1958, neither of these locomotives were preserved. (Courtesy of Conneaut Historical Railroad Museum.)

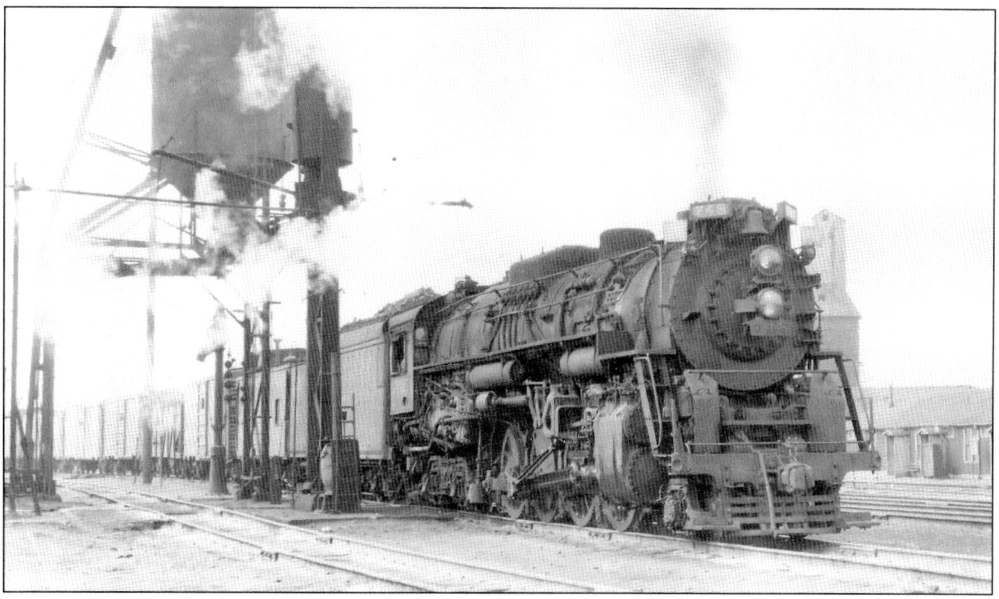

NKP S-2 NO. 748 STOPS FOR WATER WITH AN EASTBOUND FREIGHT AT CONNEAUT, MARCH 29, 1958. This 1944-built Berkshire held on longer than some, not being retired until 1960. It was sold for scrap the following year. (Courtesy of Conneaut Historical Railroad Museum.)

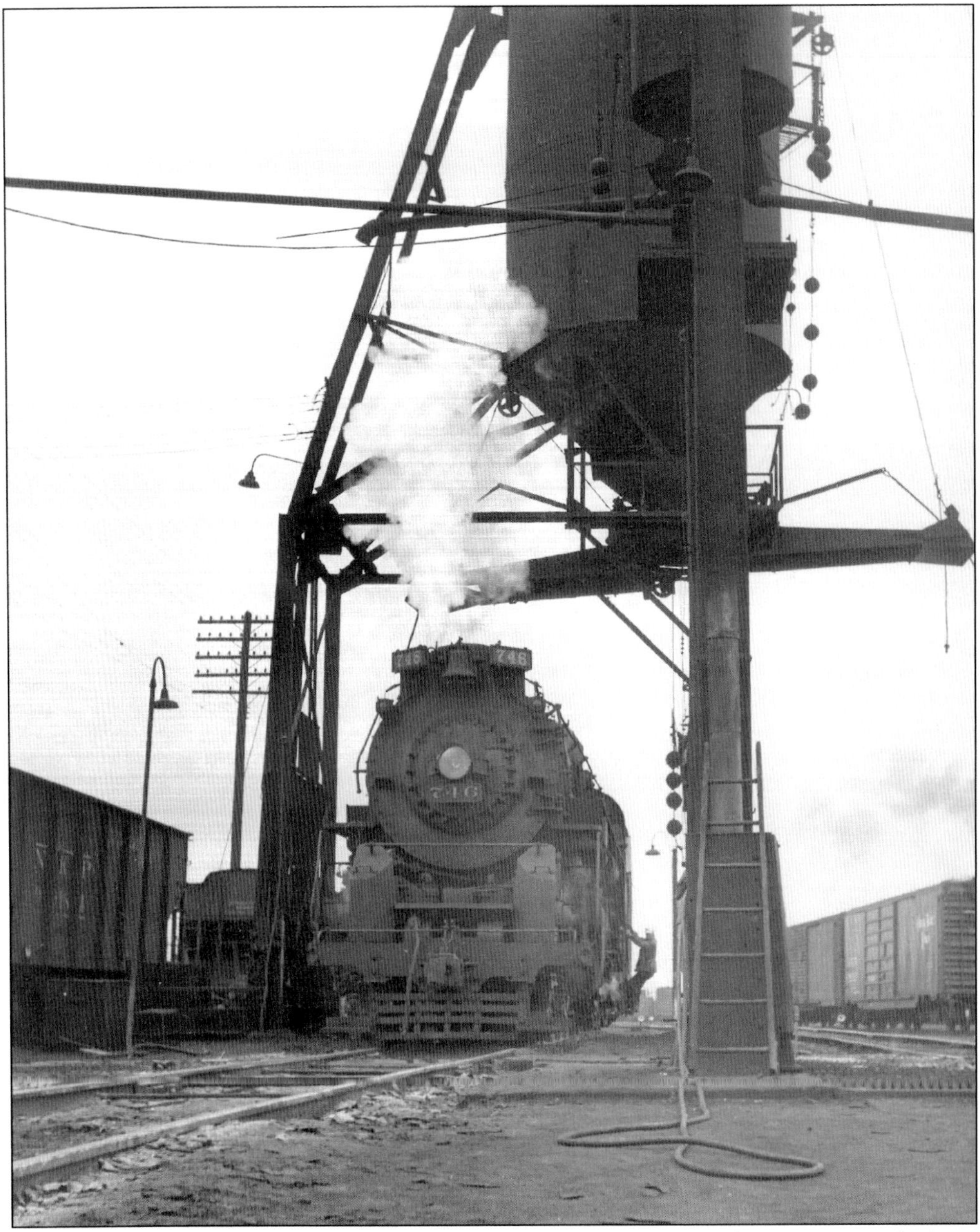

Berkshire S-2 No. 746 at Watering Tower in Conneaut. One thing Conneaut had was an inexhaustible supply of water. (Courtesy of Conneaut Area Historical Society.)

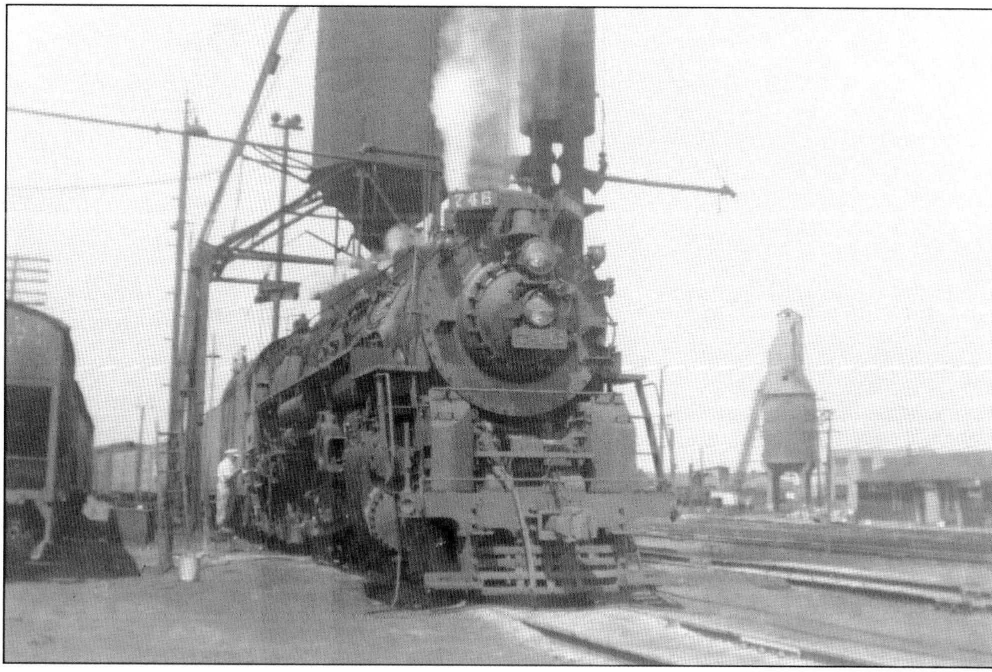

ANOTHER VIEW OF NO. 746. The locomotive is refueling for the 116-mile run to Buffalo, New York. (Courtesy of Conneaut Public Library.)

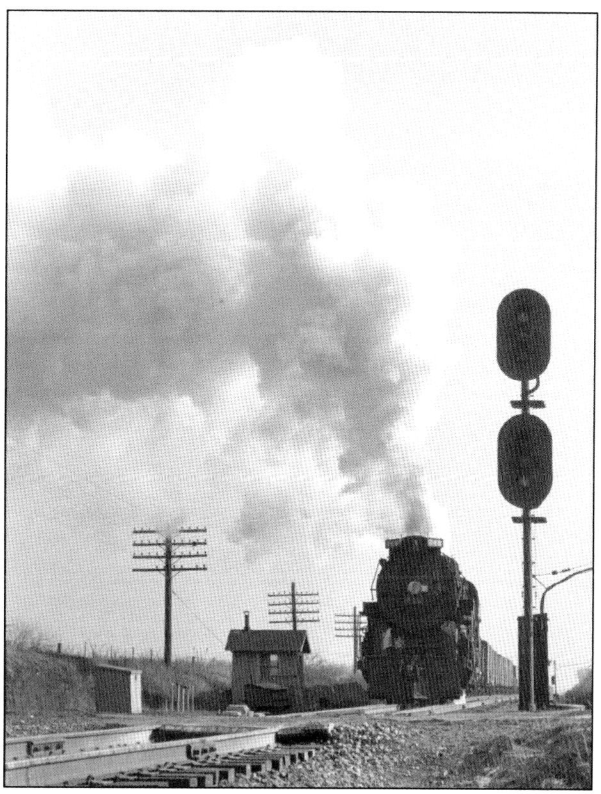

WESTBOUND S-2 NO. 742 AT WOODWORTH ROAD. Unlike the New York Central which had the luxury of a multitracked "highway," the single-track Nickel Plate depended solely upon efficient dispatching and signaling to move its fast freights to their destinations on time. (Courtesy of Conneaut Area Historical Society.)

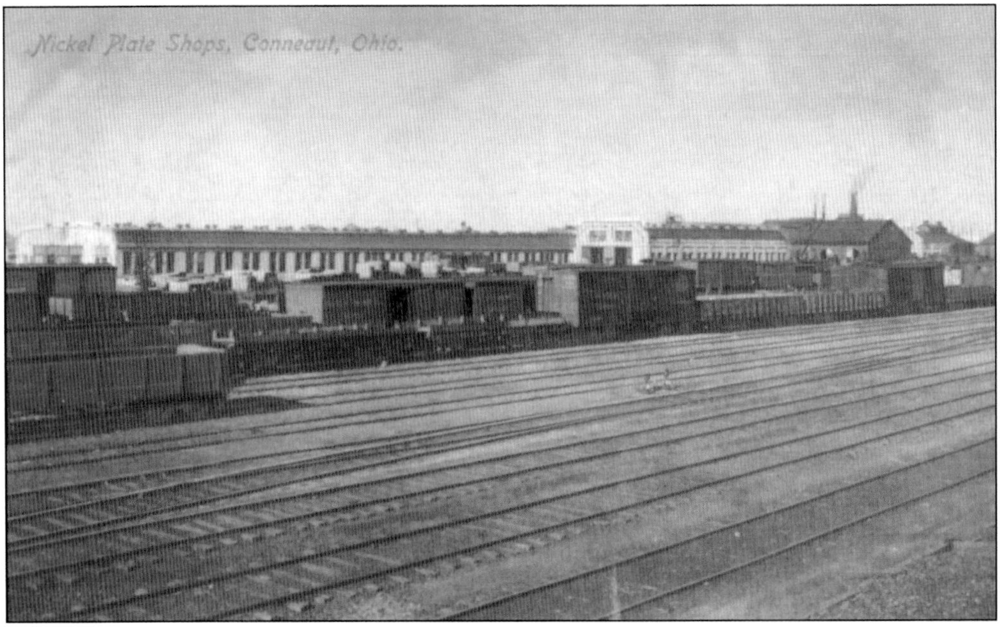

NICKEL PLATE SHOPS, VIEWED FROM YARD TRACKS. While wooden freight cars lacked the rigidity of their steel descendants, they were certainly photogenic. (Courtesy of Conneaut Area Historical Society.)

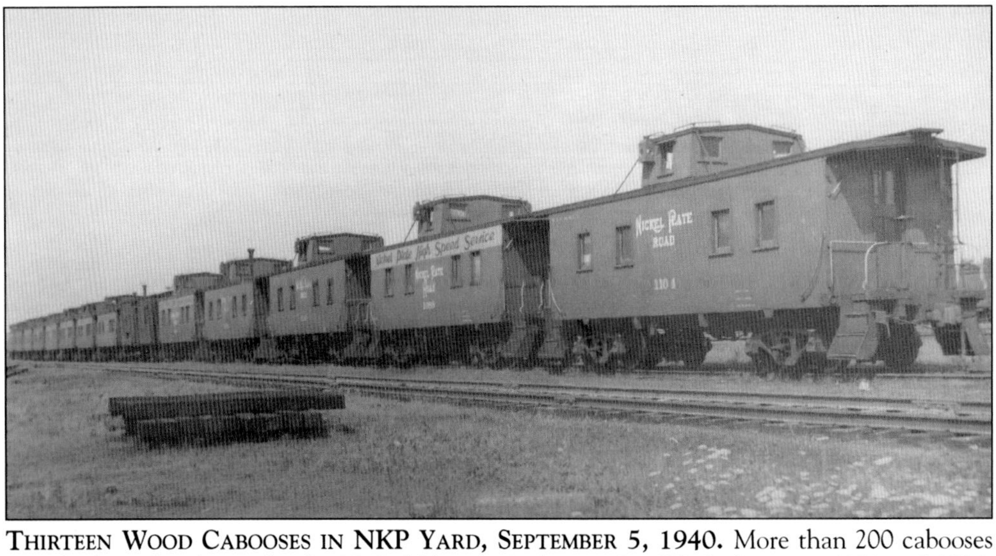

THIRTEEN WOOD CABOOSES IN NKP YARD, SEPTEMBER 5, 1940. More than 200 cabooses were built to this design for the Nickel Plate by Lafayette Car Works between 1881 and 1924. Steel cabooses, with greater structural strength and durability, gradually displaced the wooden "hacks." By the 1990s, the caboose, one of the most enduring symbols of American railroading, had vanished from the rails—an inevitable victim of crew reduction due to cost cutting. One is still occasionally seen on an inspection or work train. (Courtesy of Conneaut Historical Railroad Museum.)

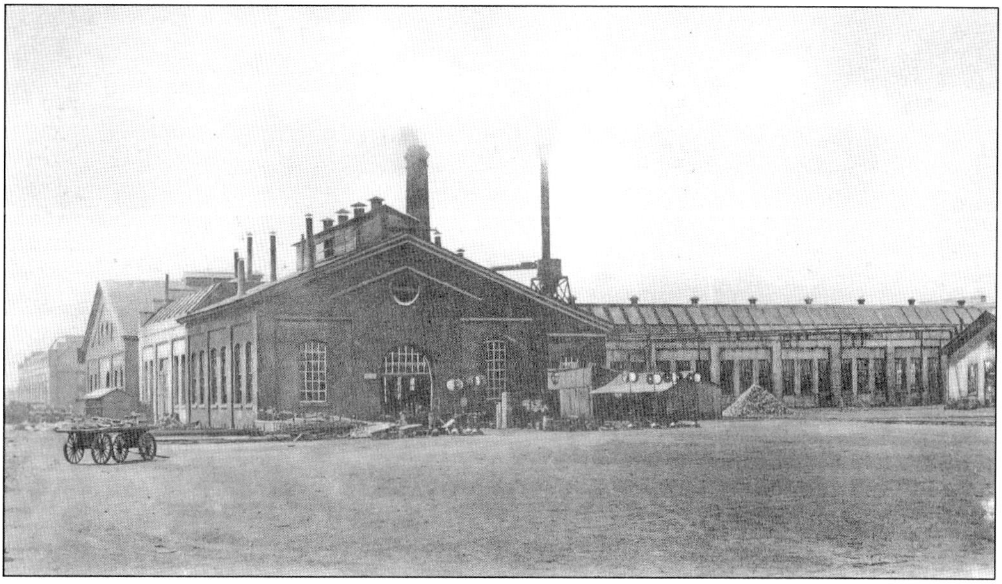

NKP SHOPS IN THE EARLY YEARS. The Conneaut population increase reflected in the censuses of 1890 and 1900 was due in part to the many new jobs created in the Nickel Plate shops and yard. (Courtesy of Conneaut Area Historical Society.)

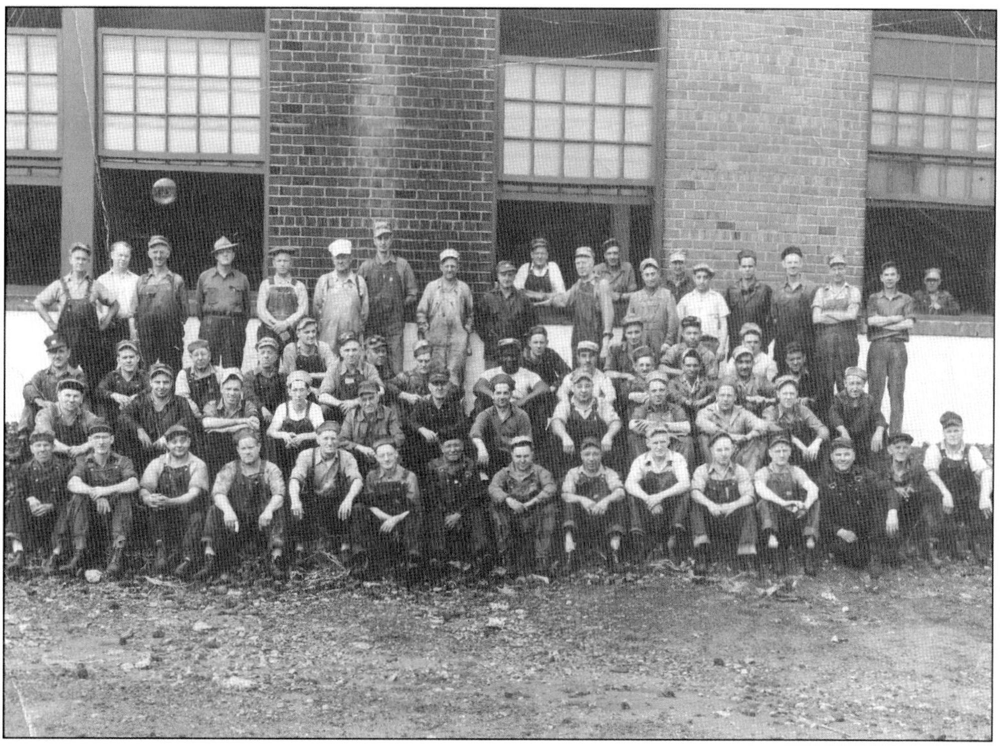

NKP ROUNDHOUSE FIRST-TRICK MAINTENANCE CREW, AUGUST 18, 1949. Many of these men, who had been responsible for keeping the railroad's magnificent steam fleet rolling, would soon be laid off as lower-maintenance diesels began to push steam locomotives from the roster. (Courtesy of Conneaut Historical Railroad Museum.).

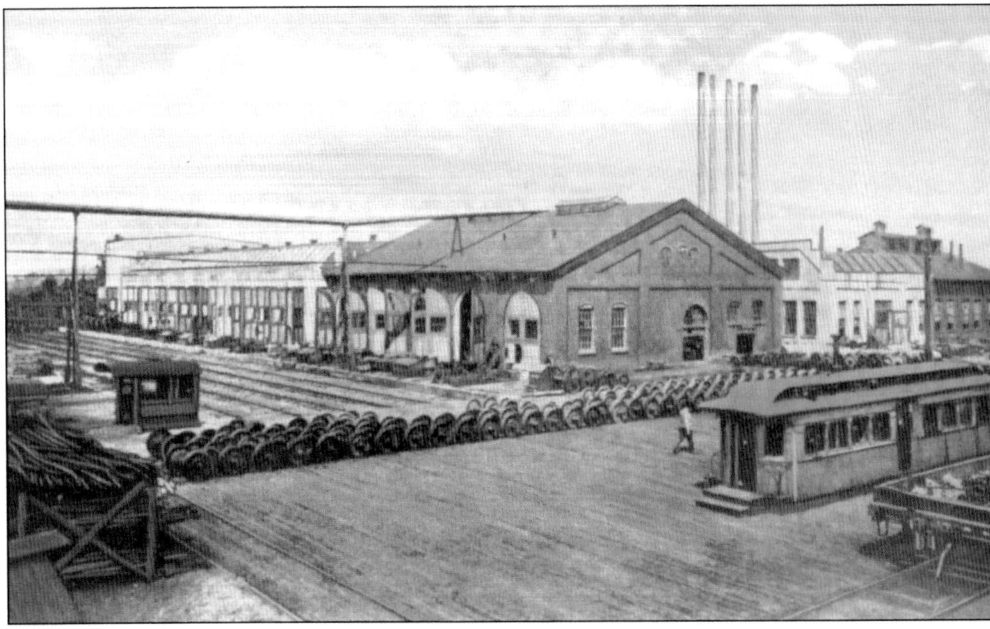

NKP BACKSHOP. At left can be seen the transfer table, which moved linearly rather than radially like a turntable to deliver locomotives or rolling stock to maintenance stalls. (Courtesy of Conneaut Area Historical Society.)

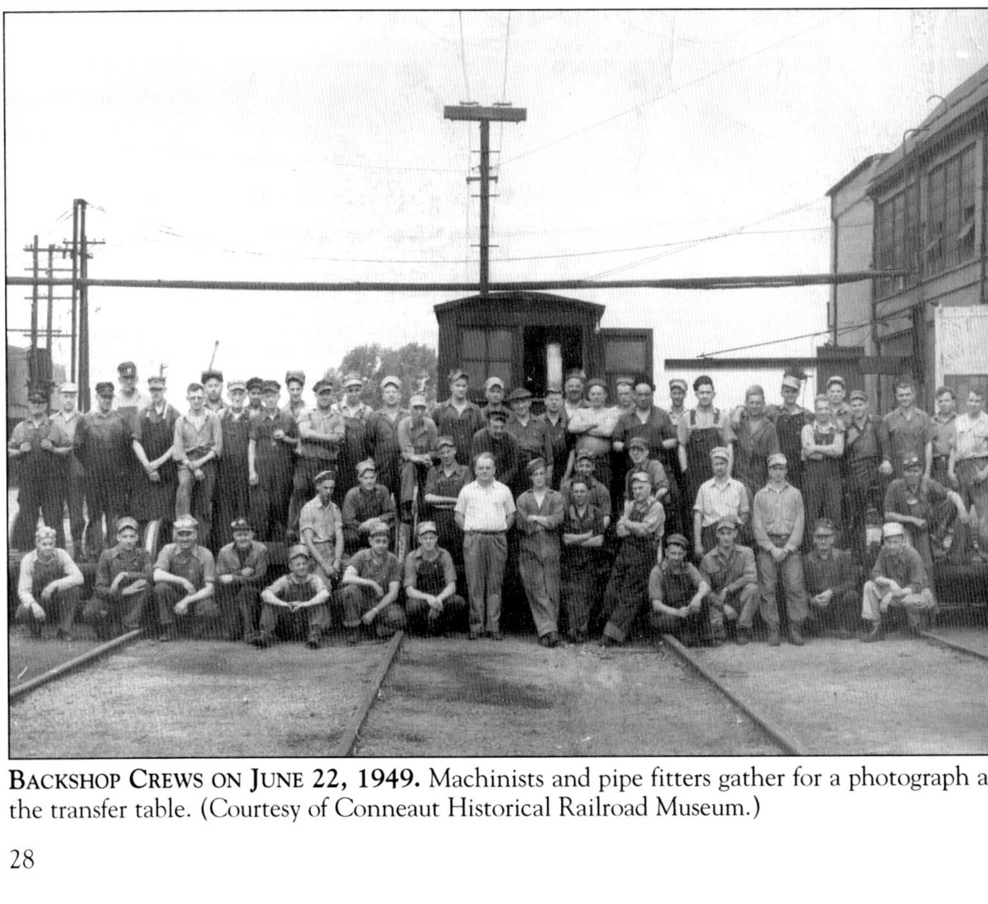

BACKSHOP CREWS ON JUNE 22, 1949. Machinists and pipe fitters gather for a photograph at the transfer table. (Courtesy of Conneaut Historical Railroad Museum.)

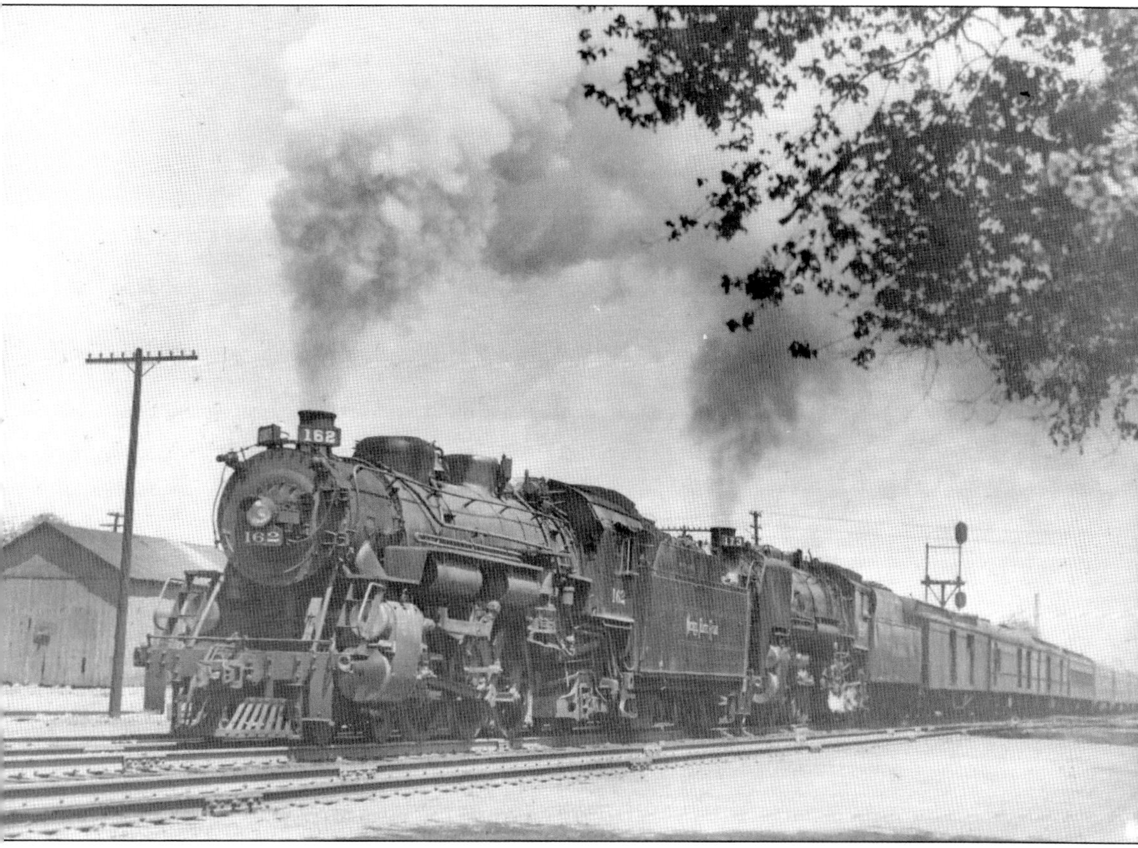

NICKEL PLATE PASSENGER TRAIN DOUBLEHEADED BY NOS. 162 AND 173, 1940. No. 162 was a 4-6-2 "Pacific" of class K-1a. Pacifics, which came in a wide variety of design variations, were the leading passenger puller in the first half of the century; in fact, nearly one-tenth of all steam locomotives ever built in America were 4-6-2s. There were six passenger trains per day on the NKP's single tracked Buffalo-Chicago line (parallel to the New York Central's great four-track boulevard) in the 1920s, and the ten-wheelers then in passenger use were having trouble coping with the increasing length of the trains. In 1922, the NKP ordered and received four K-1a Pacifics from the Lima Locomotive Works (followed by six similar K-1bs from Alco/Brooks the following year), and they did their job well for more than two decades. These magnificent passenger locomotives were quickly driven off the rails when diesels came onto the scene, and all ten of the NKP's Pacifics were scrapped between 1952 and 1954. (Courtesy of Conneaut Public Library.)

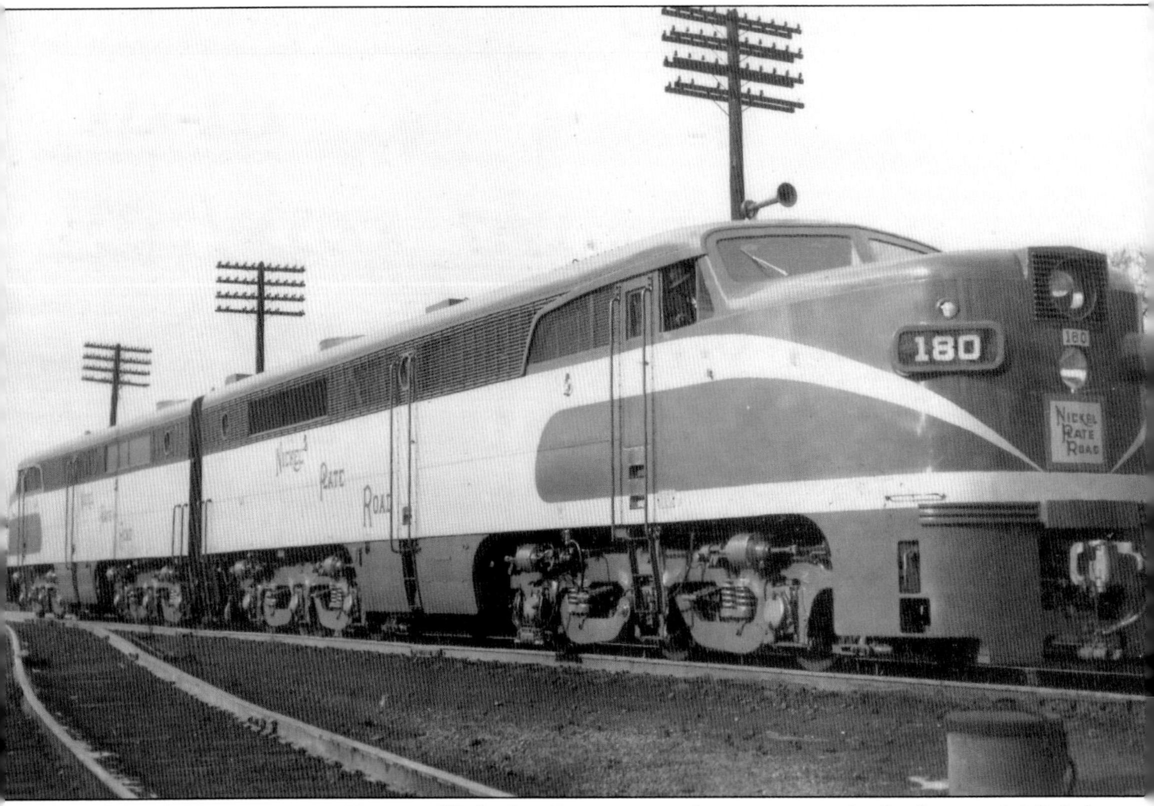

THE ARRIVAL OF THE DIESEL. With the Conneaut coaling tower in the background, Nickel Plate Nos. 180–181 are ready to make their maiden run with eastbound passenger train No. 6 on December 20, 1947. The PA1 model, one of the most recognizable examples of streamline design in the postwar American passenger train, was manufactured in Schenectady, New York by Alco. While all other NKP locomotives of that era were painted black, the PA1s sported a lively blue-and-white scheme and were nicknamed "Bluebirds." (Courtesy of Conneaut Historical Railroad Museum.)

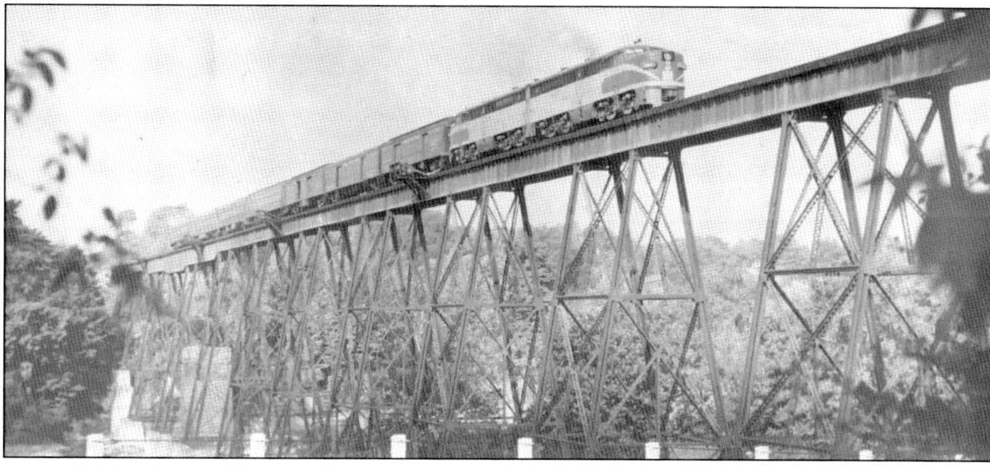

ALCO PA1S PULL A NICKEL PLATE PASSENGER TRAIN OVER CONNEAUT CREEK, C. 1950. Almost all of the PA1s were scrapped before the age of historic preservation, but the last two in existence were recently rescued in grievous condition from a scrap line in Mexico where they had been sold in 1978. One has been purchased by Conneaut-born restoration specialist Doyle McCormack. Although the unit was originally built as Santa Fe No. 62 and later ran on the Delaware & Hudson, McCormack (the son of a Nickel Plate employee) is restoring the diesel as NKP No. 190, the locomotive in which he took his first cab ride as a child. Updates on the restoration may be found on the Internet (www.nkp190.com). (Courtesy of Conneaut Public Library.)

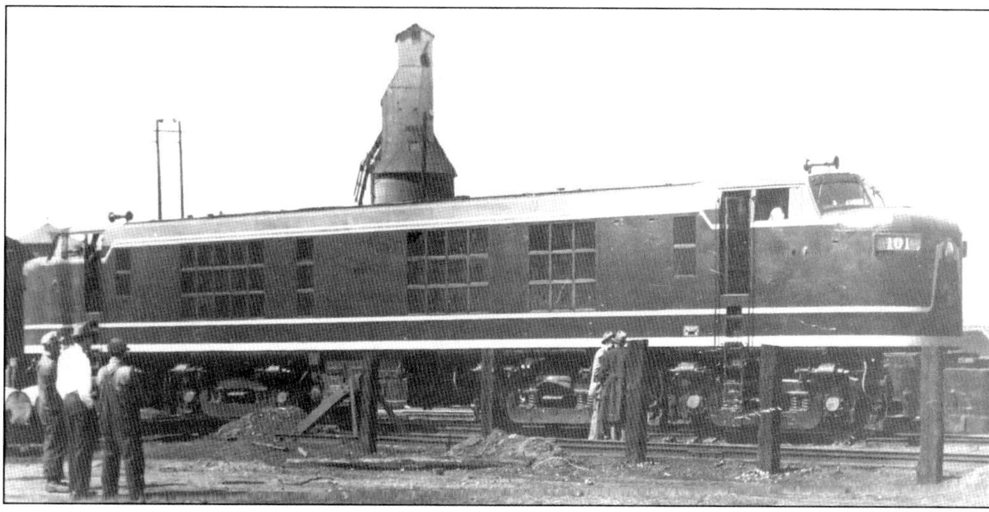

GENERAL ELECTRIC PROTOTYPE LOCOMOTIVE IN CONNEAUT. This unusual looking unit with cabs at each end was the GE 4500 Gas Turbine Electric Locomotive. Built in November 1948, No. 101 packed 4500 horsepower, but failed to attract the interest of either the Nickel Plate or the Pennsylvania Railroad while testing in 1948-49. It was repainted as Union Pacific No. 50 and tested there for nearly two years. After further testing on the Southern Pacific in 1951, No. 101 was returned to GE and scrapped in 1953. Union Pacific, the only railroad ever to use this technology in freight service, did purchase 55 gas turbine locomotives of up to 8500 hp each from 1952-61. Formidable haulers over the great distances of western mainlines, they fell out of favor because of their greedy fuel consumption and were retired in 1970. (Courtesy of Conneaut Historical Railroad Museum.)

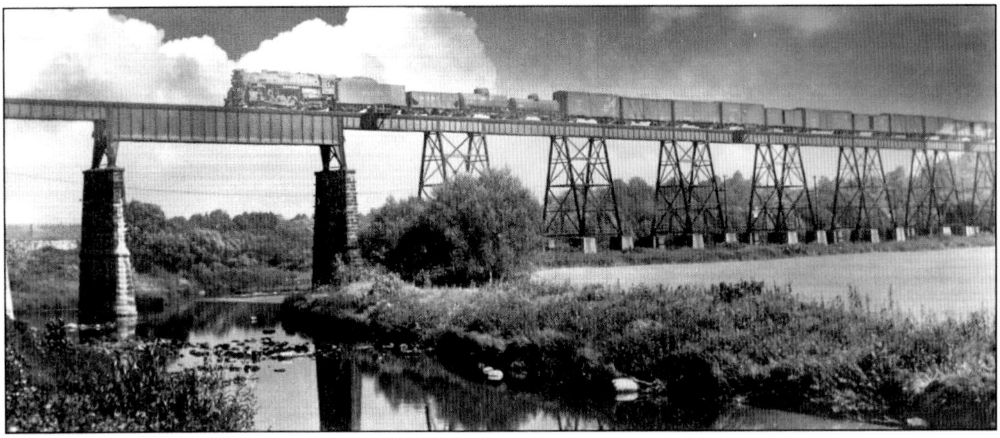

NKP S-2 No. 745 Crosses Over the Conneaut River with a Westbound Freight, September 28, 1946. Aside from No. 755 at the Conneaut Railroad Museum, five Nickel Plate Berkshires survive today, including No. 757 at the Railroad Museum of Pennsylvania; 759 at Scranton, Pennsylvania; 763 in Roanoke, Virginia; 765 at Fort Wayne, Indiana; and 779 at Lincoln Park in Lima, Ohio. (Courtesy of Conneaut Historical Railroad Museum.)

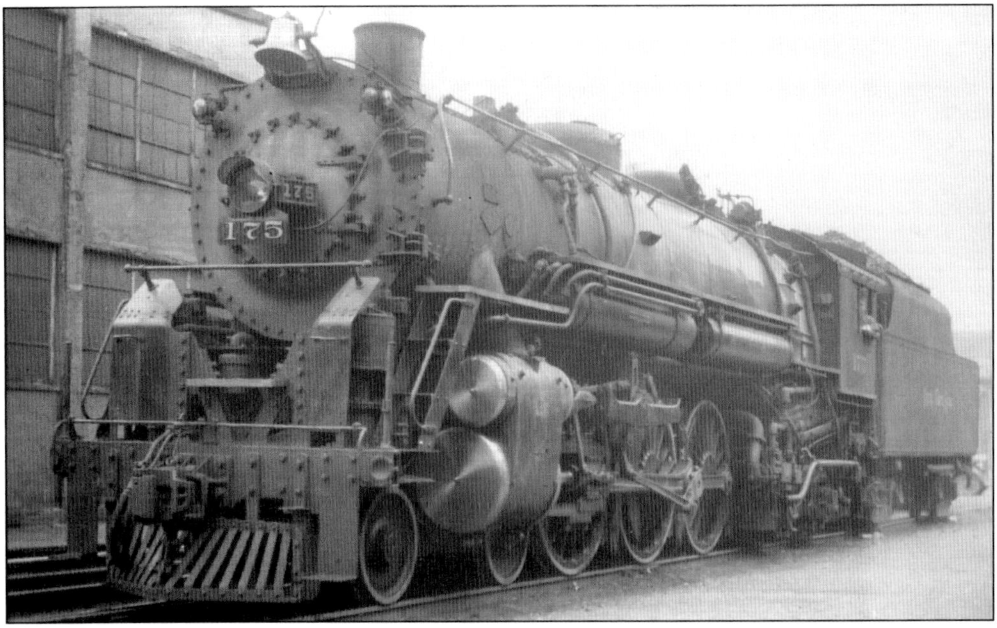

NKP No. 175 at Conneaut Shops, 1953. This locomotive was a 4-6-4 "Hudson" of class L-1b. Designed in the early 1920s by the New York Central and the American Locomotive Company to succeed the 4-6-2 Pacific, the Hudson had a four-wheel trailing truck to bear the weight of its larger firebox. They became the first-class passenger power on the Central, which ordered 275 of them from 1927-38. (The famous streamlined steam locomotives familiar from so many photographs of the *20th Century Limited* were class J-3a Hudsons.) The Nickel Plate, too, found the 4-6-4 to be a superb passenger hauler over level track. Its first four Hudsons were delivered from Alco immediately after the Central began testing its first model. The efficiency of diesels and the decline of the American passenger train reduced the need for these locomotives as the 1950s went on. The last Hudson to operate in the U. S. did so on the Nickel Plate in 1958. (Courtesy of Conneaut Area Historical Society.)

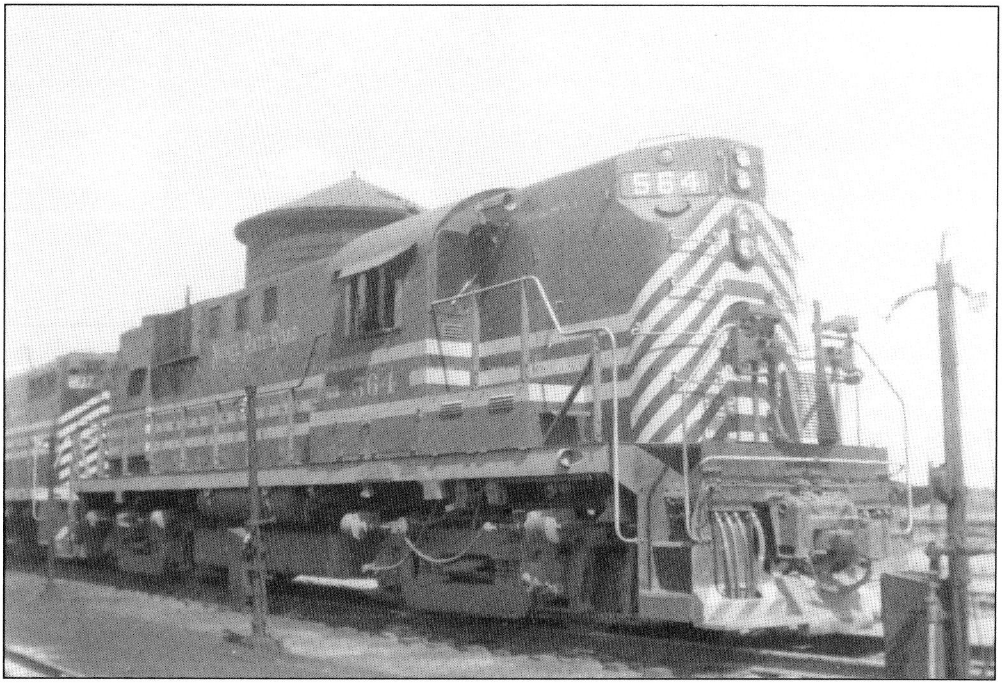

HOOD DIESELS, C. 1958. By the late 1950s, the attractive streamlined cab units, or "covered wagons" like the Alco PA1, were being superseded by utilitarian road switchers such as No. 564, an Alco RS11. (Courtesy of Conneaut Public Library.)

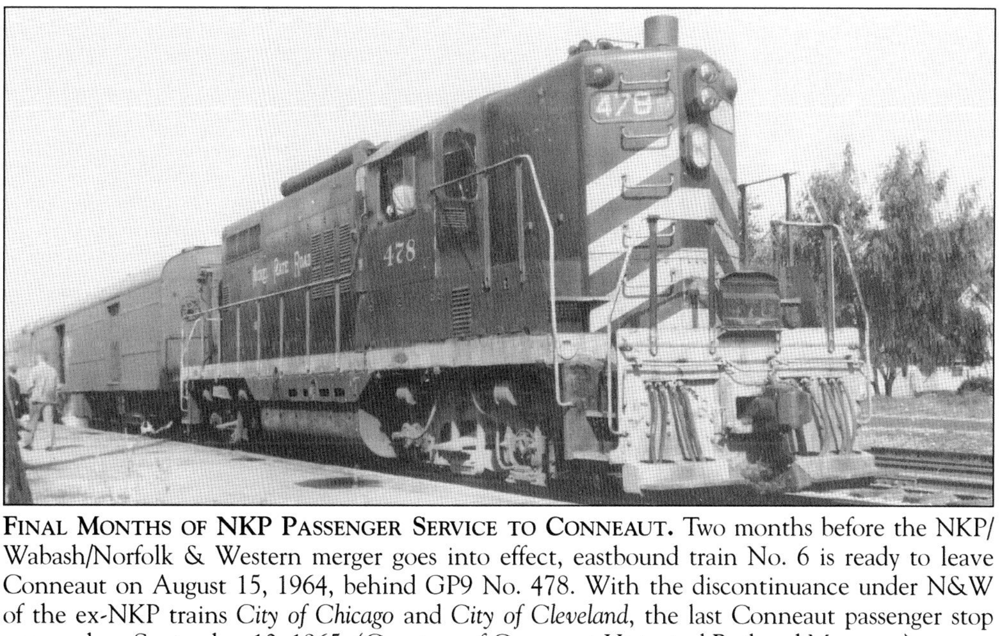

FINAL MONTHS OF NKP PASSENGER SERVICE TO CONNEAUT. Two months before the NKP/Wabash/Norfolk & Western merger goes into effect, eastbound train No. 6 is ready to leave Conneaut on August 15, 1964, behind GP9 No. 478. With the discontinuance under N&W of the ex-NKP trains *City of Chicago* and *City of Cleveland*, the last Conneaut passenger stop occurred on September 10, 1965. (Courtesy of Conneaut Historical Railroad Museum.)

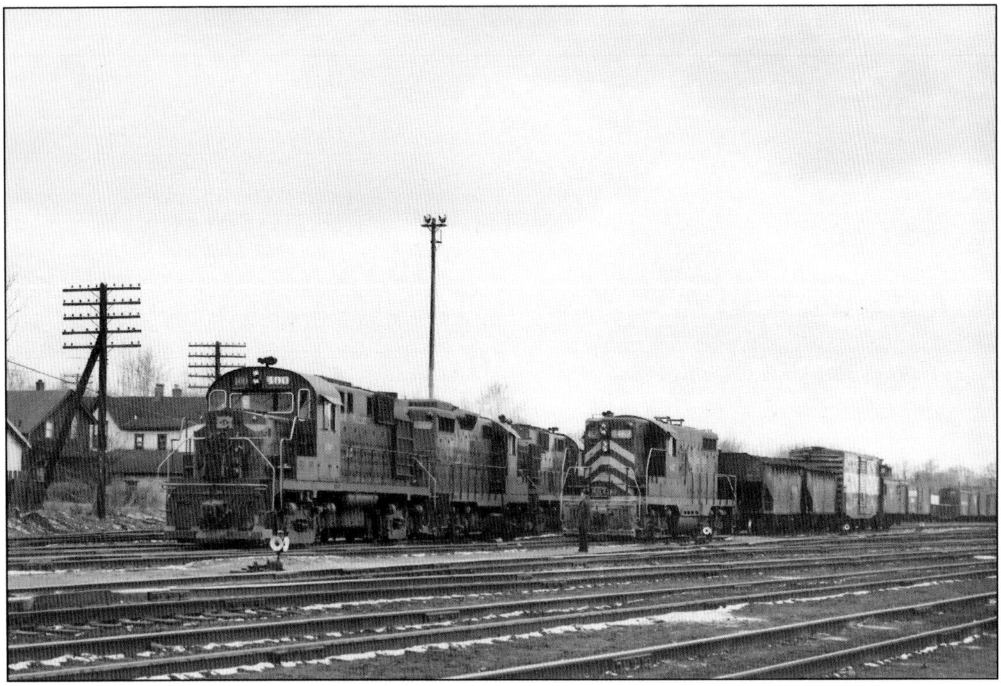

"Foreign Power" Invades the Nickel Plate, February 1964. Lehigh Valley Railroad diesels led by low-nose Alco RS11 No. 400 (at left) are inspected by J. F. Davin, Road Foreman of Engineers. Due to an agreement with the Lehigh Valley to share service between Fort Wayne, Indiana and Sayre, Pennsylvania, Lehigh Valley motive power began running over NKP rails in early 1964. (Courtesy of Conneaut Historical Railroad Museum.)

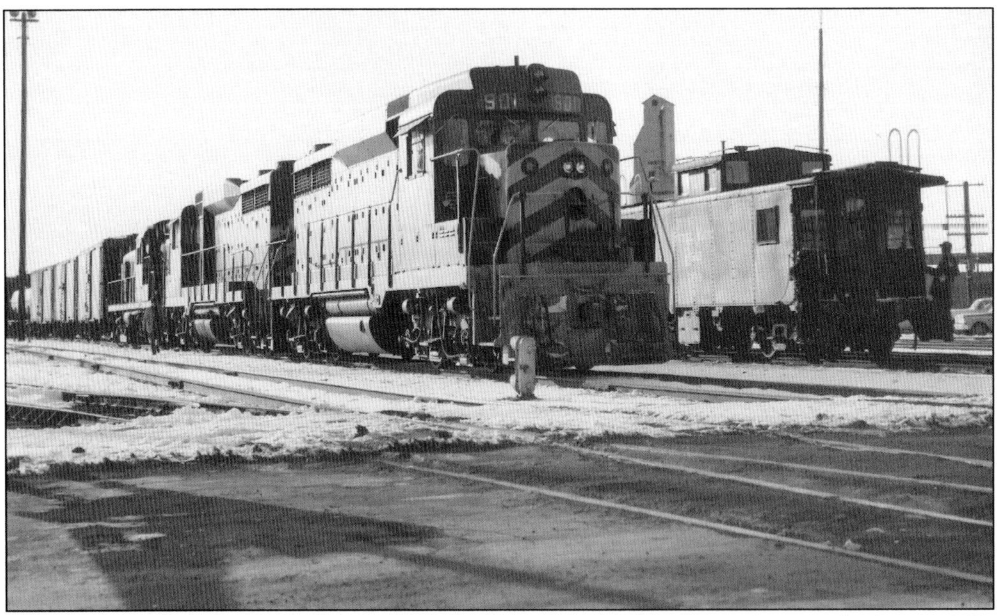

Road Switchers at Conneaut Yard in 1964. No. 901, a GP30, was built in 1962. (Courtesy of Conneaut Historical Railroad Museum.)

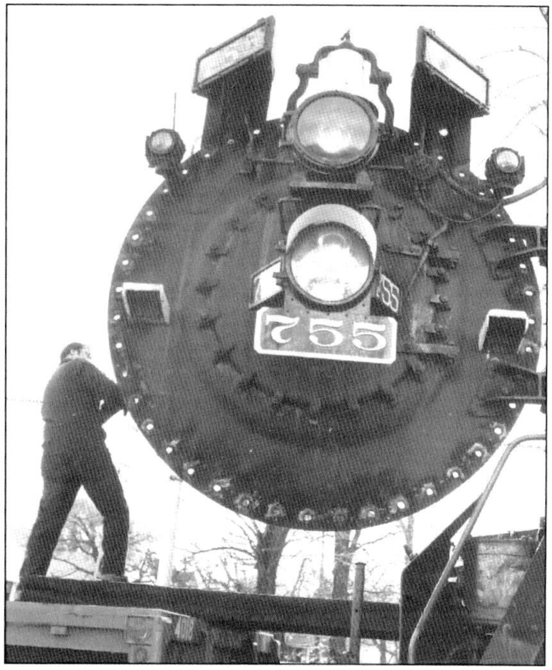

Stealing Parts. The front end of NKP S-2 class Berkshire No. 755, on stationary display at the Conneaut Historical Railroad Museum, is being opened up for the removal of superheater units. These would be installed in sister locomotive No. 759, which is bound for Steamtown in Pennsylvania (see next page). Both units were built in 1944 and retired in August 1960. (Courtesy of Conneaut Historical Railroad Museum.)

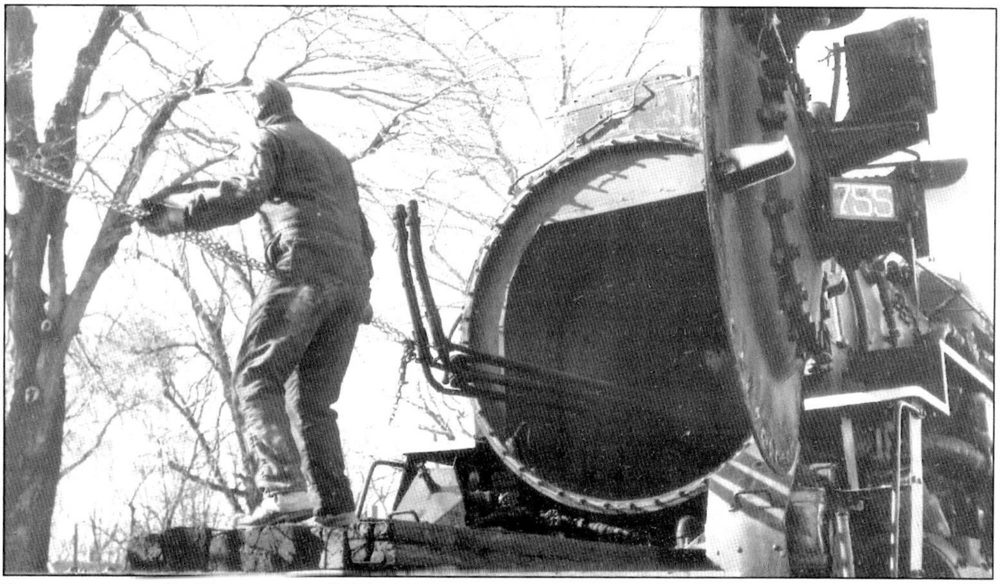

Superheater Destined for NKP 759. In October 1962, F. Nelson Blount, the owner of Steamtown USA in Bellows Falls, Vermont, acquired No. 759. The locomotive was restored to operable condition in the mid-1960s by Ross Rowland Jr., president of the High Iron Company, a group devoted to the promotion of mainline steam excursions. Seeking to mark the hundredth anniversary of the 1869 completion of the first transcontinental railroad at Promontory, Utah with a long-distance steam excursion train, Blount secured the loan of No. 759 from Steamtown in exchange for financial considerations. Norfolk & Western, which by now owned the property, arranged for Blount to lease the Conneaut roundhouse for the restoration of No. 759 to running condition. A photograph of 759 is on the next page. (Courtesy of Conneaut Historical Railroad Museum.)

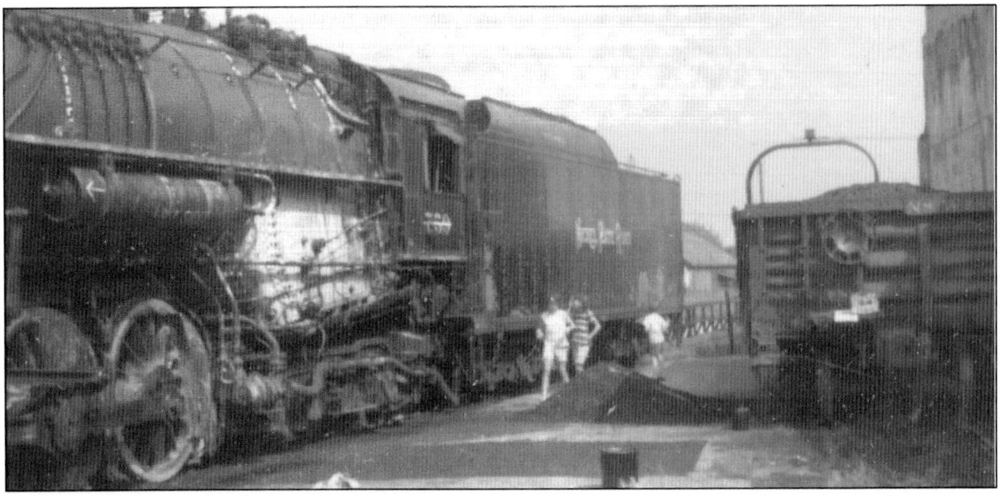

BERKSHIRE NO. 759 RUNS FOR THE FIRST TIME IN EIGHT YEARS, CONNEAUT RAILROAD MUSEUM, AUGUST 18, 1968. With much festivity, she headed for Buffalo on August 30th, pulling 15 passenger cars. No. 759 did indeed haul Blount's *Gold Spike Special* from New York City to Kansas City in May 1969, handing the train off to Union Pacific locomotives for the run to Utah. After running excursions throughout the northeast for Steamtown and other organizations in the early 1970s, No. 759 was left in the Delaware and Hudson roundhouse at Rouses Point, New York where she was unfortunately left out for the winter still full of fluids. The resulting damage from burst pipes and valves left No. 759 in an inoperable condition. She was restored at Steamtown in 1975, but it was found that more extensive repairs would be required for another mainline run, and the collapse of funding left her dead in the stall. Today she can still be restored, but a full overhaul including flues will be necessary. (Courtesy of Conneaut Historical Railroad Museum.)

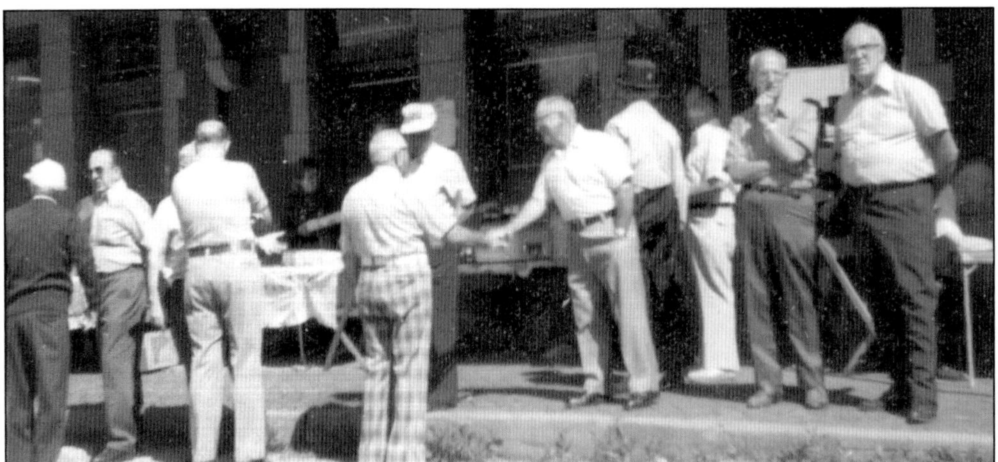

NICKEL PLATE DAY AT THE CONNEAUT HISTORICAL RAILROAD MUSEUM, 1975. The museum occupies the old New York Central depot, built in 1900 and kept in superb condition today by a dedicated group of volunteers. Dedicated on May 19, 1966, the museum houses a wide variety of interesting displays, scale models in all gauges, rare photographs, lanterns, timetables, baggage and mail carts, and a large HO scale model train layout. The biggest attraction (literally), the well-preserved Nickel Plate Berkshire locomotive No. 755 donated by the NKP in 1964, is absolutely fascinating to children. (Courtesy of Conneaut Historical Railroad Museum.)

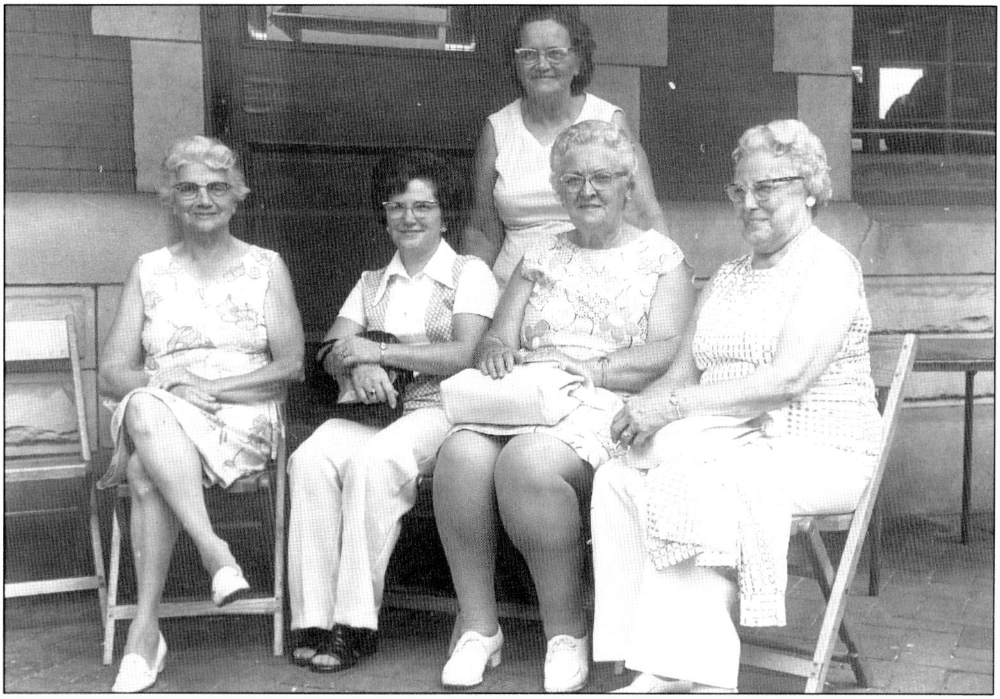

Women Who Worked on the Nickel Plate. Retired NKP employees gather at the Conneaut Railroad Museum on July 20, 1977. Pictured from left to right are telegraph operator Mrs. James McGuinn, electrician Mrs. James Schmitz, engineer Mrs. Carlton Gee, signals supervisor Pat (Mrs. Lawton) Schmitz, and Mrs. Charles Yarnell, whose husband was superintendent. (Courtesy of Conneaut Historical Railroad Museum.)

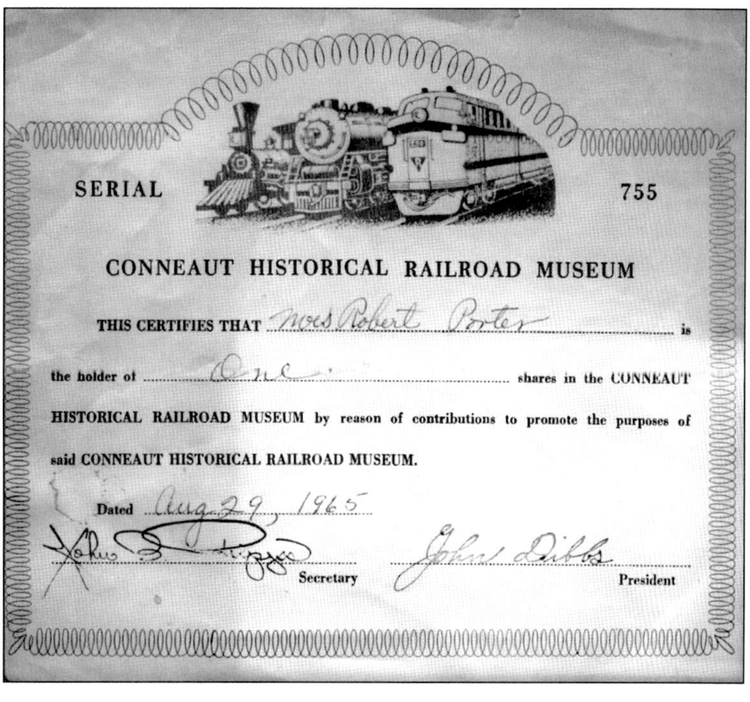

SERIAL 755

CONNEAUT HISTORICAL RAILROAD MUSEUM

THIS CERTIFIES THAT Mrs Robert Porter is

the holder of One shares in the CONNEAUT HISTORICAL RAILROAD MUSEUM by reason of contributions to promote the purposes of said CONNEAUT HISTORICAL RAILROAD MUSEUM.

Dated Aug 29, 1965

Secretary

John Dibbs
President

CHRS Share Certificate, 1965. Authenticity is added by the signature of John Dibbs, the president of the Nickel Plate Road. "Serial 755" refers to No. 755, the Berkshire steam locomotive that the NKP donated to the Museum and which is still proudly displayed on the grounds today. (Courtesy of Conneaut Historical Railroad Museum.)

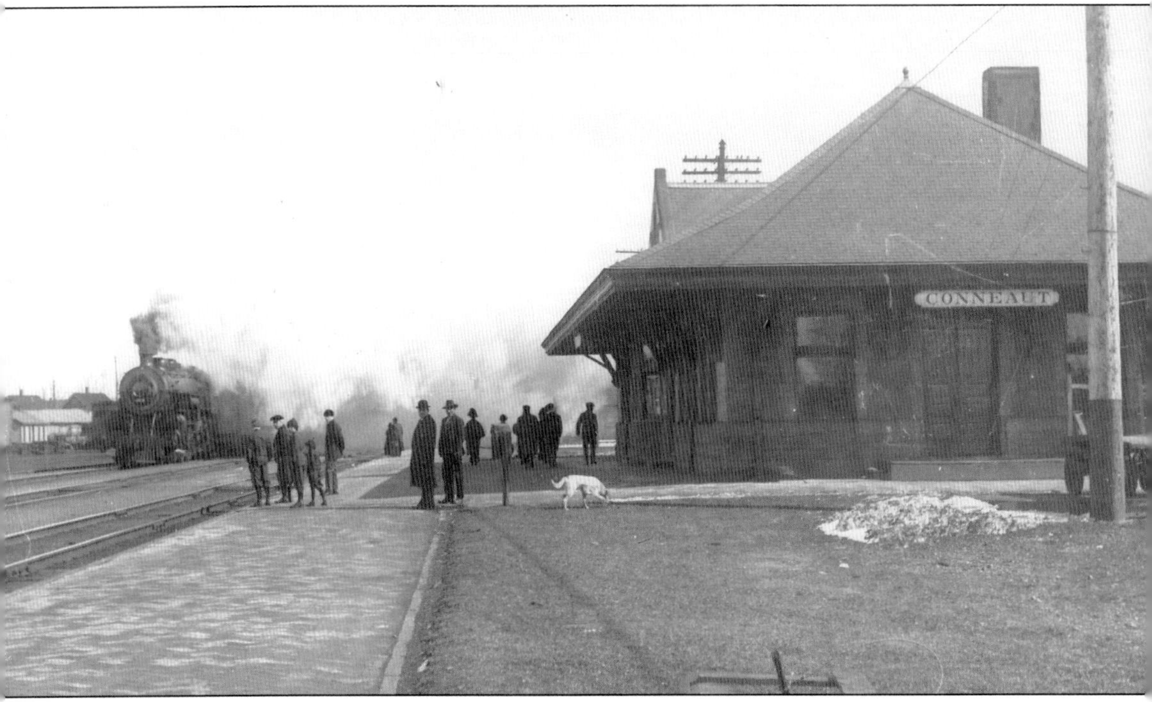

A Passenger Train Stops at the New York Central Depot in 1915. (Courtesy of Conneaut Historical Railroad Museum.)

Two

THE NEW YORK CENTRAL

In Conneaut, the New York Central Railroad was always "just passing through." Unlike the Bessemer or the Nickel Plate, both of which had major local facilities and numerous employees in town, the Central merely stopped there. Conneaut was located along the four-track Water Level Route, the venue of high-speed trains such as the famed *20th Century Limited*, traveling on a nearly gradeless line that followed the Hudson River northward from New York for many miles before turning west toward Chicago, thus avoiding the mountains that the rival Pennsylvania Railroad was forced to scale with its more direct route. In the first half of the twentieth century, many New York Central passenger trains stopped at the Conneaut depot, long coal and ore trains passed through en route to or from the Ashtabula docks, and fast freights roared by as they continue to do today on CSX.

The western portion of this mainline had been cobbled together from several smaller railroads. The main components were the Chicago-Toledo route of the Michigan Southern and Northern Indiana Railroad Company, the connection from Toledo to Erie via the Lake Shore Railway Company, and finally the Buffalo and Erie Railroad Company. In two separate mergers in 1869, the Lake Shore & Michigan Southern Railway Company was formed, uniting all of the other railroads into one continuous main and presenting the almost irresistible prospect of one more merger to create a then unprecedented direct route from New York to Chicago. Almost immediately an effort to control the LS&MS was begun by Commodore Cornelius Vanderbilt, who already ran the New York Central & Hudson River Railroad. The Commodore died in 1877 just before this goal was fulfilled, but his son William saw the process through and later acquired the brand-new Nickel Plate—this putting great competitive pressure on the Pennsylvania Railroad.

In 1905, LS&MS equipment began to bear the famous New York Central Lines oval-shaped logo. A decade later, with the NKP sold off and antitrust considerations sidestepped, the old LS&MS line through Conneaut was officially part of the New York Central. In 1900 a grand new depot was built, and for the next 67 years, Conneaut would be witness to the bustle and excitement of a high density four-track mainline that was one of America's great arteries. On such a congested main, however, there were risks.

On March 27, 1953, a terrible collision occurred just east of Conneaut. At around 10:00 p.m., near the Pennsylvania Line at milepost 112, sections of pipe fell off of a gondola in an eastbound freight on Track 4. The heavy pipe broke rail and caused an obstruction on Track 1, where passenger train No. 5, the *Mohawk*, was bearing down. As the eastbound freight cleared the scene with its crew unaware of the accident, the *Mohawk* derailed and blocked Tracks 2 and 3. By unhappy chance, not one but two additional trains—No. 12 (the *Southwestern Limited*) and a westbound freight—roared in at that moment and were caught in a fearful smashup. The casualties were grievous: twenty-one dead and over 60 injured.

Rescue workers and the Red Cross were hindered by the remoteness of the wreck's location, as well as large crowds of spectators who blocked the roads with their vehicles. Meanwhile, all four tracks were fouled, and many trains had to be rerouted over the Nickel Plate while track crews began working to clear the wreck.

The great days of the New York Central were passing. A steep decline in passenger business would bring about the end of the *20th Century Limited* in 1967, and the Central itself would disappear the following year in a long-planned merger with the rival Pennsy. The Penn Central, failing to mesh two hostile workforces and sliding into bankruptcy by 1970, was an unmitigated disaster. Conrail, its federally created successor, achieved profitability in the 1980s. In the late 1990s Conrail was conquered and divided by CSX and Norfolk Southern, with CSX taking over the old Central route through Conneaut—by now slimmed down to two tracks.

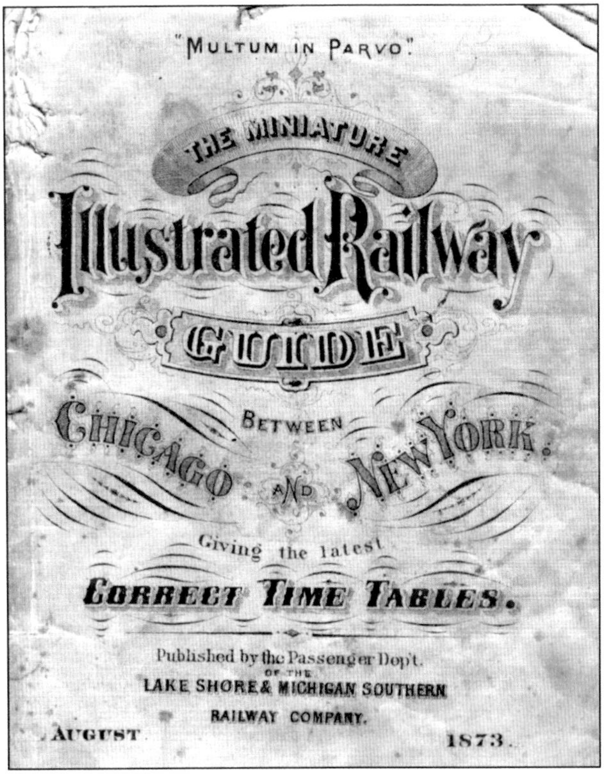

"MULTUM IN PARVO."

THE MINIATURE

Illustrated Railway

GUIDE

BETWEEN

CHICAGO AND NEW YORK.

Giving the latest

CORRECT TIME TABLES.

Published by the Passenger Dep't.
OF THE
LAKE SHORE & MICHIGAN SOUTHERN
RAILWAY COMPANY.

AUGUST 1873.

LAKE SHORE & MICHIGAN SOUTHERN TIMETABLE, 1873. The LS&MS was consolidated in 1869 from three existing railroads. It was purchased in September of that year by Commodore Cornelius Vanderbilt, owner of the New York Central & Hudson River Railroad, who nearly became the first railroad magnate to gain control of a continuous route between New York and Chicago. Vanderbilt died in 1877, but his son William would further the Commodore's efforts to dominate the entire region, purchasing controlling stock in the rival Nickel Plate in 1882, its first year of operation. (Courtesy of Conneaut Historical Railroad Museum.)

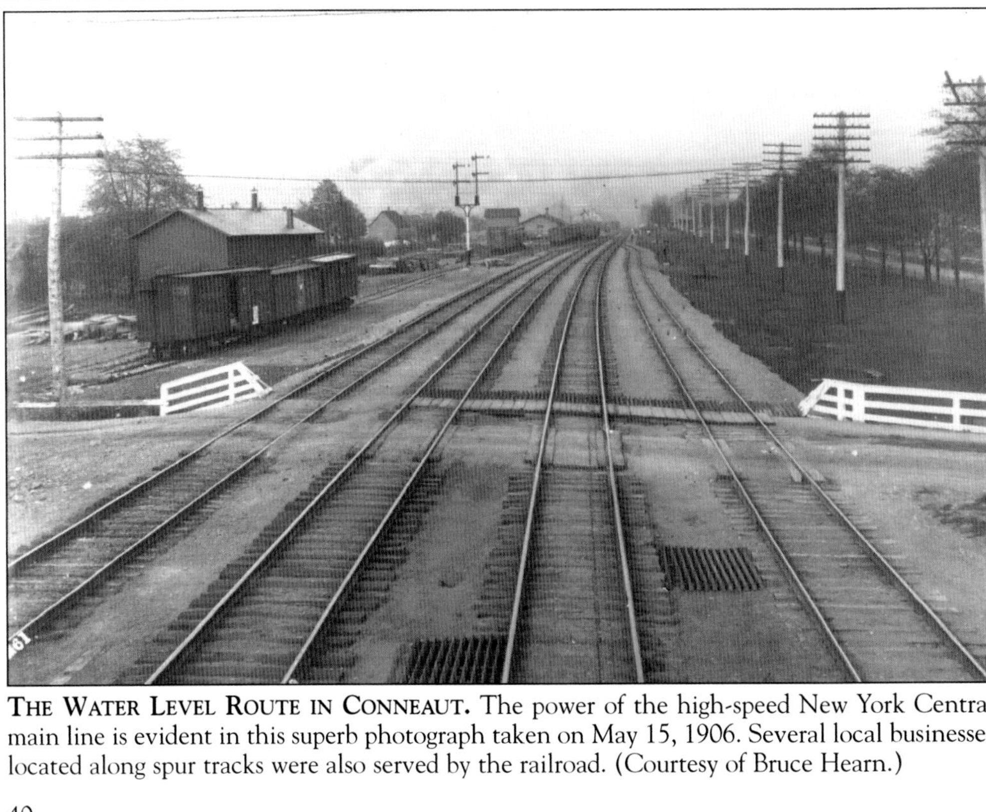

THE WATER LEVEL ROUTE IN CONNEAUT. The power of the high-speed New York Central main line is evident in this superb photograph taken on May 15, 1906. Several local businesses located along spur tracks were also served by the railroad. (Courtesy of Bruce Hearn.)

NEW YORK CENTRAL TIMETABLE. The great *20th Century Limited* made its first run—and its first "fly-by" at Conneaut—on June 15, 1902. Running daily at high speeds between New York and Chicago, offering every luxury and frequented by the rich and famous, it was the premiere passenger train in America. (Courtesy of Conneaut Historical Railroad Museum.)

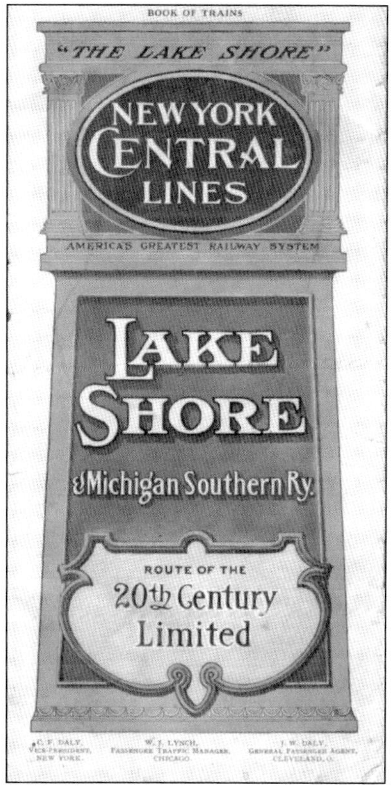

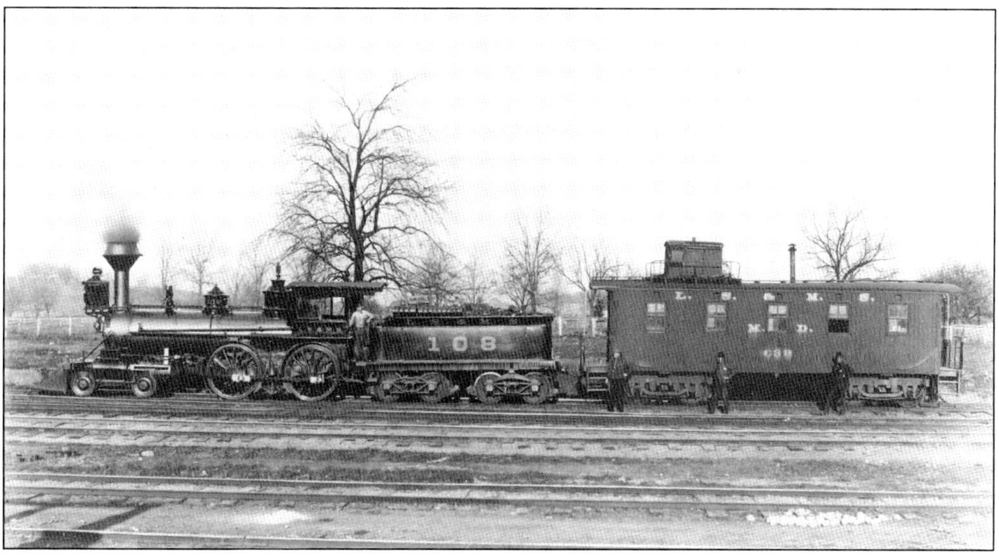

LAKE SHORE & MICHIGAN SOUTHERN NO. 108. The 4-4-0 "American" locomotive was a popular freight and passenger workhorse in the early years of all three of Conneaut's railroads. Fancier in design than most other locomotives, 4-4-0s were soon surpassed by more powerful models. (Courtesy of Conneaut Historical Railroad Museum.)

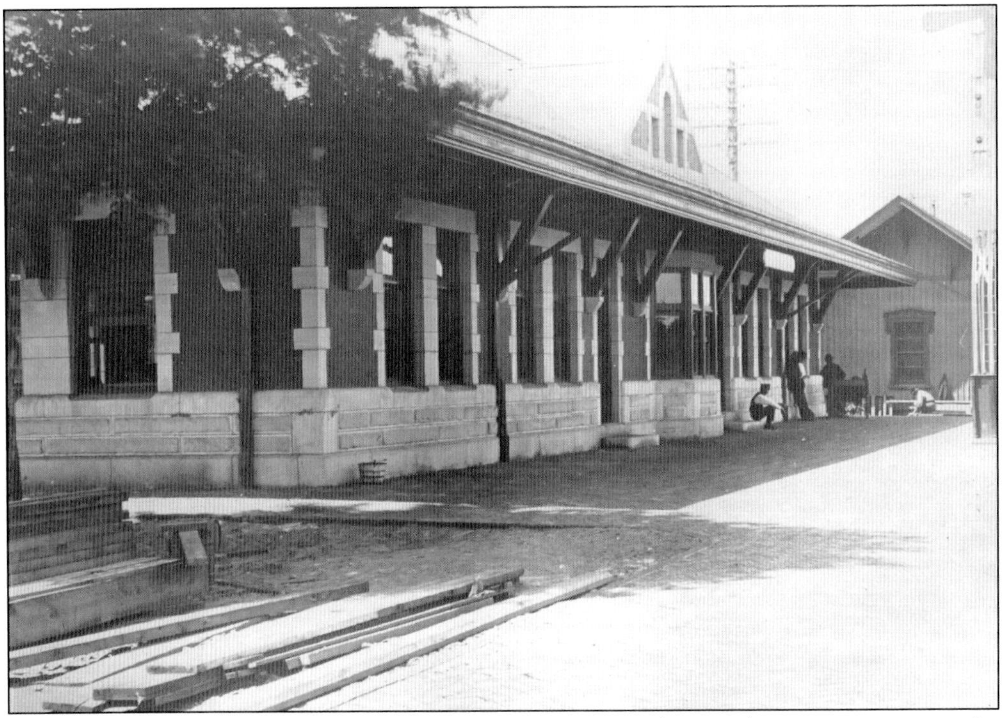

LS&MS Depot Under Construction, 1900. Its wooden predecessor is seen in the background here and on the right side in the photograph below. (Courtesy of Conneaut Historical Railroad Museum.)

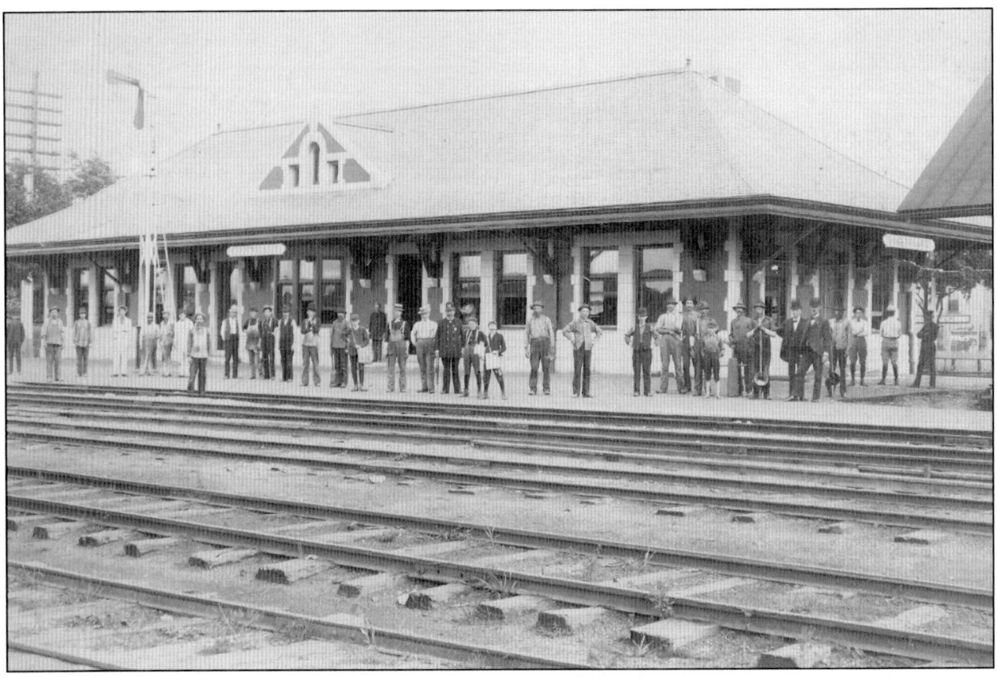

Passengers Wait at the Depot. Passenger trains, both local and express, were very frequent in the early decades of the twentieth century. (Courtesy of Conneaut Historical Railroad Museum.)

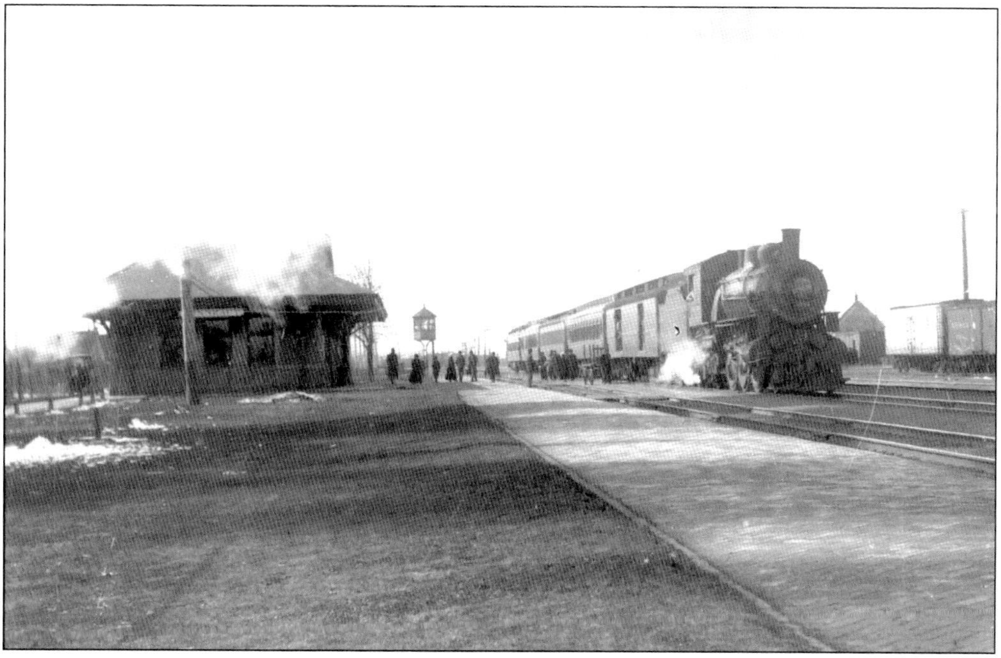

New York Central Train at the Depot in 1915. The Central was advised by the Justice Department in 1914 that since it had now absorbed the Lake Shore & Michigan Southern, it held the reins of too many railroads operating between Buffalo and Chicago. The Nickel Plate was thus sold off by the NYC on July 3, 1916. (Courtesy of Conneaut Historical Railroad Museum.)

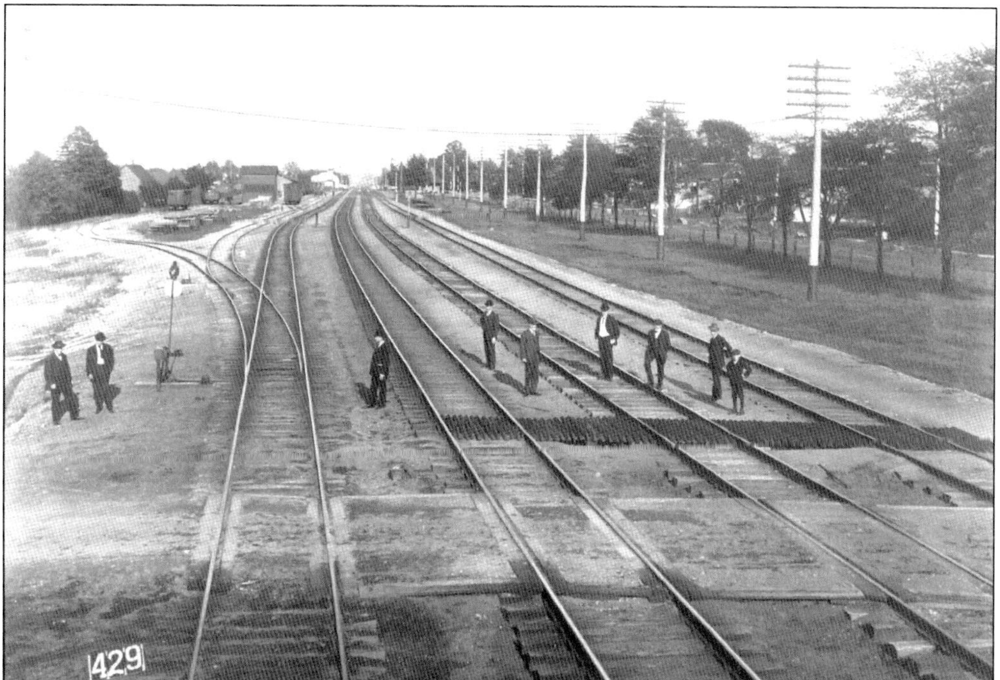

Inspecting the Four-Track Main Line, September 12, 1907. Another superb image of the superhighway along which the Great Steel Fleet traveled. (Courtesy of Bruce Hearn.)

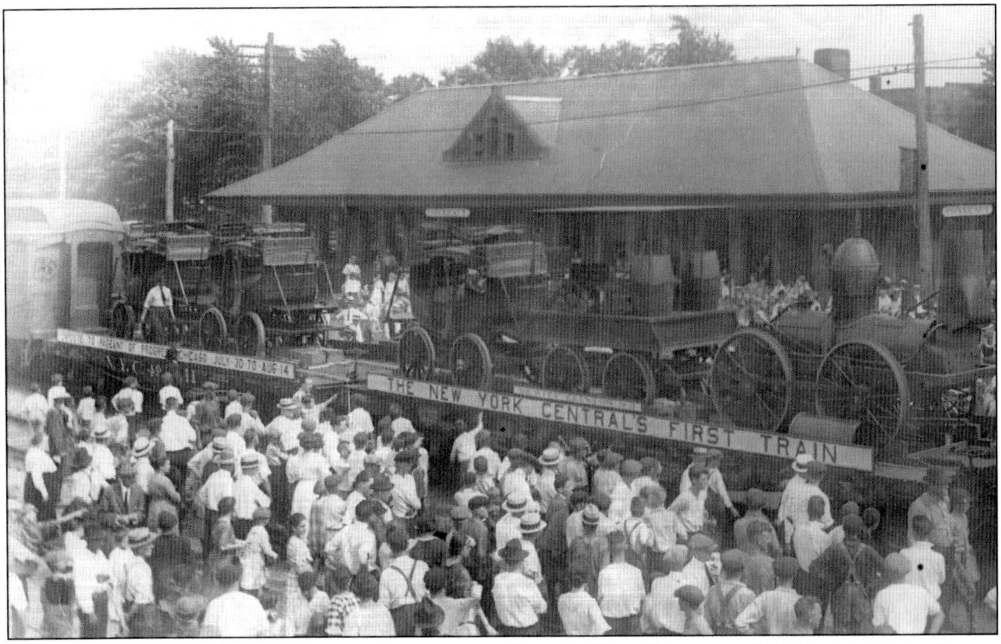

A Historic Locomotive Visits Conneaut. The *DeWitt Clinton*, an 0-4-0 with 54-inch cast iron drivers, was one of the great steam locomotives in the annals of American railroading. Among the first to be manufactured in America instead of England, the *DeWitt Clinton* was built by the West Point Foundry. When she entered service on the Mohawk & Hudson Railroad on August 9, 1831, it was the first locomotive to pull a passenger train in the state of New York. At the time of this photograph, taken at the New York Central depot in 1921, the locomotive was en route to the "Pageant of Progress" in Chicago, the first of the great exhibitions on that city's Navy Pier. More than a million visitors saw the *DeWitt Clinton* there. (Courtesy of Conneaut Historical Railroad Museum.)

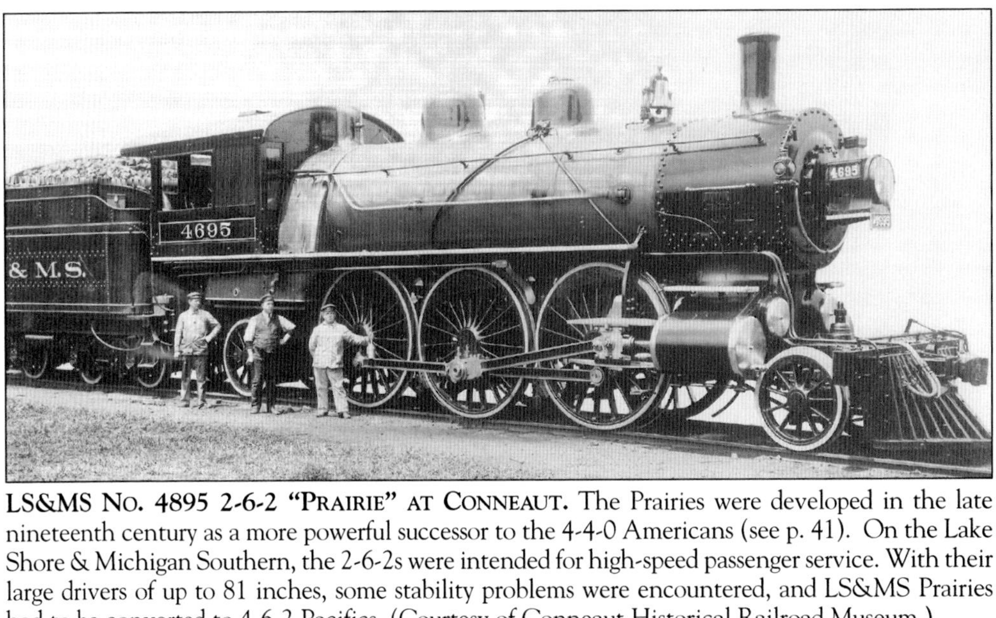

LS&MS No. 4895 2-6-2 "Prairie" at Conneaut. The Prairies were developed in the late nineteenth century as a more powerful successor to the 4-4-0 Americans (see p. 41). On the Lake Shore & Michigan Southern, the 2-6-2s were intended for high-speed passenger service. With their large drivers of up to 81 inches, some stability problems were encountered, and LS&MS Prairies had to be converted to 4-6-2 Pacifics. (Courtesy of Conneaut Historical Railroad Museum.)

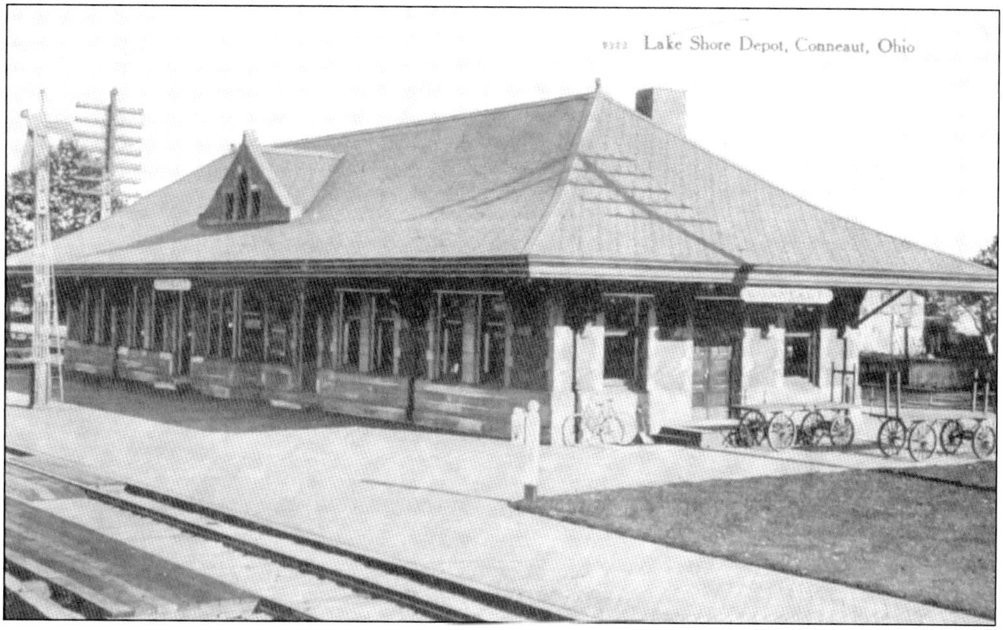

Two Classic Postcard Views of the Depot. The structure has been beautifully preserved as the home of the Conneaut Historical Railroad Museum. (Both courtesy of Conneaut Area Historical Society.)

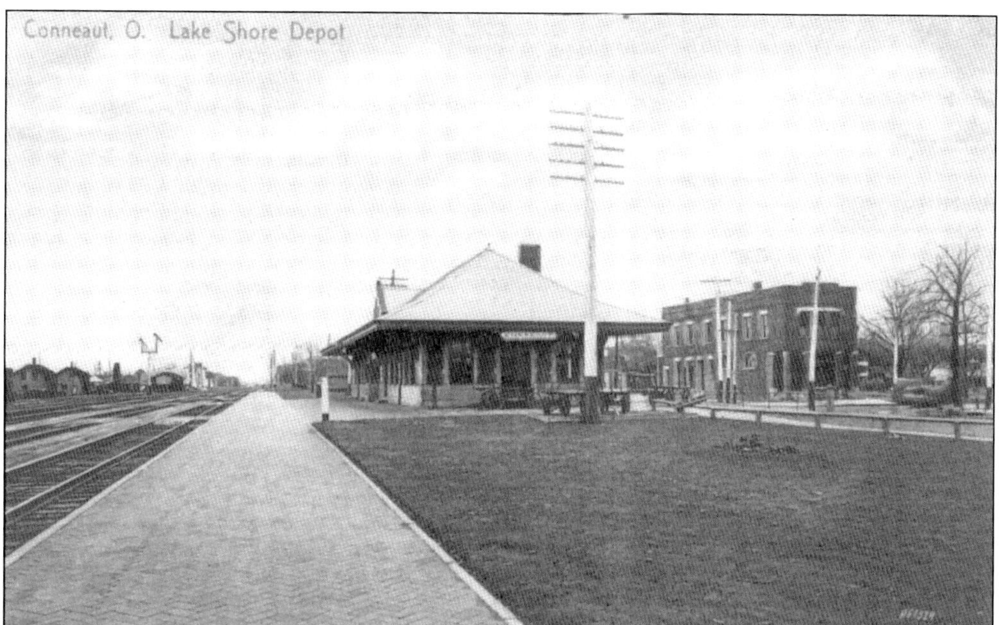

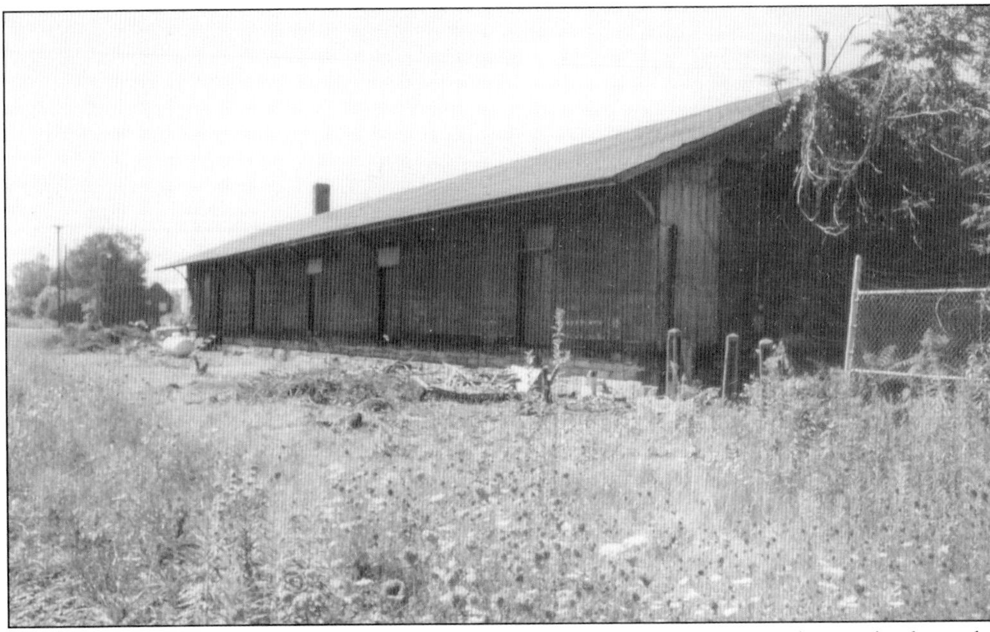

The Old Railway Express Agency Building. Built in 1873 across the tracks from the LS&MS depot, this building is now being refurbished to serve as the home of the Conneaut Area Historical Society. (Courtesy of Conneaut Area Historical Society.)

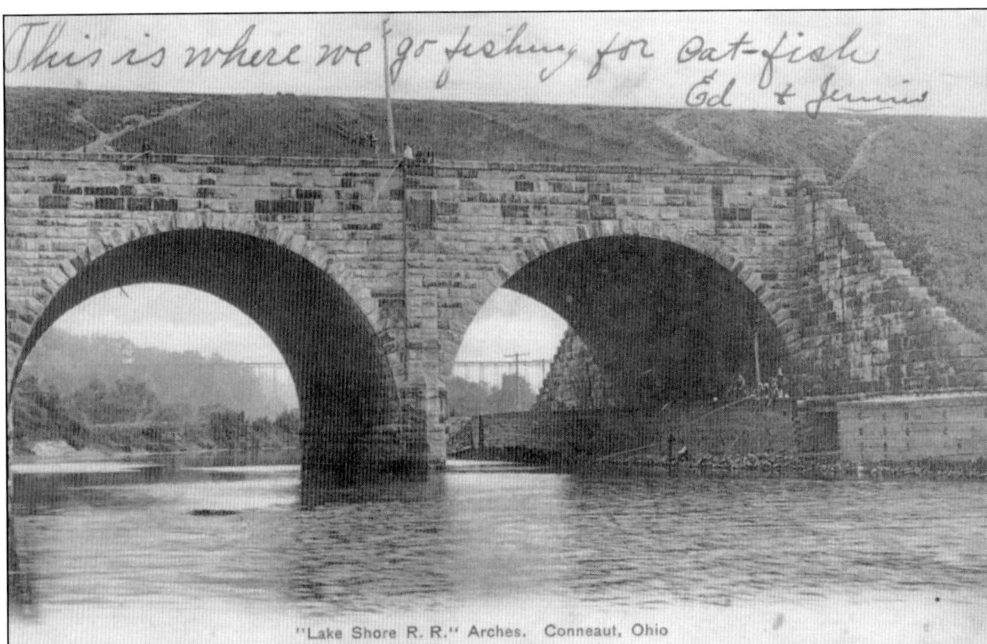

Lake Shore & Michigan Southern Stone Railroad Bridge. A fine view of the right-of-way of all three of Conneaut's great railroads. In this postcard photograph looking south, the old (pre-1930) Nickel Plate bridge is seen in the distance, and the Bessemer & Lake Erie track is on the right-hand bank. (Courtesy of Conneaut Area Historical Society.)

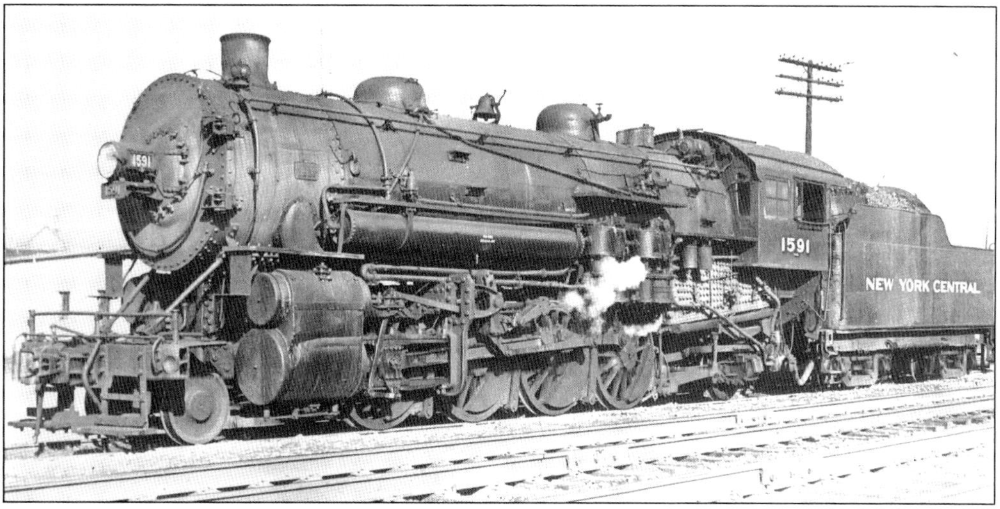

ONE OF THE NEW YORK CENTRAL "MIKADOS." On November 21, 1946, 2-8-2 No. 1591 (built as a class G5 2-8-0 at Brooks Locomotive Works of Dunkirk, New York in December 1905 and converted in October 1915) was photographed in Conneaut. At one time the Central had 1,350 Mikados in service on the entire system, including the 15 which were classified as H-5r, originally built for the Indiana Harbor Belt. With a starting tractive effort of 48,570 lbs., NYC Mikados were intended for mainline freight service, but most were displaced in that role by the 4-8-2 "Mohawks" (below). They hung on in the yards and on way freights or branch lines, and in fact the last steam locomotive to be retired by the New York Central was a 2-8-2. None, however, have been preserved. (Courtesy of Conneaut Historical Railroad Museum.)

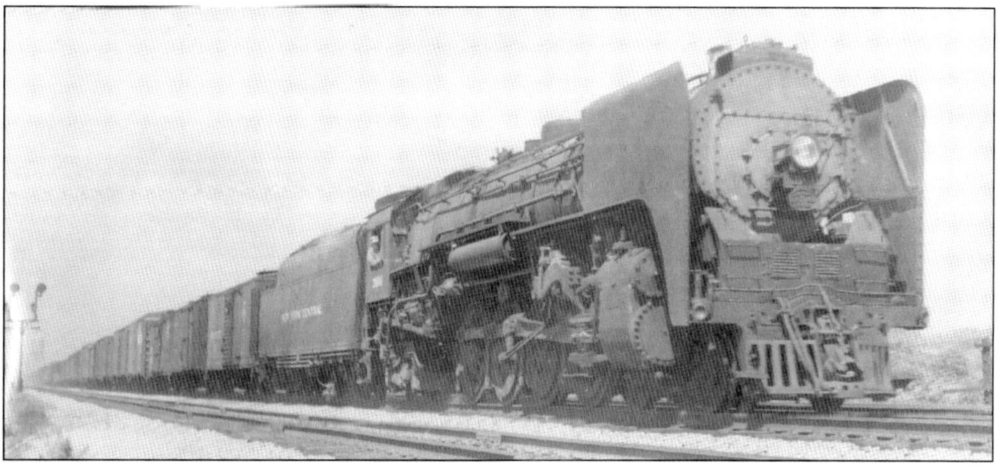

MOHAWK WITH AN EASTBOUND FREIGHT PASSING THROUGH CONNEAUT, JUNE 17, 1947. The 4-8-2 "Mountain," as its name suggests, was designed to conquer steep grades. Purchased by the Chesapeake & Ohio in 1911, it eliminated the need for doubleheading on heavy C&O passenger trains. Its design was altered for different railroads over the next few years, and the New York Central placed an order in 1916 for Mountains with enlarged drivers, bigger boilers, and greater power. By 1944, the Central had purchased 600 of the 4-8-2s, which it renamed "Mohawks." They were most often used on fast freights, as in this photograph. No. 3101 was one of 25 class L-4a Mohawks, built at Lima in 1942-43, that occasionally doubled as passenger power. (Courtesy of Conneaut Historical Railroad Museum.)

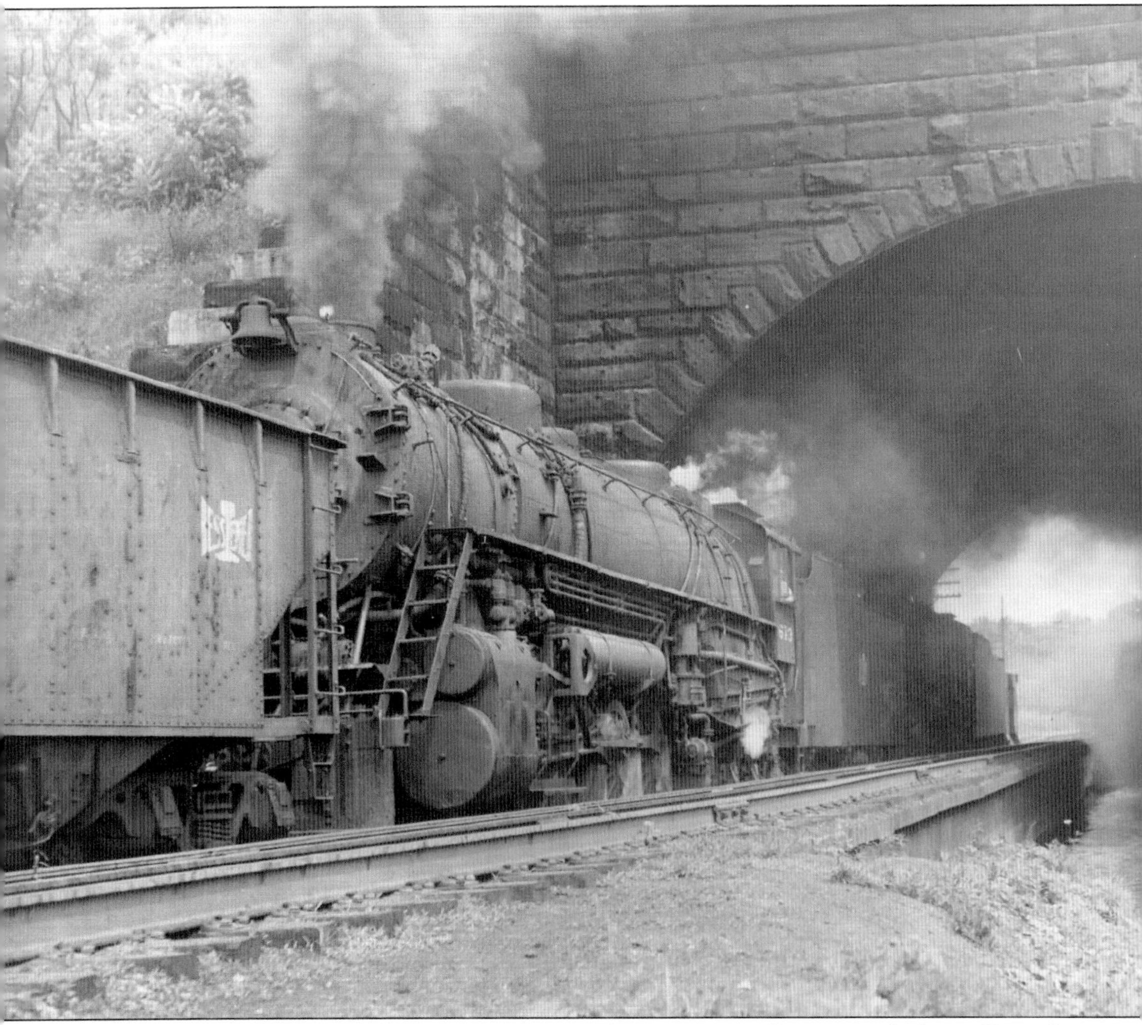

2-10-4 "TEXAS" TYPE LOCOMOTIVE WITH A SOUTHBOUND BESSEMER & LAKE ERIE ORE TRAIN, UNDER THE ARCHES OF THE NEW YORK CENTRAL BRIDGE. (Courtesy of Conneaut Historical Railroad Museum.)

Three

The Bessemer & Lake Erie in Conneaut Harbor

The Bessemer & Lake Erie Railroad ran north–south, in contrast to the east–west mainlines of the town's other two railroads. While the Nickel Plate brought boom times to Conneaut by building a division point roundhouse and servicing facility there, the Bessemer served an equally vital purpose in the city's economic development, connecting Conneaut Harbor with the steel mills of southwestern Pennsylvania. Conneaut was far behind neighboring Ashtabula in creating such a boat-to-rail connection; the first ore boat had called at Ashtabula Harbor in 1873 to transfer its load to freight cars of the new Pittsburgh, Youngstown & Ashtabula Railroad. Conneaut would have to wait nearly two more decades for a coal carrier to reach it. An attempt in 1889 by the Nickel Plate Road to build a dock in the harbor came to nothing.

Suitable for use only by smaller boats in the early nineteenth century, Conneaut's harbor underwent a series of enlargements. As the Pittsburgh, Shenango and Lake Erie Railroad (the predecessor of the B&LE) began to lay tracks from Albion, Pennsylvania to Conneaut in 1891, it was also improving the piers and dredging the harbor deeper with funds appropriated by the U. S. Congress in anticipation of the big boats' arrival. The Bear Creek Railroad (founded in 1865 and later called the Shenango and Allegheny Railroad Company) had grown steadily from its inception as a 21-mile short line, and on August 15, 1892, the renamed Pittsburgh, Shenango & Lake Erie reached the port of Conneaut. The first ore boat to unload there was the steamer *Charles J. Kershaw*, on November 6, which brought more than 1100 tons of red Mesabi iron ore. The *Kershaw* was followed soon afterward by two other vessels, and on November 18, the Conneaut Terminal Railroad Company was formed to oversee construction of all of the trackage, buildings, and infrastructure needed to meet the demands of the coming ore trade. It was soon leased and operated by the PS&LE, and in 1893, it became part of the railroad.

In 1894, an idea was put forth to send PS&LE freight cars across Lake Erie on carferries to interchange with the Grand Trunk Railway in Port Dover, Ontario. In July of the following year, the United States and Ontario Steam Navigation Company was formed by the railroad to move the carferry concept forward, and on August 22, the service was begun. Carferries with their heavy and unstable loads were inherently very dangerous to operate, but the Conneaut fleet had special misfortune. One of the boats was destroyed by fire at Conneaut in 1904, and the *Marquette & Bessemer No. 2* was tragically and mysteriously lost (as described on p. 67). The carferry service ended in August 1932.

Soon the entire operation came to the attention of Andrew Carnegie, who built the Butler and Pittsburgh line to connect the PS&LE to his steel mills and in 1897, merged the two into the Pittsburg, Bessemer & Lake Erie. Four years later, the railroad (now incorporated as the Bessemer & Lake Erie) was sold to U. S. Steel. The Bessemer & Lake Erie name has lasted for more than a century, unlike Conneaut's other major railroads that disappeared during a series of large mergers in the 1960s. In 2001, the B&LE was acquired by Great Lakes Transportation, which was recntly bought in turn by Canadian National.

Over the decades, as the ore trade approached its peak, the railroad purchased ever more powerful locomotives to haul trains that grew to a mile in length. Photographs of many of these are seen here. The story of the Bessemer & Lake Erie in Conneaut is also, of course, the story of a harbor filled with a fascinating array of specialized machinery designed to speed the transfer of ore, gravel, and coal between boats and rail cars. Thus, images of boats and docks, as well as lighthouses and other maritime elements, are included.

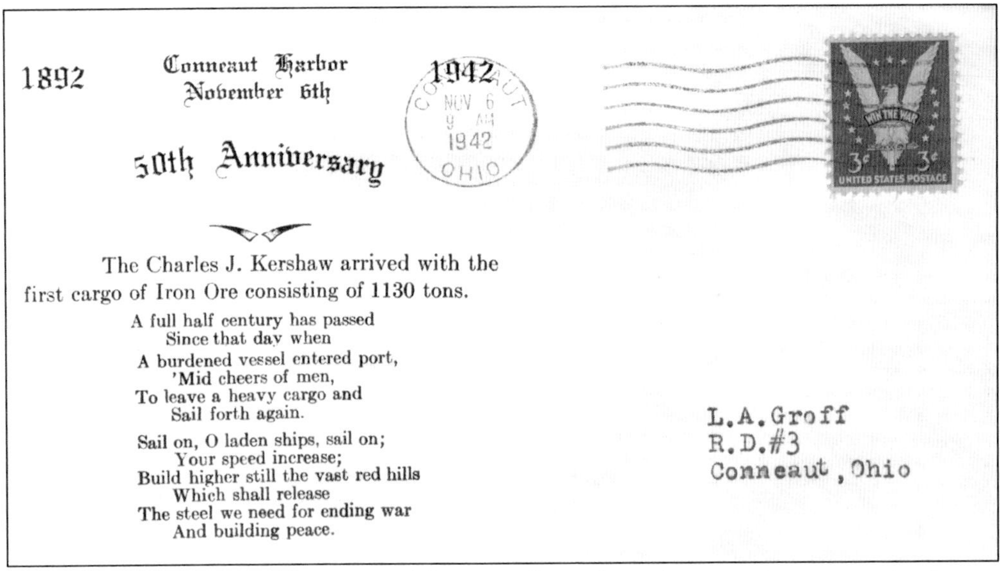

THE ORE BOAT ERA BEGINS IN THE HARBOR. Once the rail connection was made, the ore and coal shipping business began to grow in leaps and bounds. (Courtesy of Conneaut Area Historical Society.)

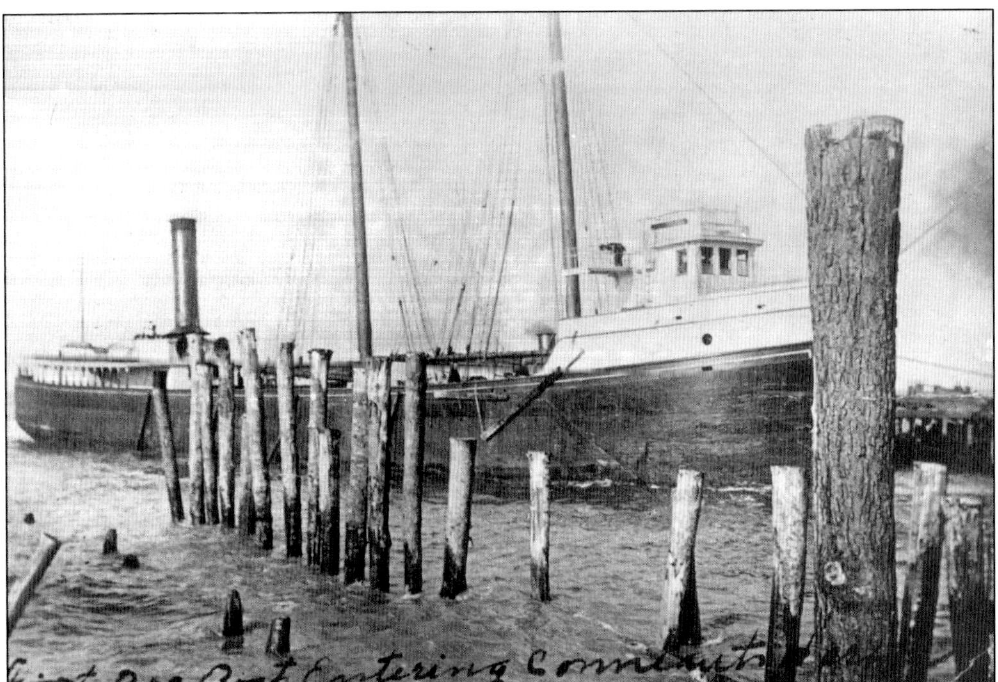

THE CHARLES J. KERSHAW ENTERING PORT FOR THE FIRST TIME, NOVEMBER 6, 1892. In those days, shovels and wheelbarrows were the means by which ore was transferred to railway hoppers. (Courtesy of Conneaut Historical Railroad Museum.)

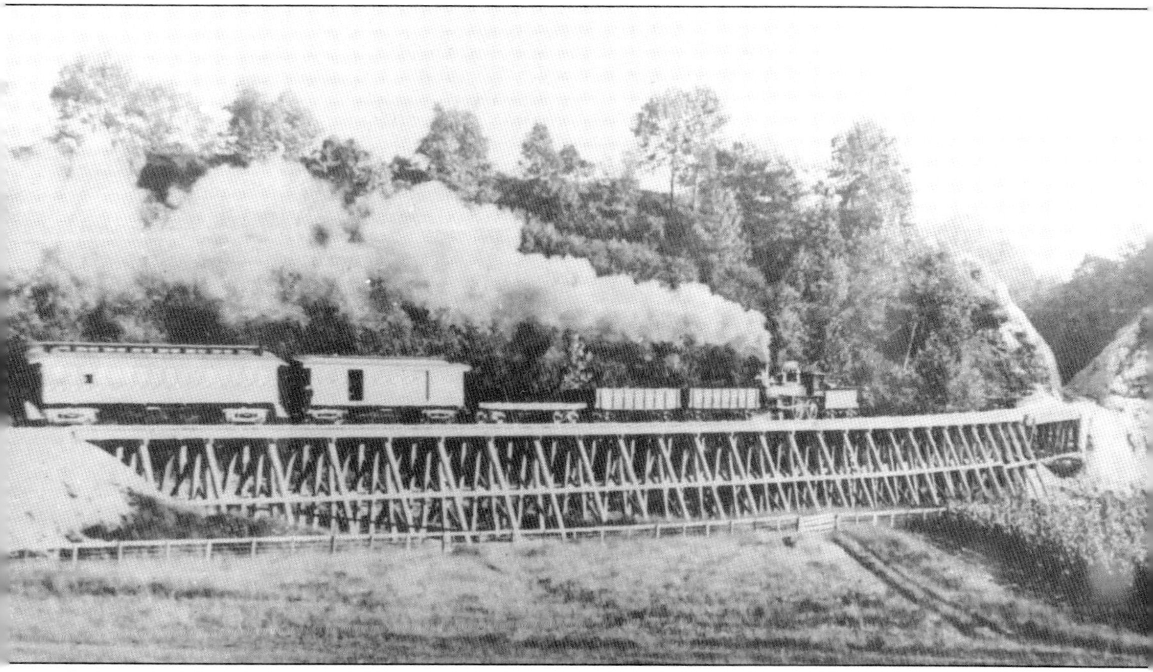

Bessemer & Lake Erie No. 3 Backs with a Mixed Train Over the Old Wooden Trestle at Conneaut Creek in 1892. Because of the blending of equipment rosters during mergers, the B&LE had two No. 3s, both 4-4-0 Americans. This locomotive is the *H.K. Wicks*, the original Shenango and Allegheny Railroad No. 3, which was the first locomotive on the system to be built by the Pittsburgh Locomotive Works (1876). Turned over to the Pittsburg, Bessemer and Lake Erie in 1888, her number was changed to 201 by the Bessemer & Lake Erie in 1900, and she was retired and scrapped in Greenville, Pennsylvania 11 years later. With tractive power rated at 10,530 lbs., the "eight-wheeler" was used in all types of service at the time of this photograph, but five years later the 4-4-0s had been displaced by heavier freight-hauling brutes and were designated as passenger locomotives only. Their ornate brass trim and long pilots distinguished them from more utilitarian freight power. (Courtesy of Conneaut Historical Railroad Museum.)

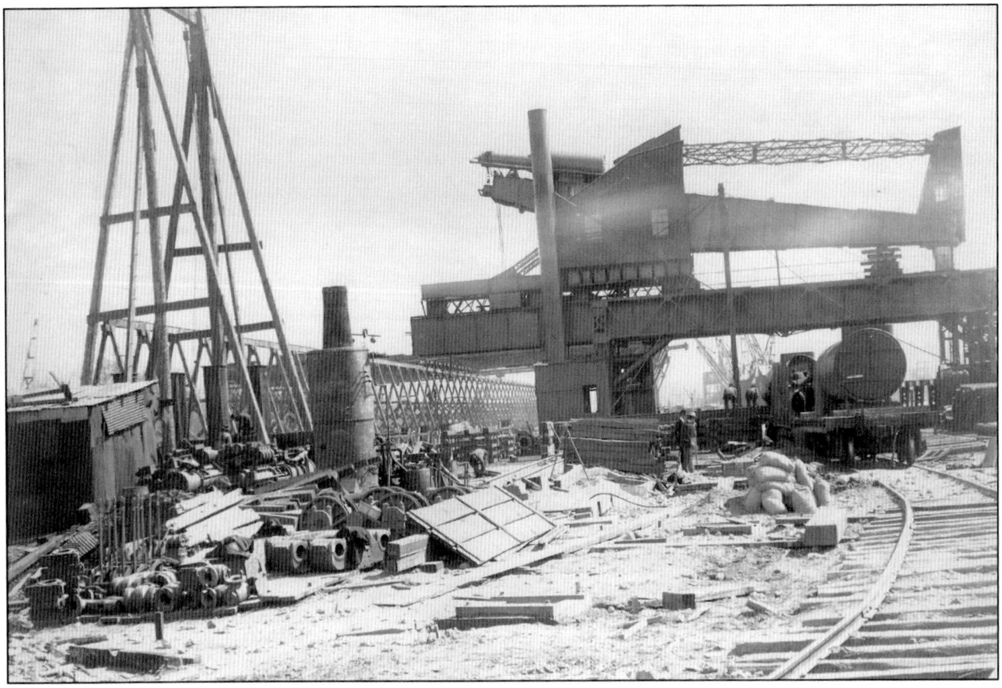

PITTBURGH & CONNEAUT DOCK, LOOKING SOUTH, APRIL 25, 1900. The construction of a Hulett Ore Unloader. (Photo by Naef & Joslin, Conneaut, courtesy of Special Collections, Cleveland State University.)

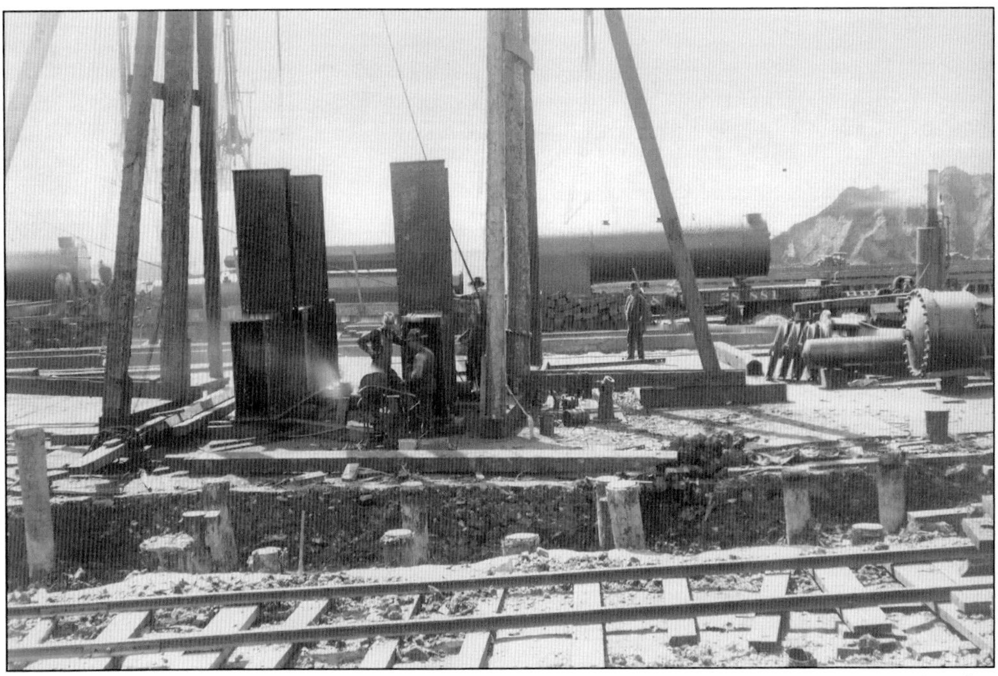

P&C DOCK COMPANY'S CONSTRUCTION OF TWO HULETT UNLOADERS, 1900. In this westward view, the hastily laid temporary ties under the rails illustrate the speed of harbor development. (Naef & Joslin, courtesy of Special Collections, Cleveland State University.)

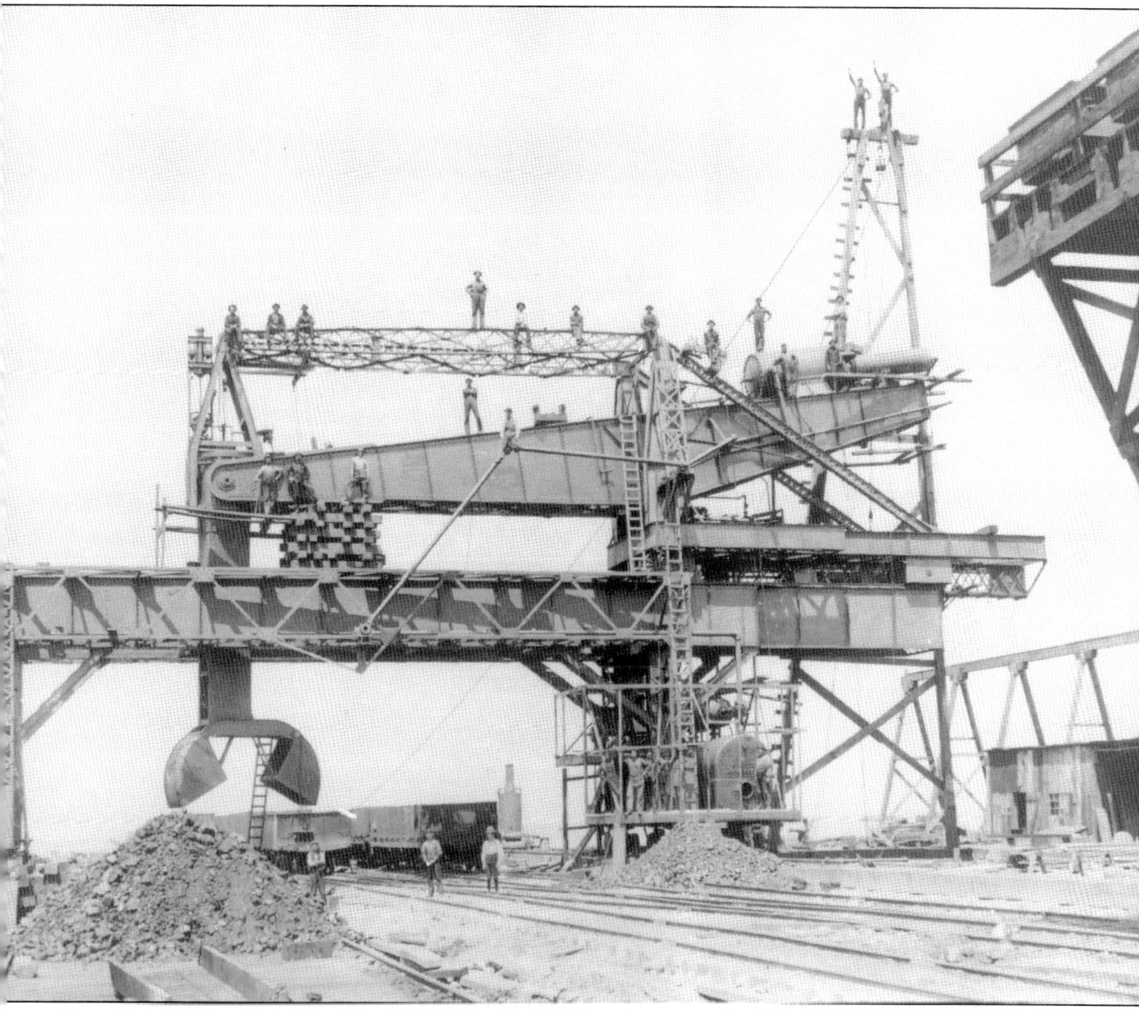

THE FIRST HULETT ORE UNLOADER IN CONNEAUT, 1899. George H. Hulett of Conneaut invented the unloader to speed up the pace of a dock operation that could not keep up with the efficiency and capacity of its boats and trains. Until late in the nineteenth century, men with shovels and wheelbarrows were the only means by which iron ore could be loaded and unloaded. Hulett, who was an ordinary businessman for the first half of his career, began designing and building coal and ore handling machinery in 1890. He invented the Hulett Unloading Machine while employed by the McMyler Manufacturing Company, for which he had previously built other unloaders such as the McMyler Car Dumper Machine (see pp. 57, 62). The Hulett Unloader, a sophisticated and highly maneuverable crane with a large grab bucket, was unrivaled in its ability to dig into the hold of an ore boat with pinpoint accuracy and take a "bite" of up to 17 tons. Where it once took 12 hours for a hundred men to unload a 5000-ton boatload of ore, the same tonnage could be processed by a single Hulett Unloader in 2 1/2 hours with no more than 25 workers. (Courtesy of Ashtabula Marine Museum.)

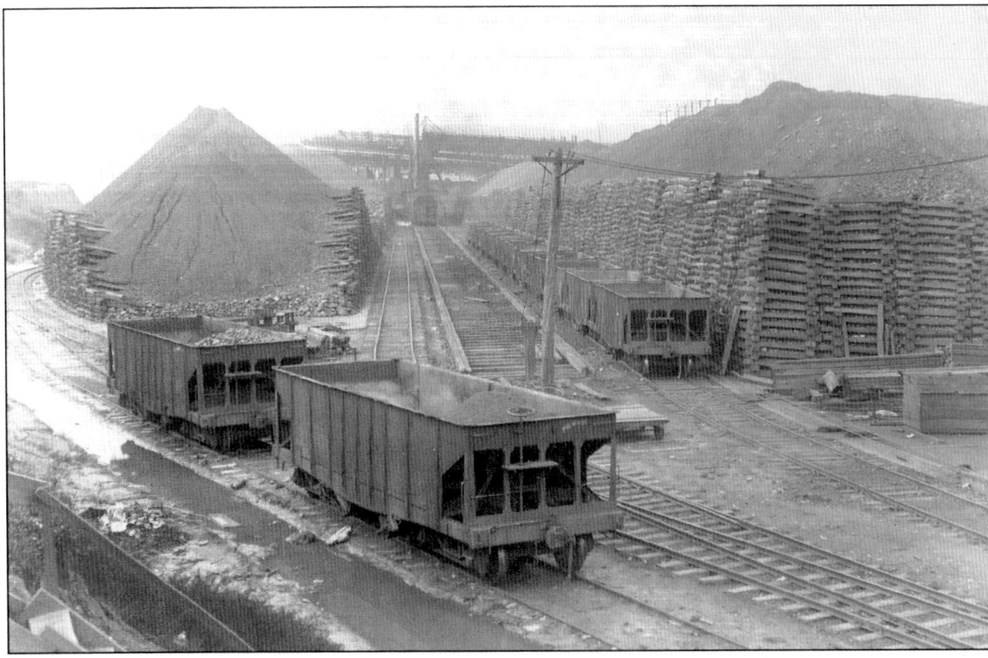

BESSEMER & LAKE ERIE HOPPER CARS AT THE HARBOR, C. 1900. These were new 40-ton steel hoppers, built in the 1890s to cope with ever-increasing loads as the iron ore business soared. (Naef & Joslin, courtesy of Special Collections, Cleveland State University.)

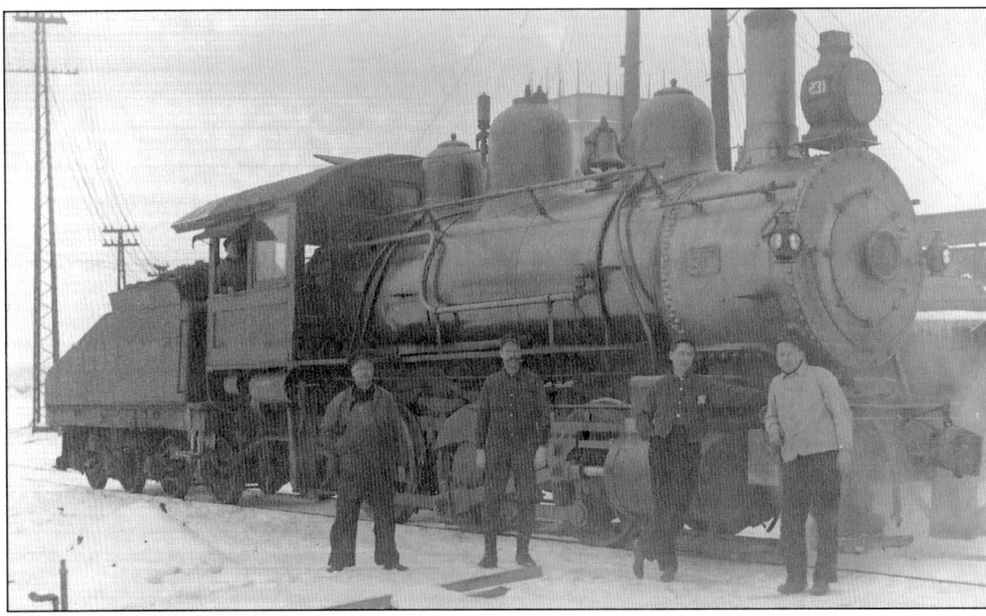

B&LE WINTER SCENE: 0-6-0 NO. 231 WITH CREW AT CONNEAUT HARBOR YARD. The six-wheelers were first introduced in 1894 to replace 4-4-0 Americans in switching service. Thirteen were purchased specifically to work in the yards, but after about 1911, they began to dwindle and were replaced by worn-out road locomotives. S2A-class No. 231 (old No. 10), with 28,721 lbs. tractive power was built in 1899 by the Pittsburgh Locomotive Works. (Courtesy of Conneaut Historical Railroad Museum.)

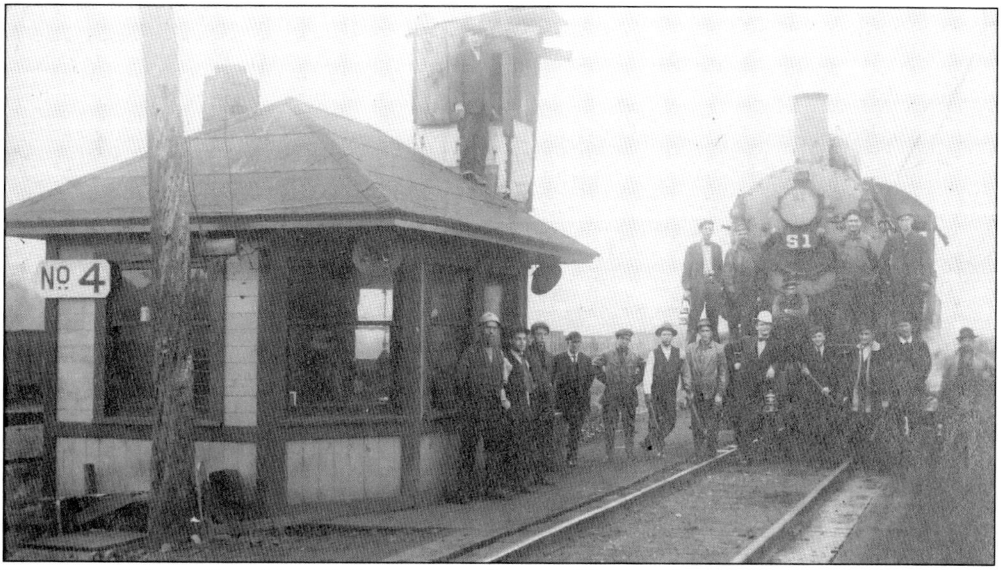

BESSEMER & LAKE ERIE NO. 51 POSES WITH CREWS. The speedy growth of the Conneaut iron ore business in the 1890s required longer and longer trains and increasingly powerful locomotives. With a hefty 28,414 lbs. of tractive power, No. 51 was one of three class M3A locomotives built for the Bessemer by Brooks Locomotive Works, a predecessor to Alco. (Courtesy of Conneaut Historical Railroad Museum.)

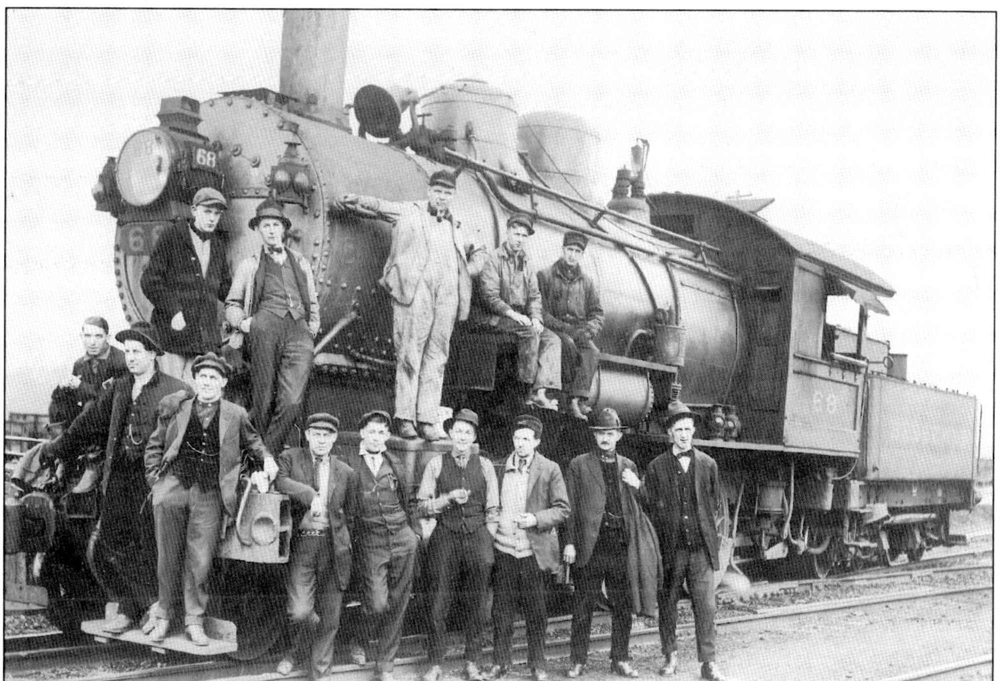

B&LE (PS&LE) NO. 68, ANOTHER BROOKS-BUILT M3A MOGUL. The second generation of Moguls, built by three different makers during 1897–8, were purchased by the Bessemer to improve on the ten-wheelers.(Courtesy of Conneaut Historical Railroad Museum.)

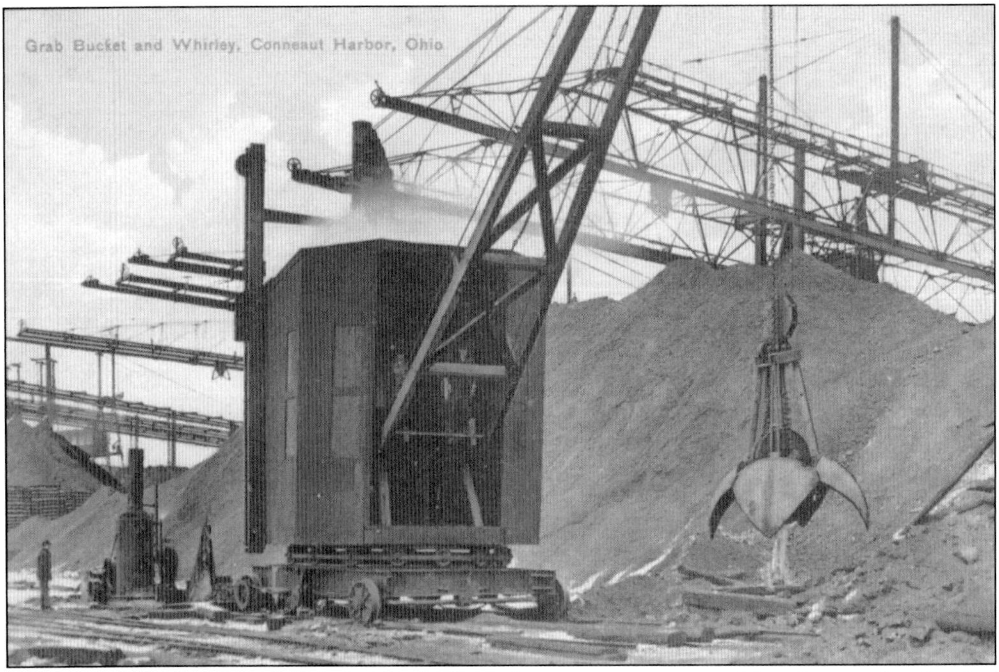

McMyler Corporation "Whirlies." These distinctive cranes could grab a modest load of ore from a boat, spin around, and deposit it into a hopper or gondola car—or reverse the process with coal or limestone. (Courtesy of Conneaut Area Historical Society.)

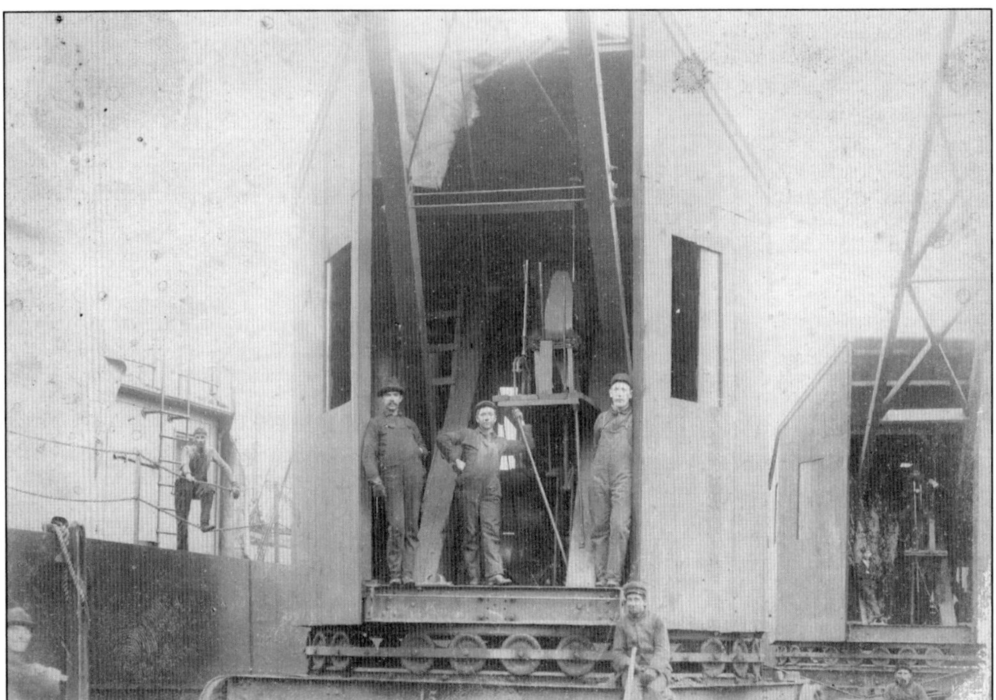

Whirly Operators. An inscription on the back of the photograph says, "The Whirlies that Mike Foley operated at Conneaut Harbor." (Courtesy of Conneaut Historical Railroad Museum.)

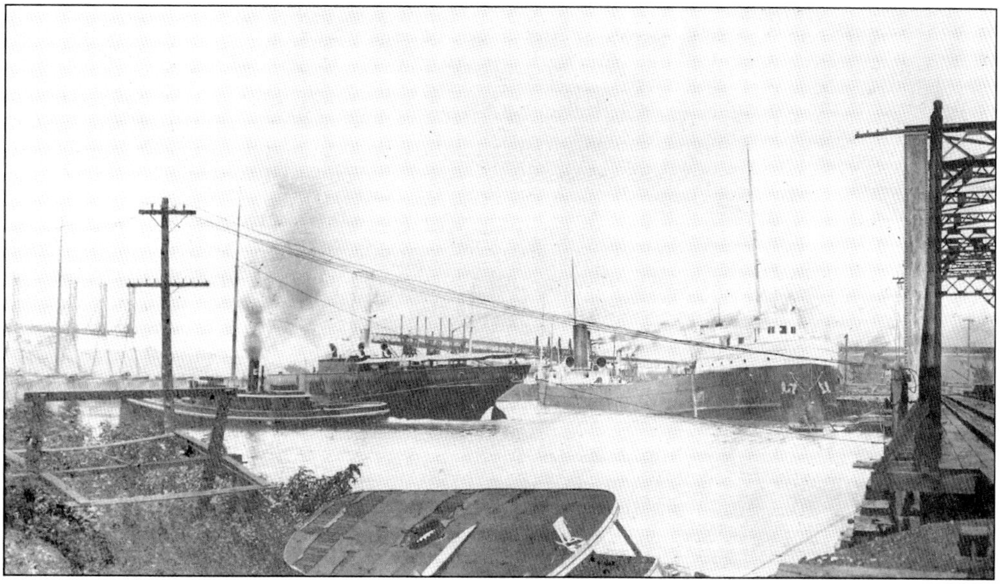

Conneaut Harbor in 1901. The four-track railroad swing bridge (page 65) is seen at left. (Courtesy of Conneaut Historical Railroad Museum.)

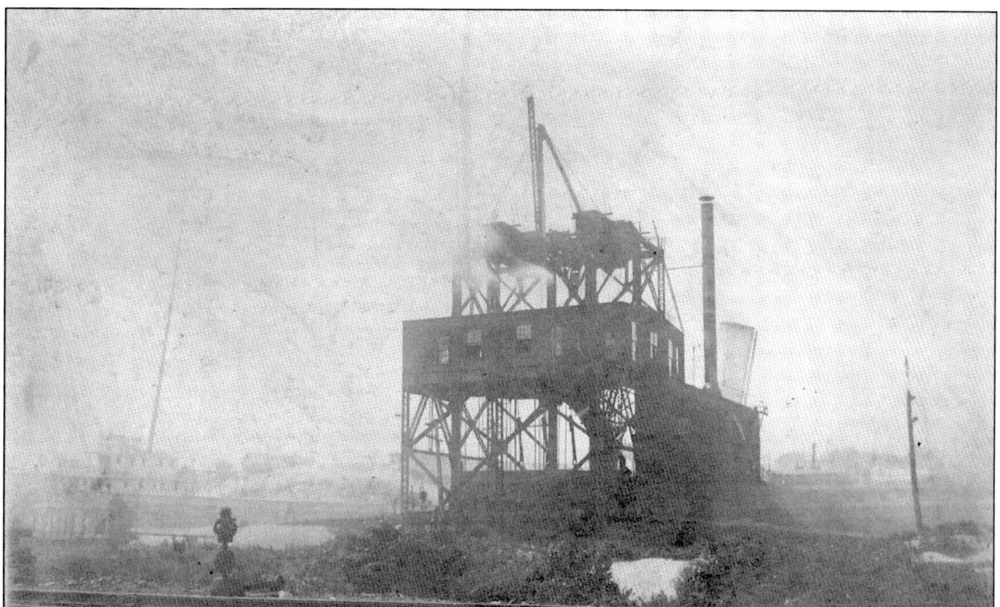

Original Steam Powered Car Dumper, c. 1901. If the Hulett Ore Unloaders facilitated moving material from boats to trains, the car dumper went in the opposite direction. Taking a broadside approach, Hulett's car dumper lifted up a hopper car full of coal, rolled it on its side, and poured the coal into a funnel-shaped apron that led down a chute into the hold of the boat. The process, from pick-up to set-down, took about two minutes. (Courtesy of Conneaut Historical Railroad Museum.)

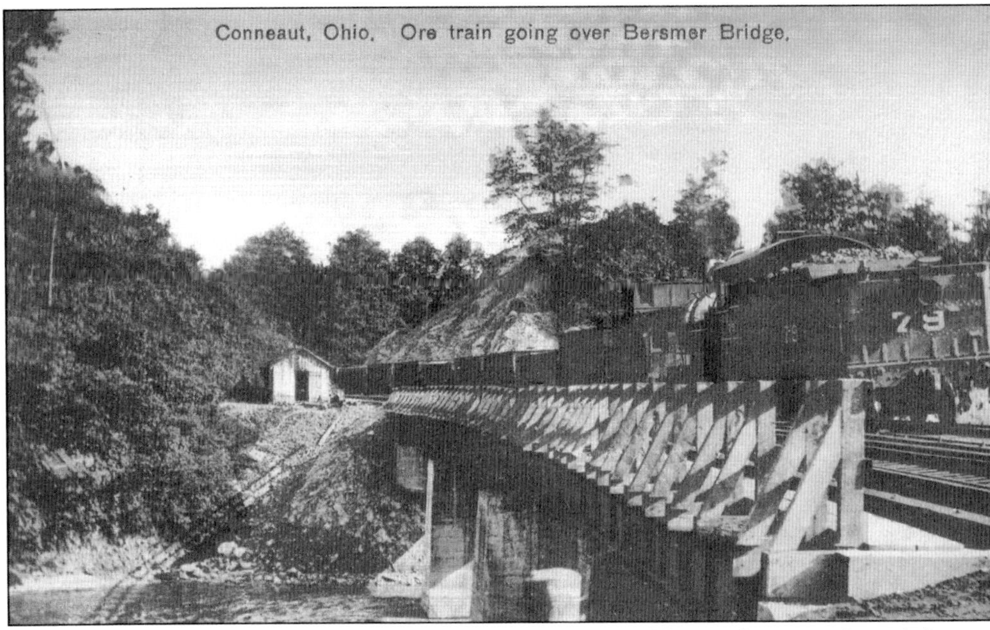

2-8-0 C1A-CLASS "CONSOLIDATION" NO. 79 IN ORE TRAIN HELPER SERVICE. Consolidations, with tractive effort of 38,398 lbs., were purchased for heavy road service in 1898 as successors to the Moguls seen on page 55. One of their frequent duties was to push on the caboose of a heavy ore train going uphill. (Courtesy of Conneaut Area Historical Society.)

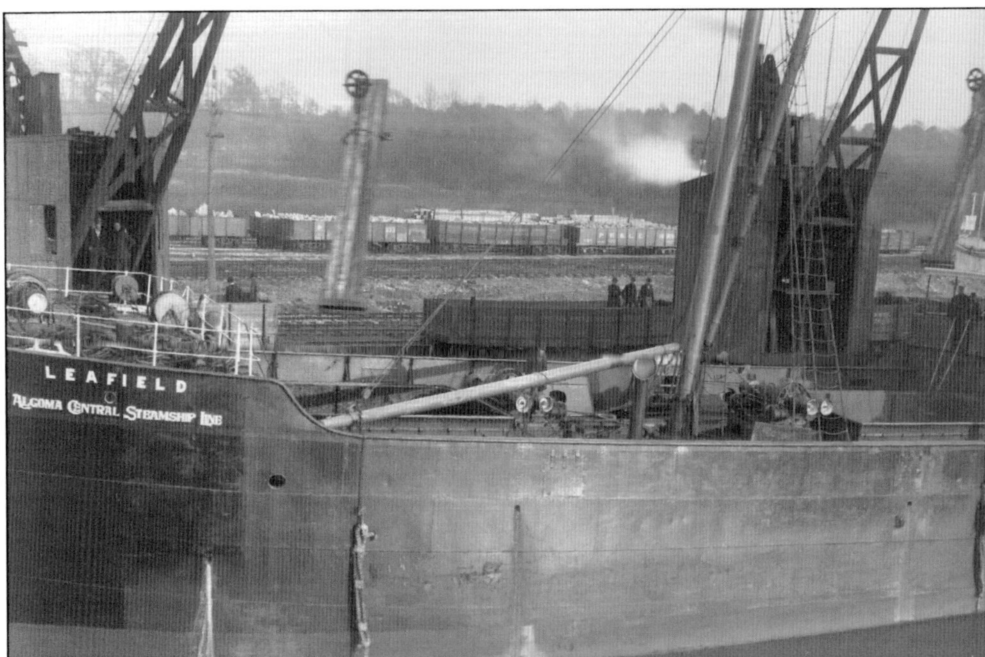

ALGOMA CENTRAL STEAMSHIP *LEAFIELD* WITH PITTSBURG, BESSEMER, AND LAKE ERIE WOODEN GONDOLAS, C. 1900. The steel-hulled *Leafield* was one of the first four boats built for the Algoma Central, a company that operated trains and boats in the Great Lakes. (Naef & Joslin, courtesy of Special Collections, Cleveland State University.)

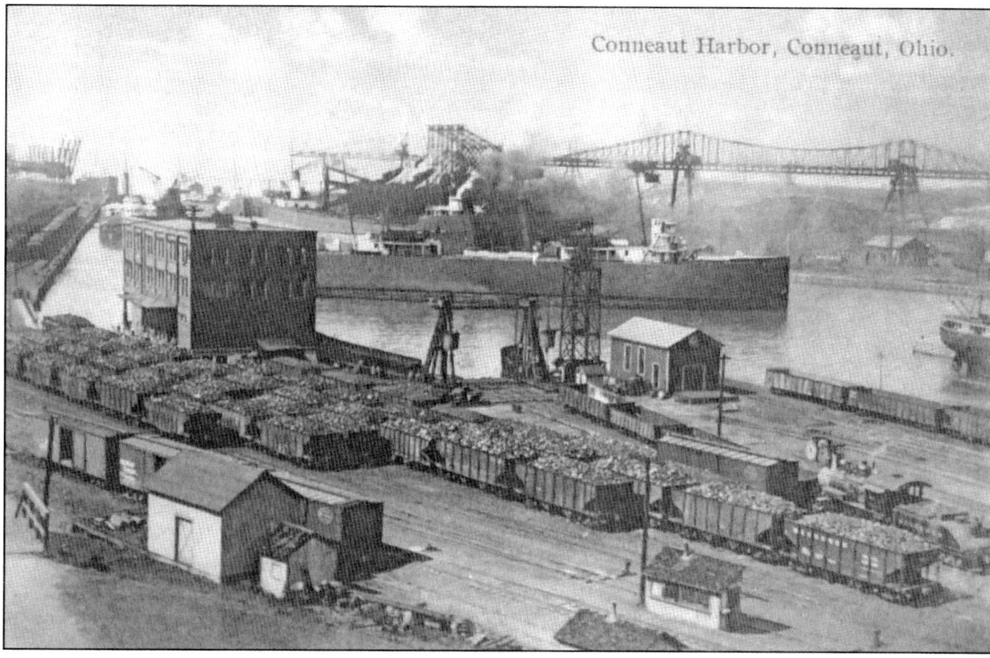

CONNEAUT HARBOR IN THE EARLY 1900S. At center is the carferry dock. (Courtesy of Conneaut Area Historical Society.)

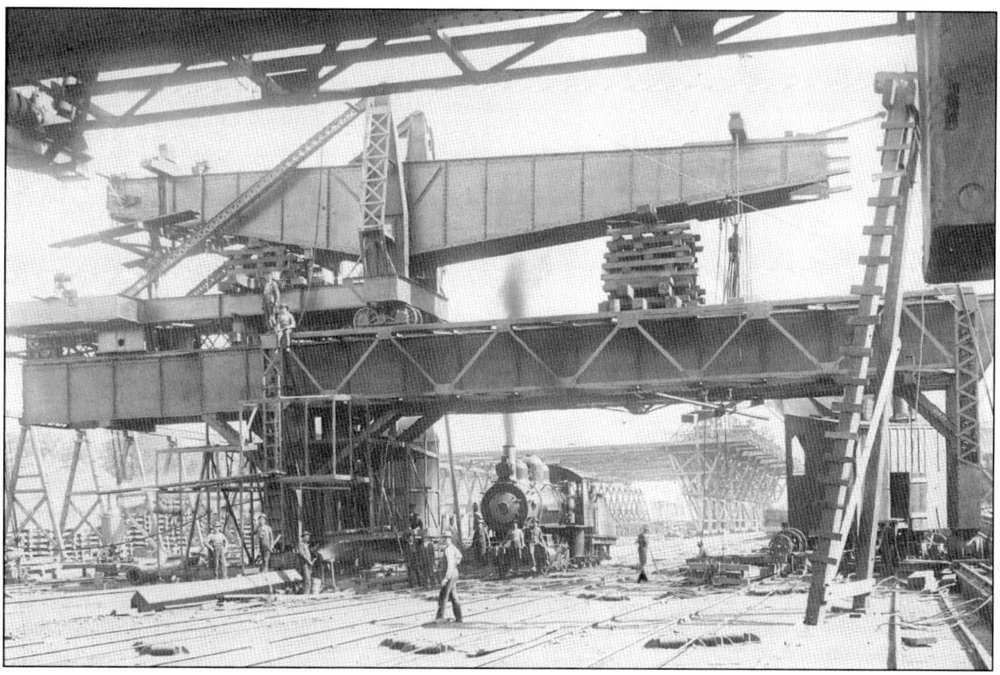

ERECTING A STEAM POWERED HULETT ORE UNLOADER IN CONNEAUT HARBOR, JUNE 22, 1901. The first Huletts were all run by steam engines and were later converted to utilize electric power and hydraulics. Hulett Ore Unloaders were put into service at many Great Lakes ports; they were unsuitable for saltwater harbors because they were unequipped to adjust for the tides. (Courtesy of Conneaut Historical Railroad Museum.)

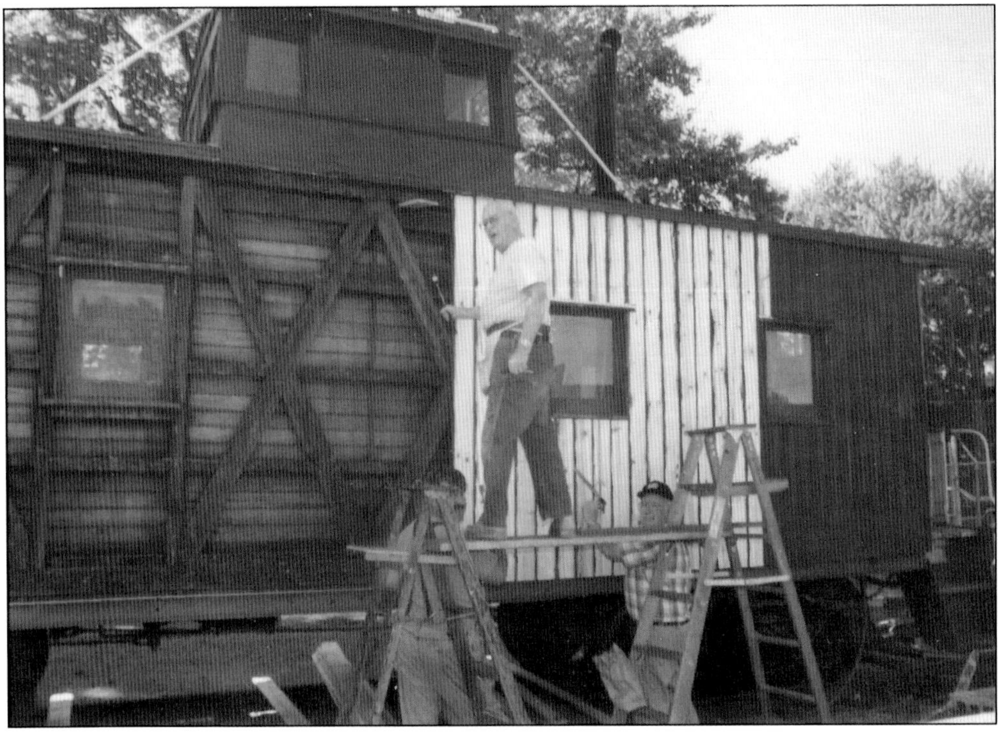

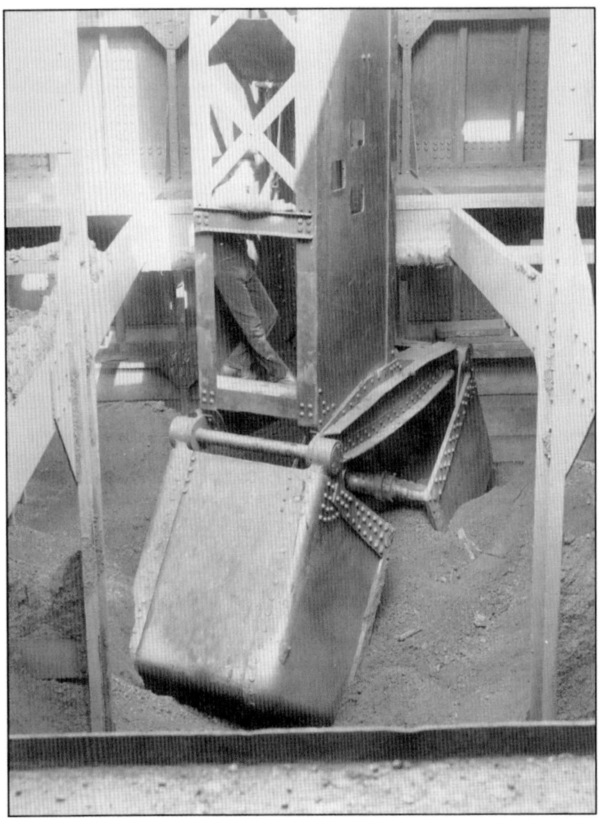

RESTORATION OF A VINTAGE B&LE WOOD CABOOSE. In this 1997 photo, an old Bessemer car is rebuilt and repainted for the Conneaut Railroad Museum. On the scaffold is Robert Leach; Below are Ron Brundage (left) and Norm Gross. (Courtesy of Conneaut Historical Railroad Museum.)

HULETT CONTROL CAB, C. 1900. The operator stood right on top of the grab bucket. The movement of the digging leg was so complex that it took five years of practice for an operator to be considered fully trained. (Naef & Joslin, courtesy of Special Collections, Cleveland State University.)

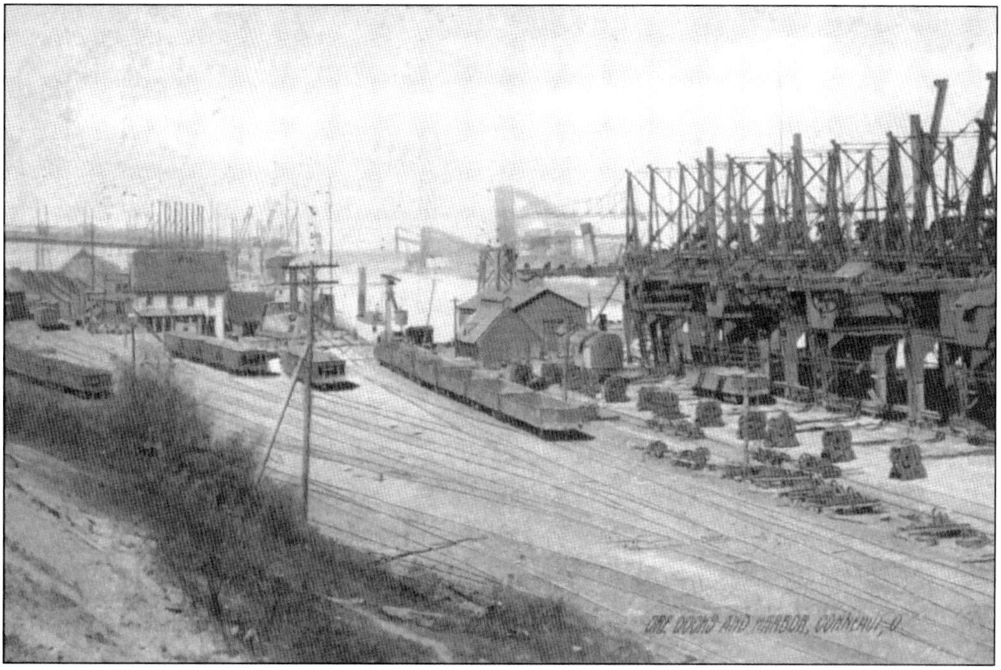

BESSEMER & LAKE ERIE ORE DOCKS AT CONNEAUT HARBOR. The B&LE harbor yards at their height had over 30 miles of rail in 80 tracks. In addition to loading, unloading, and assembling of trains, substantial locomotive and car maintenance was done here. (Courtesy of Conneaut Area Historical Society.)

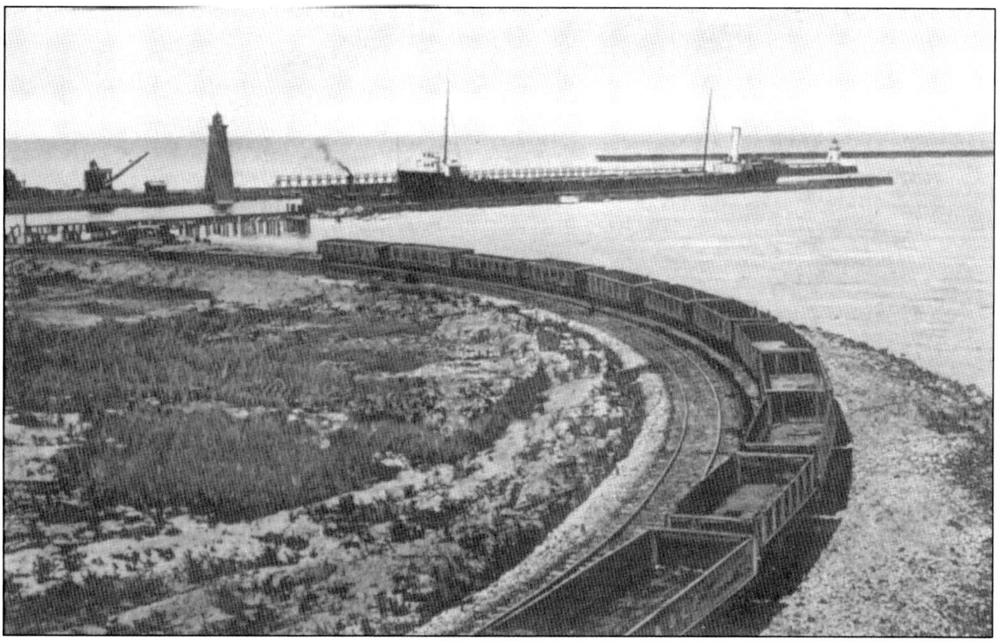

HOPPER CARS AT THE HARBOR ENTRANCE. Both the East and West Pier lighthouses are seen behind the loop of track on which cars are loaded and unloaded. (Courtesy of Conneaut Area Historical Society.)

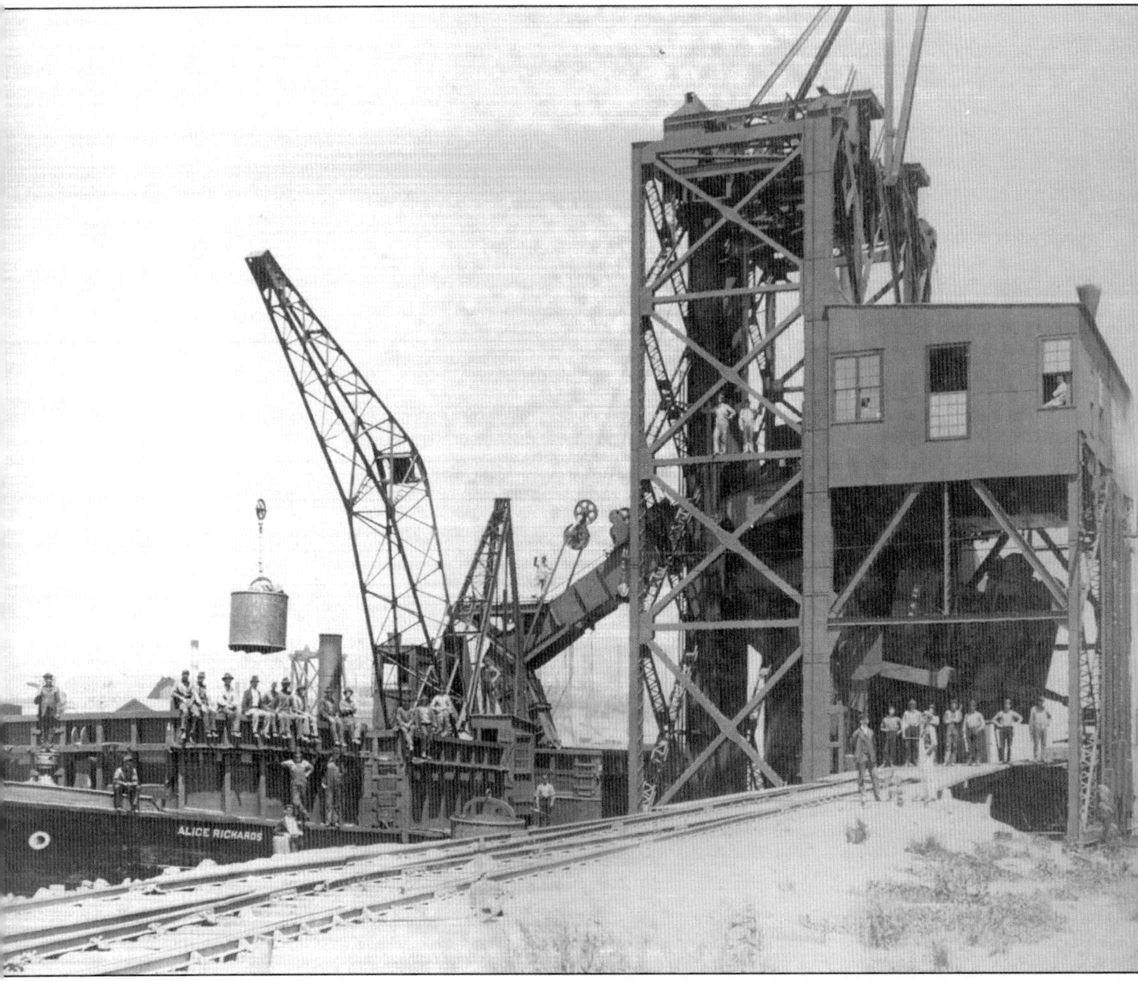

HARBOR CREWS AT MCMYLER CAR DUMPER, C. 1900. The machine was designed by Conneaut's own George Hulett. (Naef & Joslin, courtesy of Special Collections, Cleveland State University.)

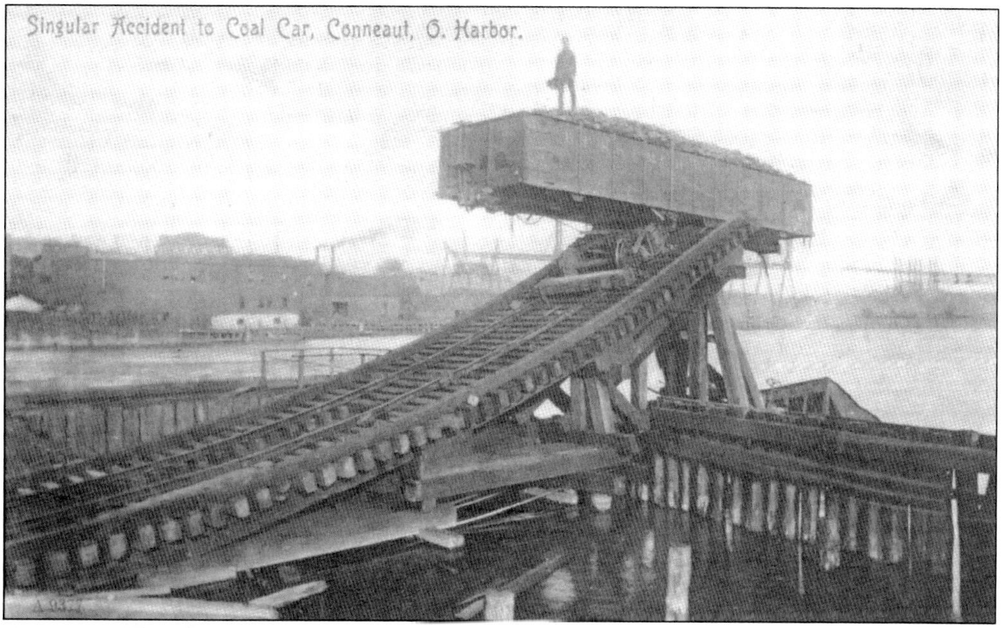

ONE CAR TOO MANY. This disaster was precipitated by putting two hoppers, instead of one, into the backup track for a car dumper. Something had to give! (Courtesy of Conneaut Historical Railroad Museum.)

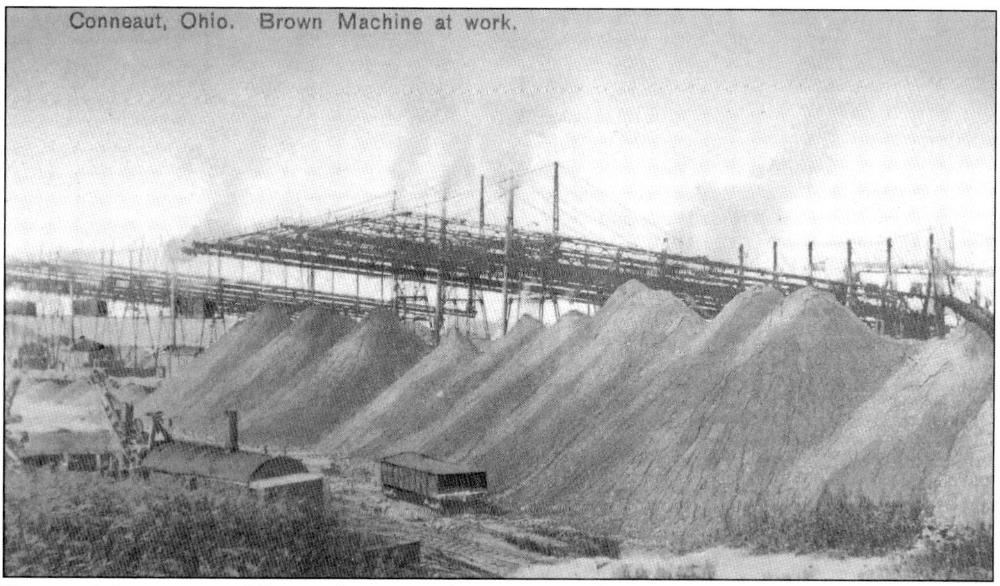

BROWN MACHINE AT WORK. George Hulett was not the first man to make his mark in the field of ore handling. Alexander E. Brown (1852-1911), an inventor and manufacturer who was the son of ore pioneer Fayette Brown, devoted much of his early career to increasing the tempo of ore and coal transfer. He invented the cable-wired Brown Rig, which hoisted a bucket from a ship's hold and conveyed it to the dock or storage piles. Despite the limitations of relatively small tubs, the Brown Rig and the other machines he invented reduced unloading time dramatically, especially because several rigs could work side by side at the same boat. (Courtesy of Conneaut Area Historical Society.)

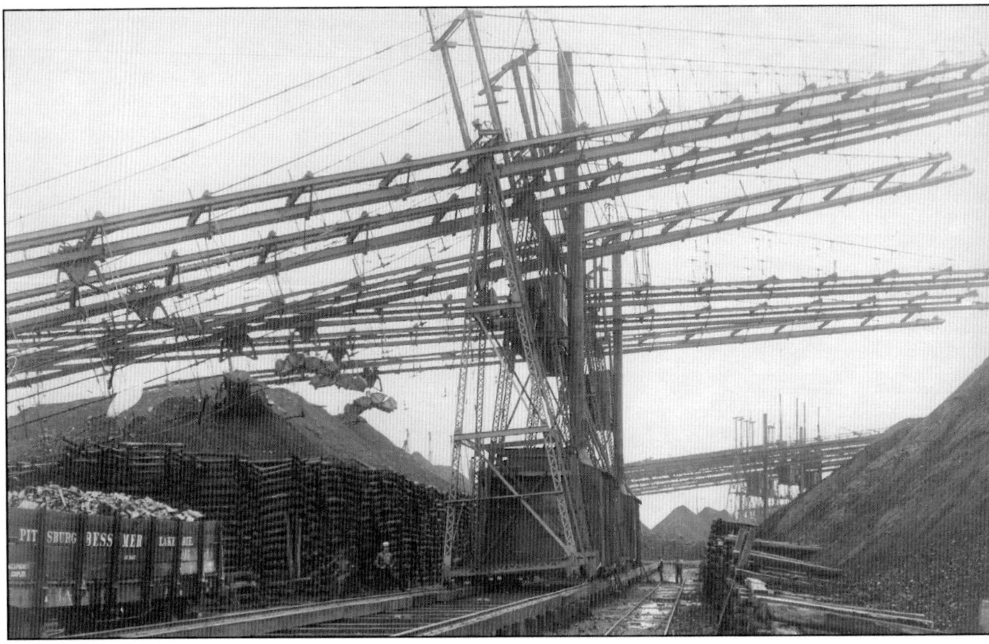

Bringing in Ore Bridge Sections During Construction. Note the old "Pittsburg" spelling on the vintage wooden gondola. (Naef & Joslin, courtesy of Special Collections, Cleveland State University.)

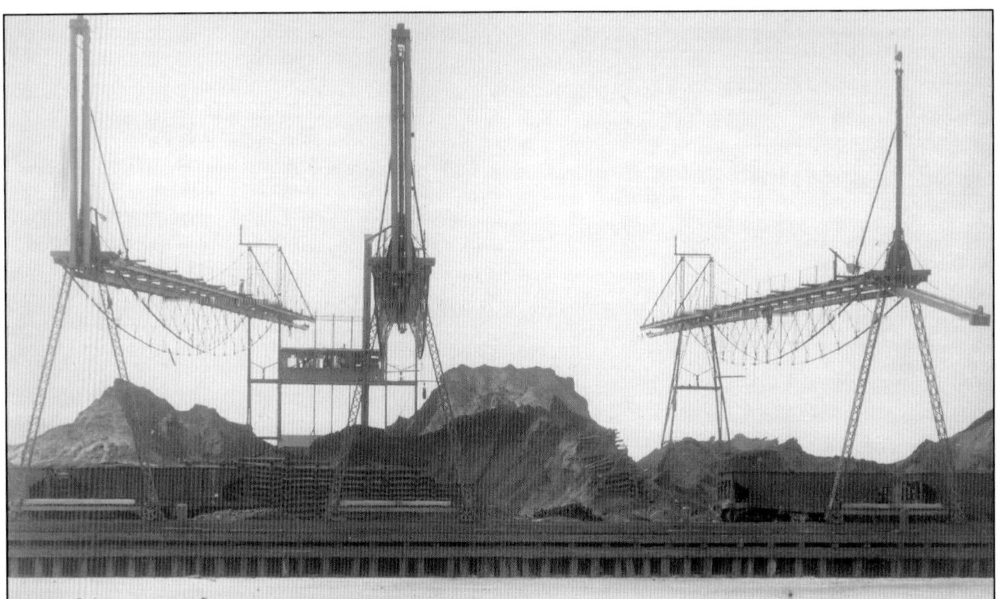

Dock 1 Looking West, Brown Ore Bridges, March 20, 1900. Many generations of equipment have been used here, but loading and unloading continued unabated. (Naef & Joslin, courtesy of Special Collections, Cleveland State University.)

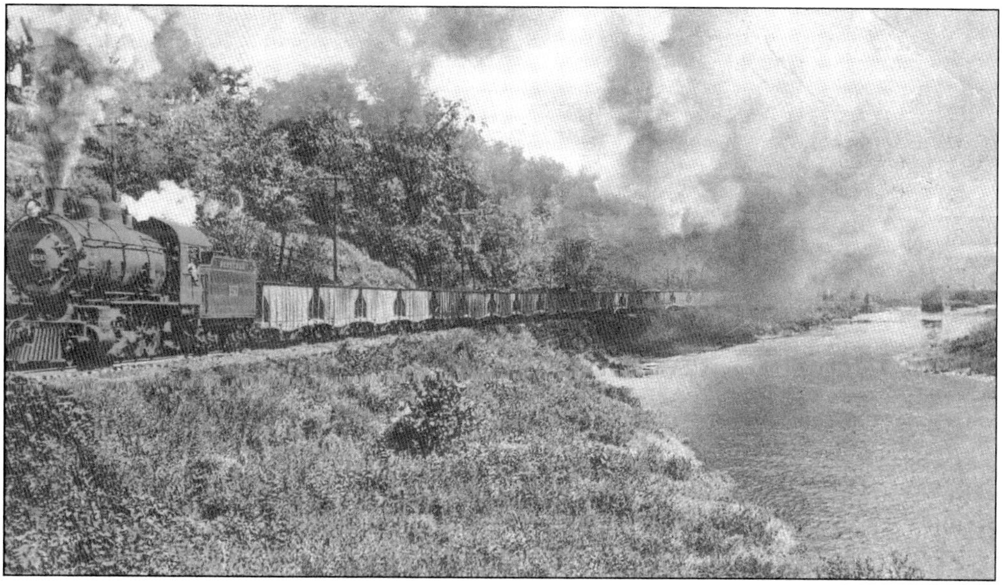

Bessemer & Lake Erie Ore Train Leaving Conneaut Yards. "Drag" type 2-8-0 Consolidation No. 150 is doing exactly what it was designed to do—hauling a heavy consist of hoppers at moderate speed toward a series of tough grades in the hills to the south. Nos. 150-159 were a later generation of Consolidations, built from 1900-13. (Courtesy of Conneaut Area Historical Society.)

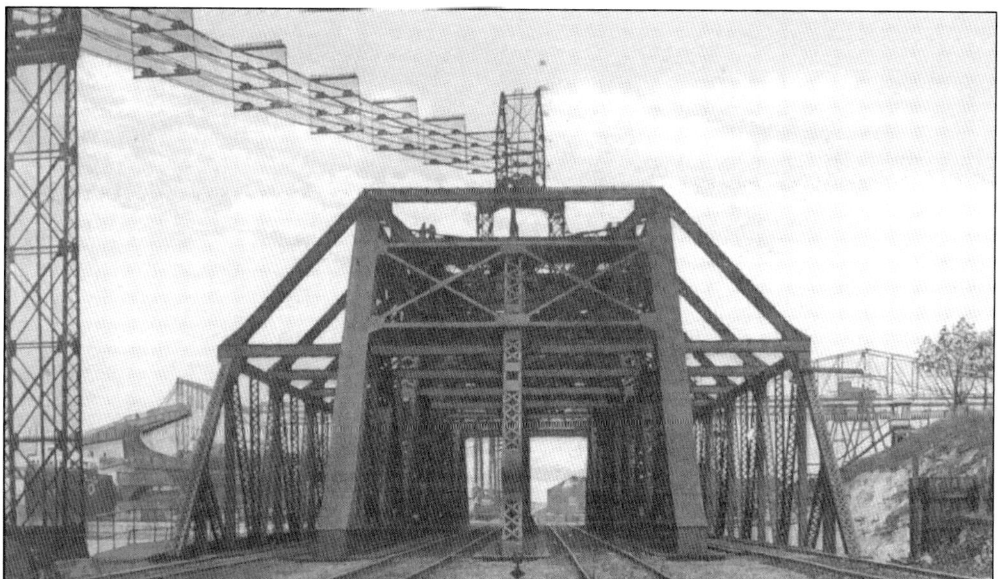

Unique Bessemer & Lake Erie Swing Bridge at Conneaut Harbor. The bridge, still in place and thought to be the world's only four-track bridge of this type, has never in fact swung fully open. Given its width, it is difficult to imagine that anything larger than pleasure craft could pass through. (Courtesy of Conneaut Area Historical Society.)

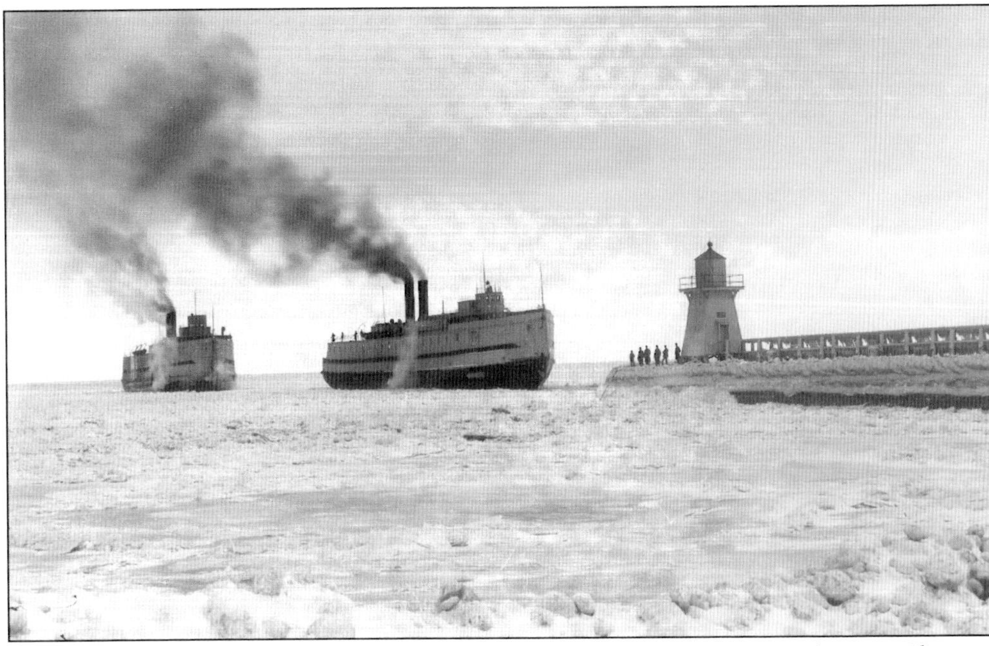

CARFERRIES IN THE ICE OFF OF EAST PIER LIGHTHOUSE, 1899. As winter closes in, *Shenango No. 1* uses her bow propeller to break ice for the trailing *Shenango No. 2*. (Courtesy of Conneaut Area Historical Society.)

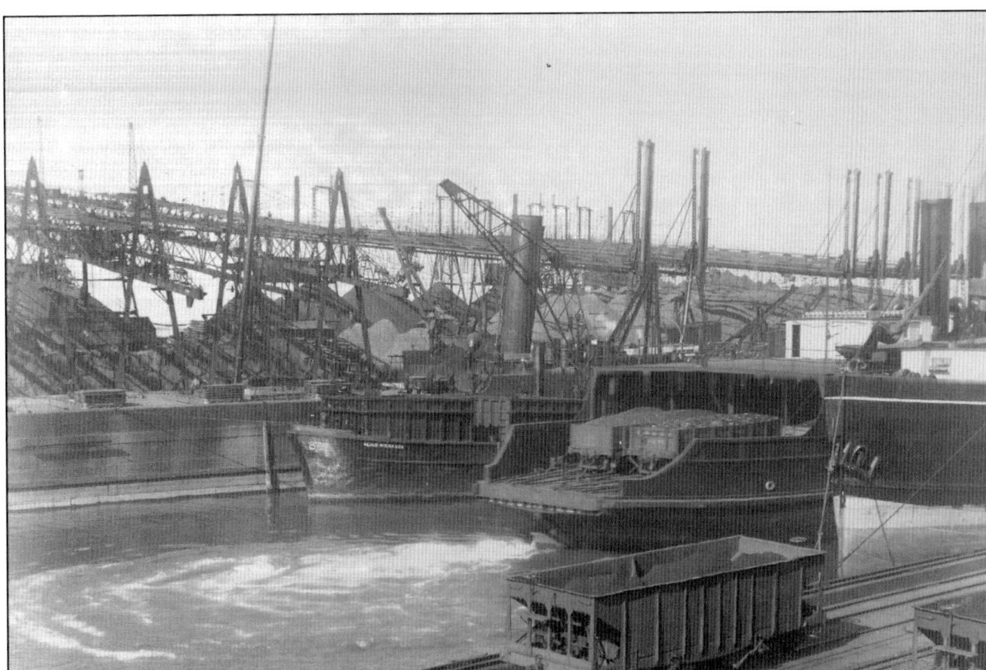

CONNEAUT CARFERRY, C. 1900. Beginning on August 22, 1895, these boats carried loads of up to 32 railroad hopper cars full of coal from the Bessemer & Lake Erie. Crossing the lake to Port Dover, Ontario, the ferries would deliver the cars to the Grand Trunk Railway. (Naef & Joslin, courtesy of Special Collections, Cleveland State University.)

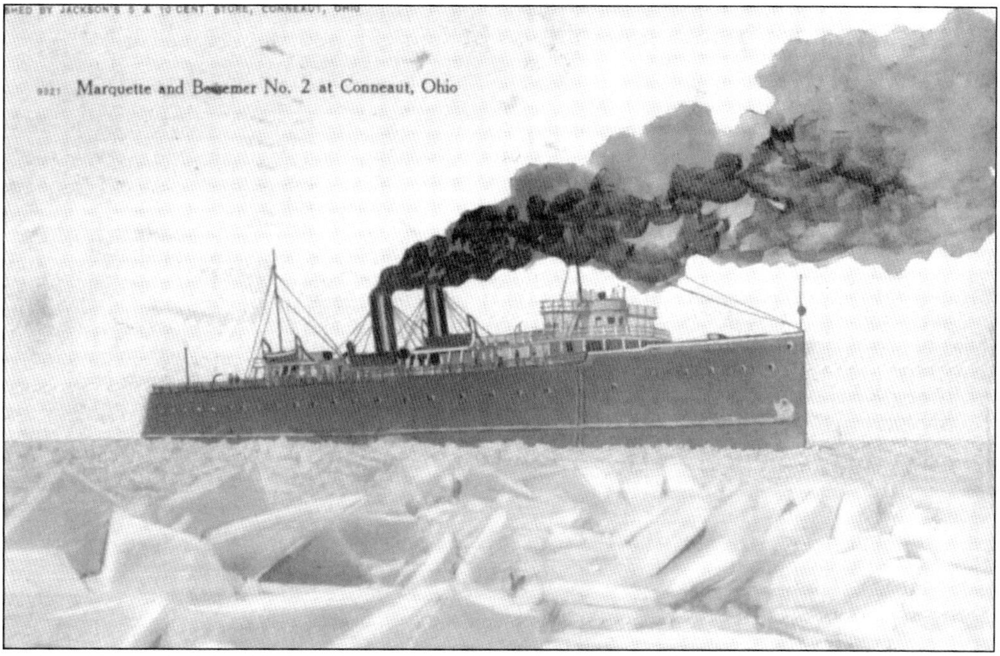

TWO VIEWS OF THE *MARQUETTE & BESSEMER* NO. 2. This carferry met a disastrous end after only four years of service. On the morning of December 7, 1909, she steamed from Conneaut into a dangerous storm with a full load of coal hoppers and was never seen again, although several crew members were found frozen to death in a lifeboat, and the body of the captain was later washed ashore. Exceedingly dangerous to operate, the Conneaut carferries were retired in 1932. (Both courtesy of Conneaut Area Historical Society.)

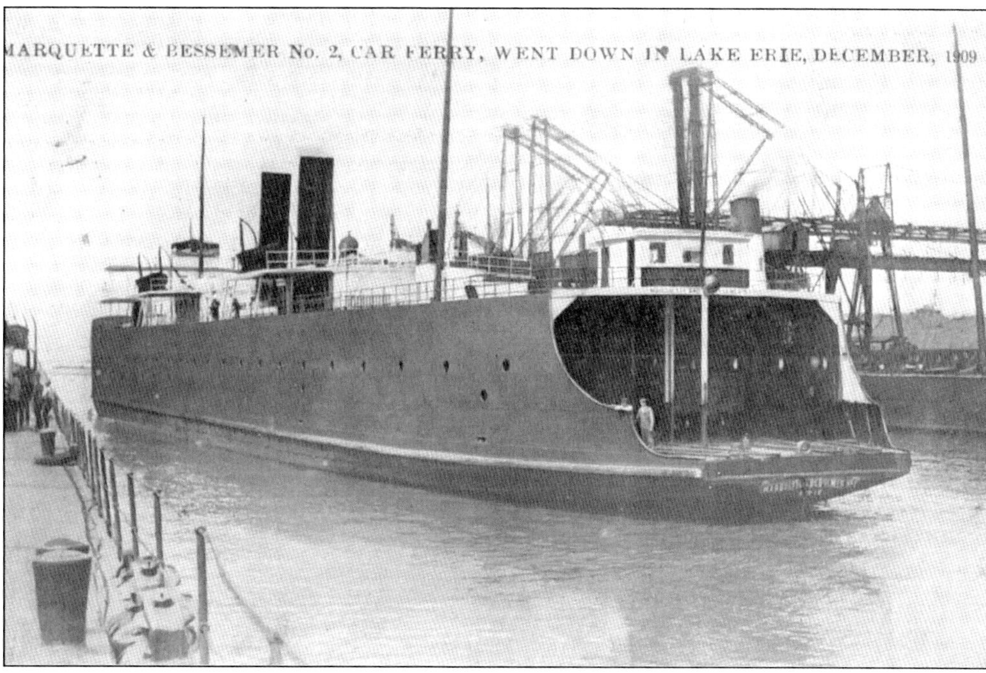

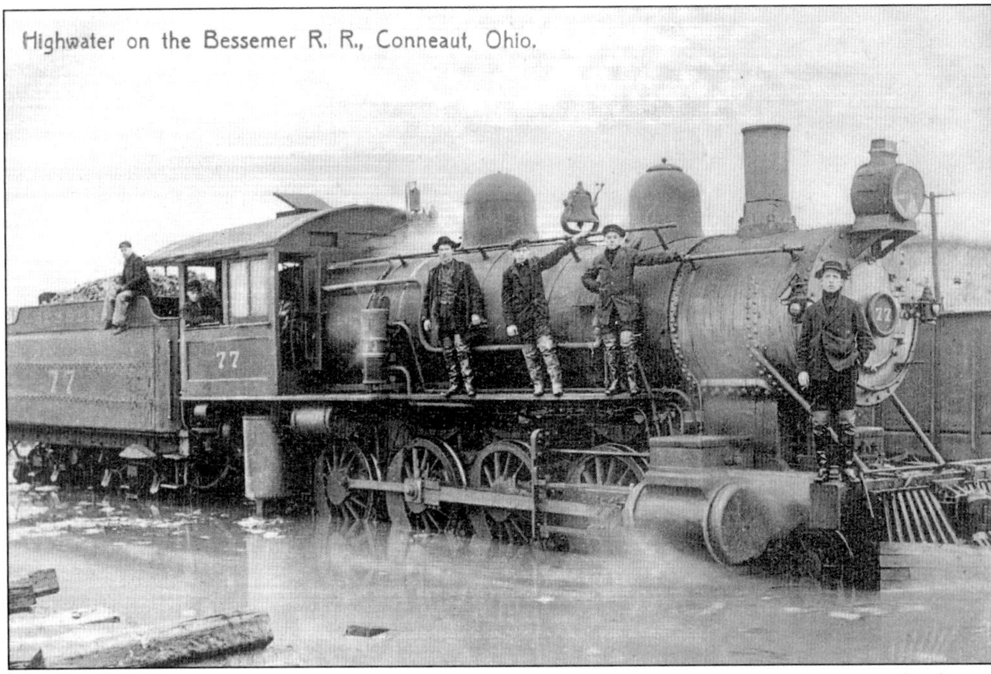

HAZARDS OF THE RIVERBANK: FLOODING ON BESSEMER & LAKE ERIE TRACKS. The heavy Mogul locomotives such as those seen on page 55 were eventually overmatched as the ore trains grew still heavier. In 1898, the railroad again moved to acquire heavier, more powerful locomotives, purchasing newly designed 2-8-0 Consolidations with tractive power in excess of 38,000 pounds from several builders. Sixty-one were bought, including class C1A No. 77 from the Pittsburgh Locomotive Works. (Courtesy of Conneaut Area Historical Society.)

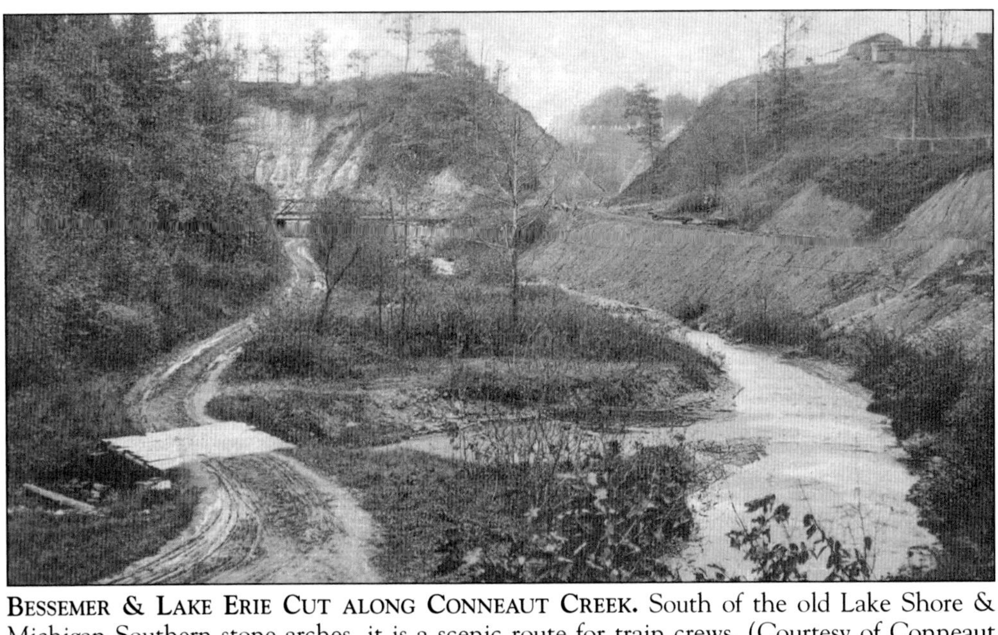

BESSEMER & LAKE ERIE CUT ALONG CONNEAUT CREEK. South of the old Lake Shore & Michigan Southern stone arches, it is a scenic route for train crews. (Courtesy of Conneaut Area Historical Society.)

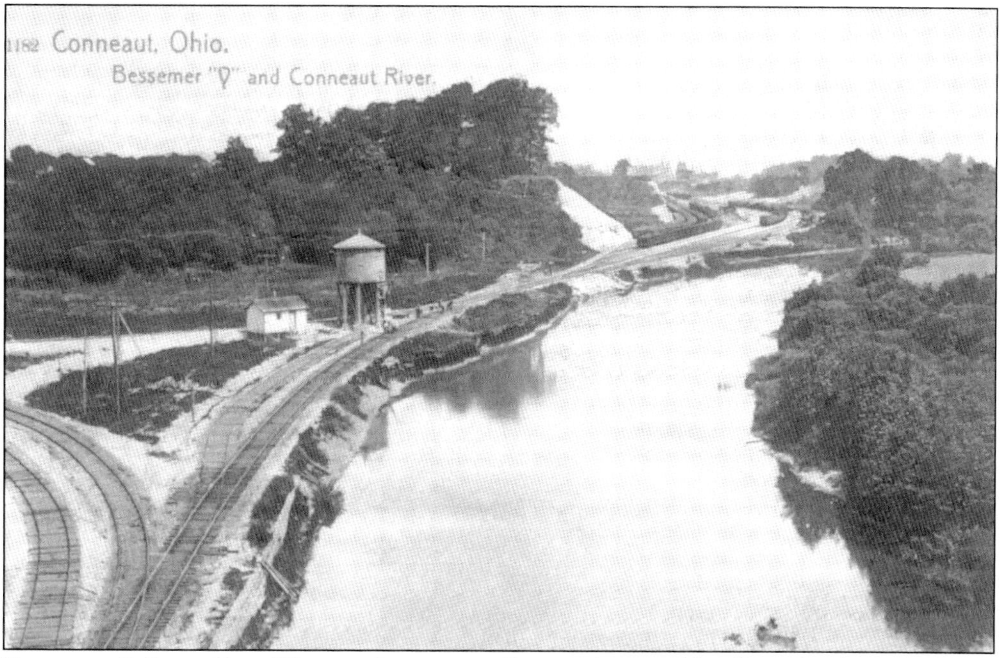

BESSEMER & LAKE ERIE WYE AT CONNEAUT CREEK. A turntable allows for the reversing of a single locomotive in the yard, and a triangle of trackwork called a "wye" makes this same thing possible out on the mainline, something particularly important near the end of a line. For operators of steam locomotives, which ran backwards only grudgingly, a wye made life considerably easier. (Courtesy of Conneaut Area Historical Society.)

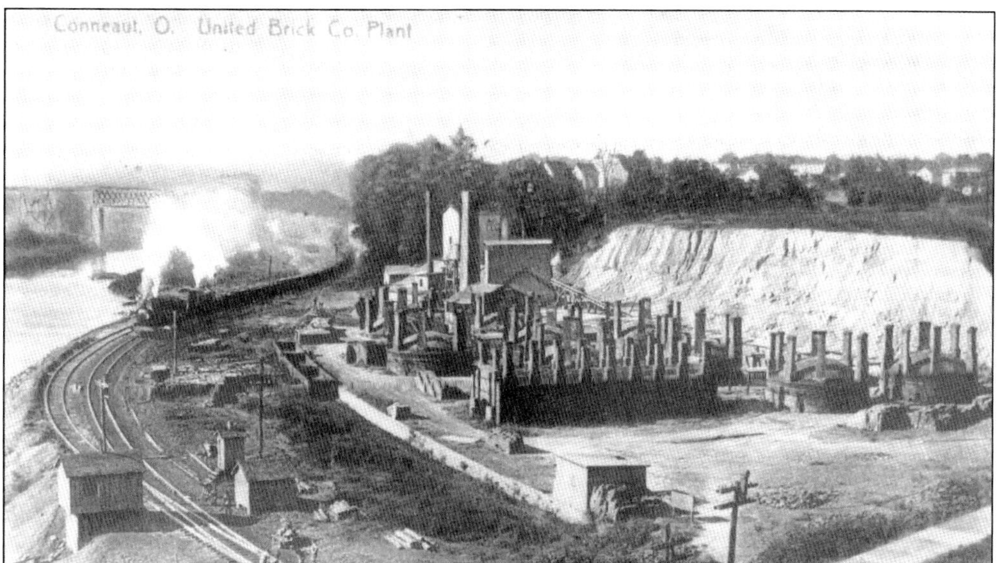

UNITED BRICK COMPANY PLANT ALONG THE B&LE. There were three brick plants located at Conneaut Creek: United Brick, Harper Norton, and Conneaut Block. (Courtesy of Conneaut Area Historical Society.)

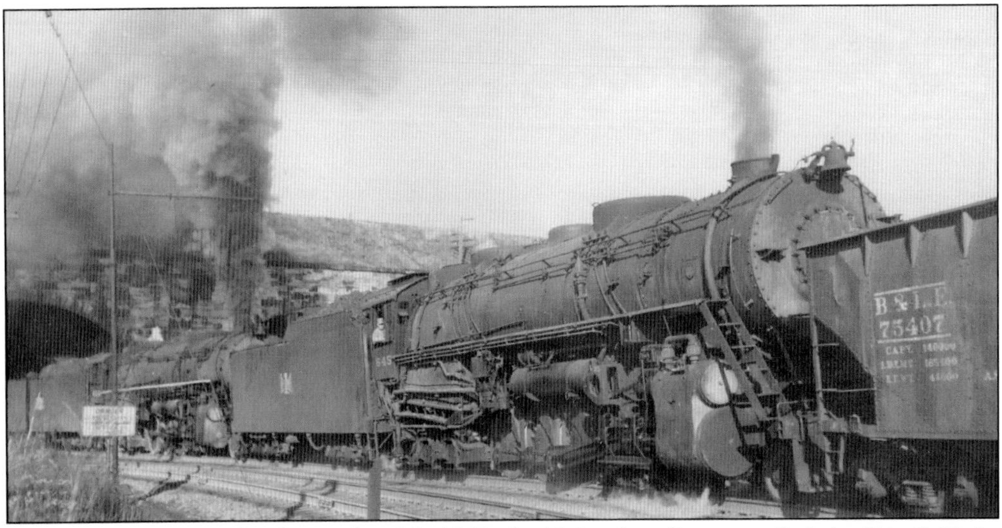

A SHOW OF FORCE. On September 25, 1949, doubleheading Bessemer & Lake Erie 2-10-4s, Nos. 645 and 616, pause with a northbound coal train at the New York Central arches, the entrance to the industrial harbor area. The 2-10-4 "Texas" type locomotives, purchased beginning in 1929, were the last and most powerful in a distinguished line of B&LE steam power. Forty-seven of these locomotives, which had a prodigious tractive effort of 96,700 lbs. (increased to 109,935 lbs. with the use of special trailer boosters), would have continued in service for many years if their retirement had not been mandated in 1952 by the efficiency and crew cost savings of diesels. (Courtesy of Conneaut Historical Railroad Museum.)

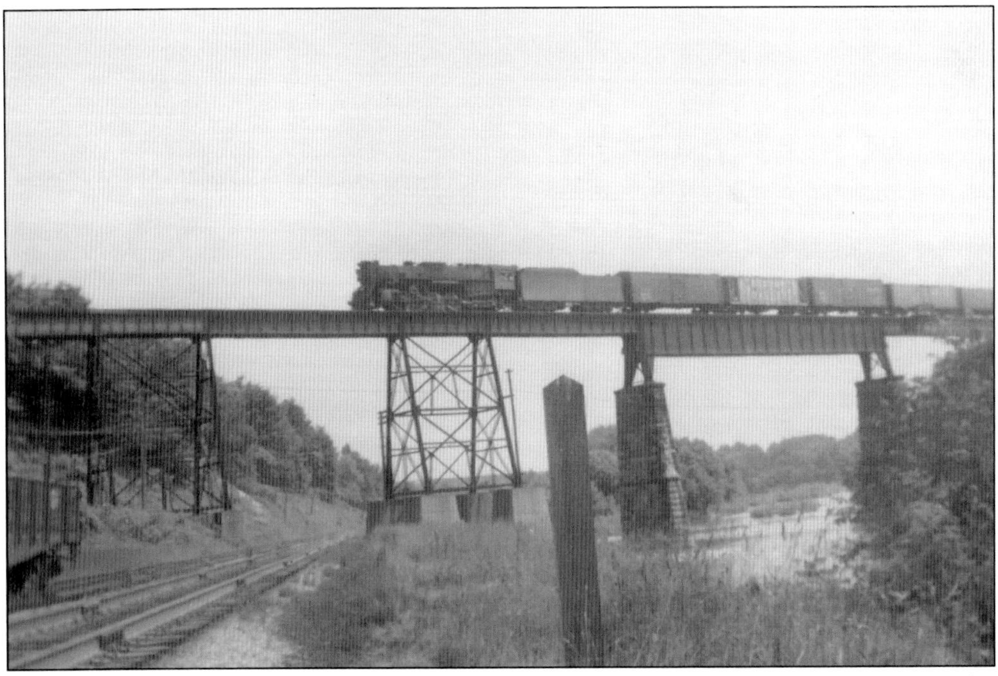

NICKEL PLATE FREIGHT TRAIN ON THE BRIDGE OVER THE BESSEMER & LAKE ERIE, C. 1950. While the NKP passes 109 feet over Conneaut Creek, a gondola of the B&LE is seen on the tracks below. (Courtesy of Conneaut Public Library.)

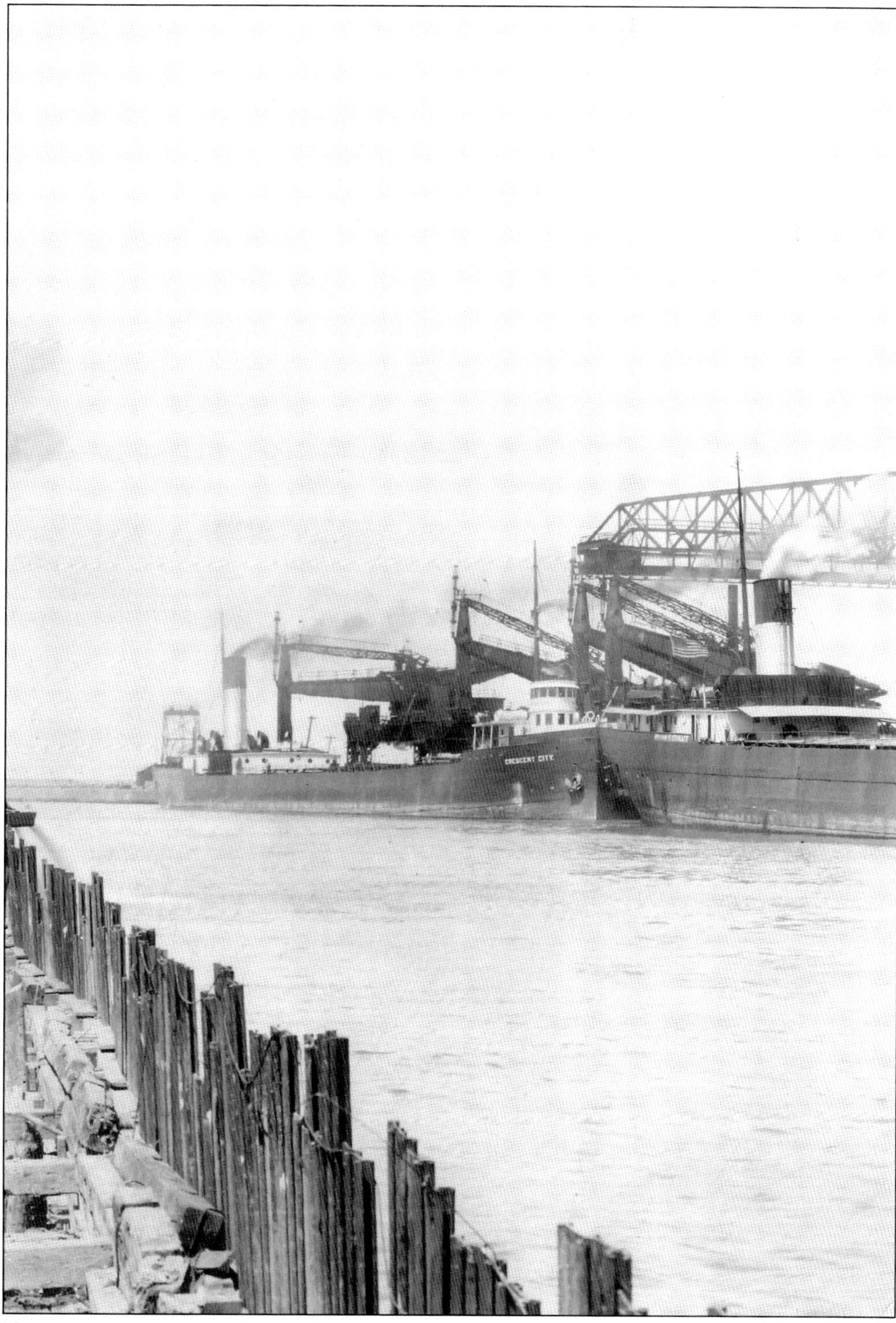

HULETTS UNLOADING IRON ORE IN CONNEAUT HARBOR. This is the left half (and unfortunately the only surviving portion) of a photograph that was folded and torn into two pieces. (*Cleveland Press*, courtesy of Special Collections, Cleveland State University Library.)

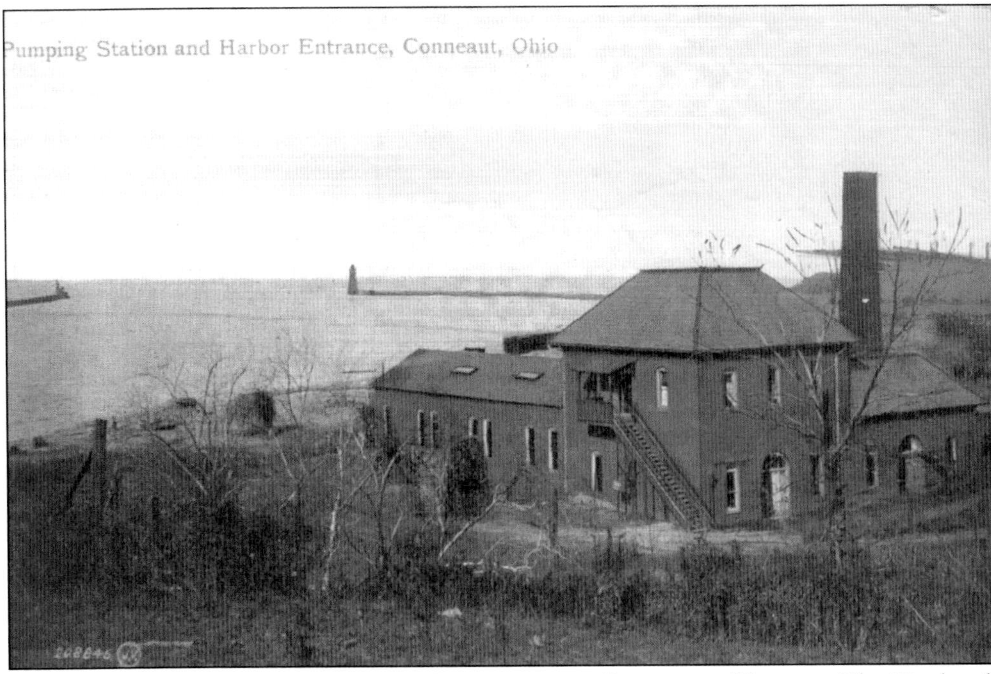

PUMPING STATION OVERLOOKING THE ENTRANCE TO CONNEAUT HARBOR. The Pittsburgh & Conneaut Dock Company is located to the left of this scene. (Courtesy of Conneaut Area Historical Society.)

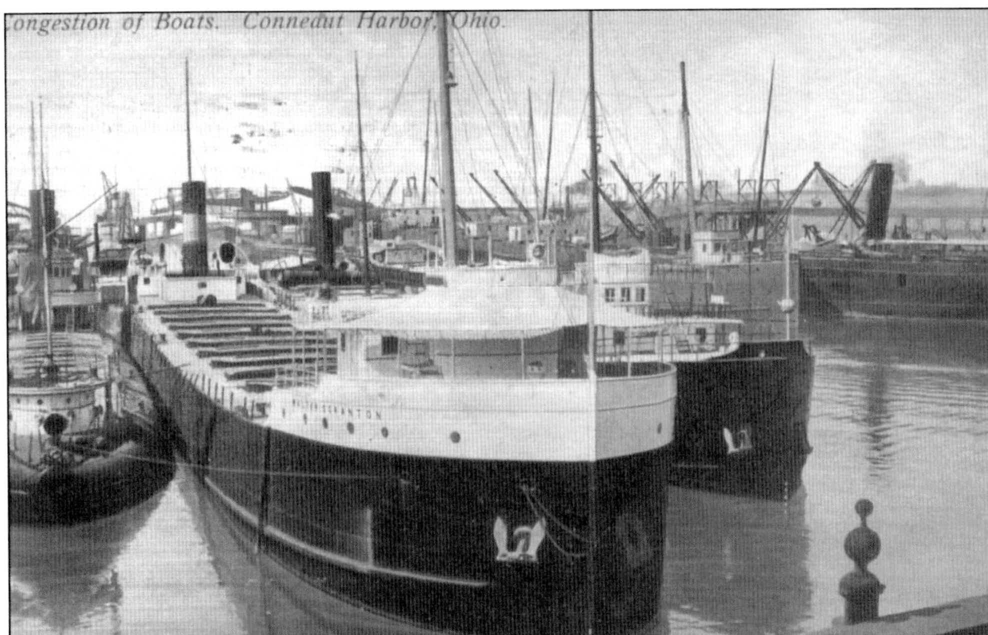

ORE BOATS IN CONNEAUT HARBOR. A distinctive "whaleback" boat is on the left. (Courtesy of Conneaut Area Historical Society.)

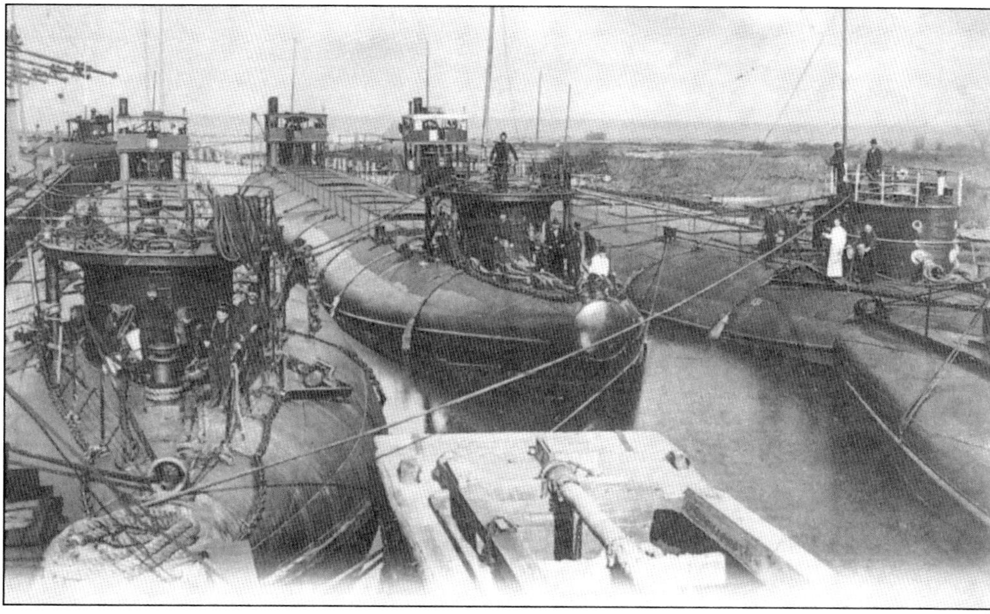

WHALEBACK STEAMERS AT BESSEMER DOCK. Nineteen whaleback freighters, one passenger vessel, and 23 "consorts" were built in Duluth, Minnesota and later in West Superior, Wisconsin by Captain Alexander McDougall from 1889-98. Their novel and inexpensive design was very influential on Great Lakes shipbuilding of that era. Although its rounded deck allowed efficient operation in heavy seas, the exposed center of the whaleback made bow-to-stern communications difficult under such conditions. (Courtesy of Conneaut Area Historical Society.)

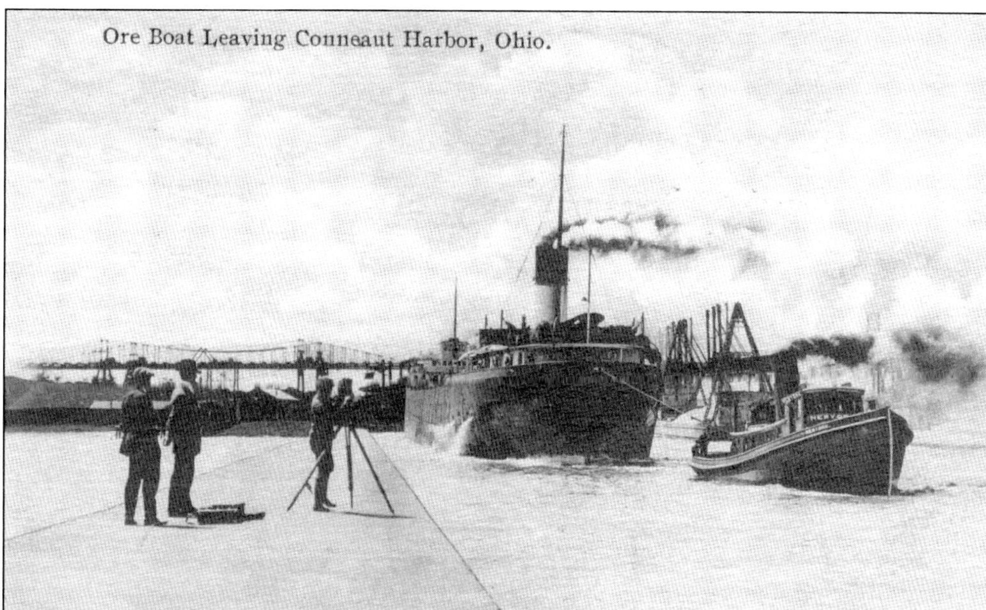

ORE BOATS SEEN FROM EAST PIER. The tug will pull the big boat until it clears the breakwater. (Courtesy of Conneaut Area Historical Society.)

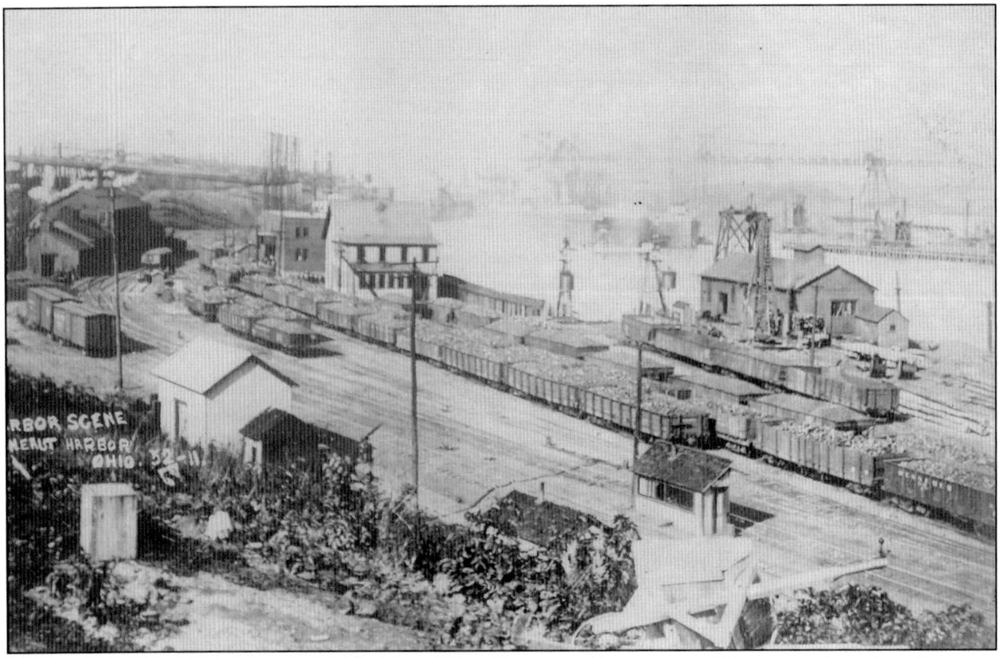

CONNEAUT HARBOR IN THE EARLY TWENTIETH CENTURY. The wooden freight cars date this scene at approximately one hundred years ago. (Courtesy of Conneaut Historical Railroad Museum.)

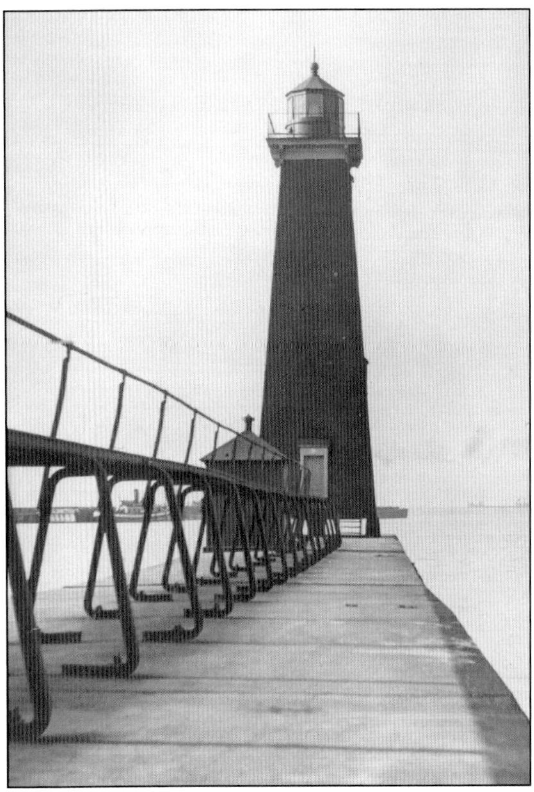

OLD WEST PIER LIGHTHOUSE (UNDATED). Today Conneaut Harbor has a modern, fully automated light. (Courtesy of Conneaut Area Historical Society.)

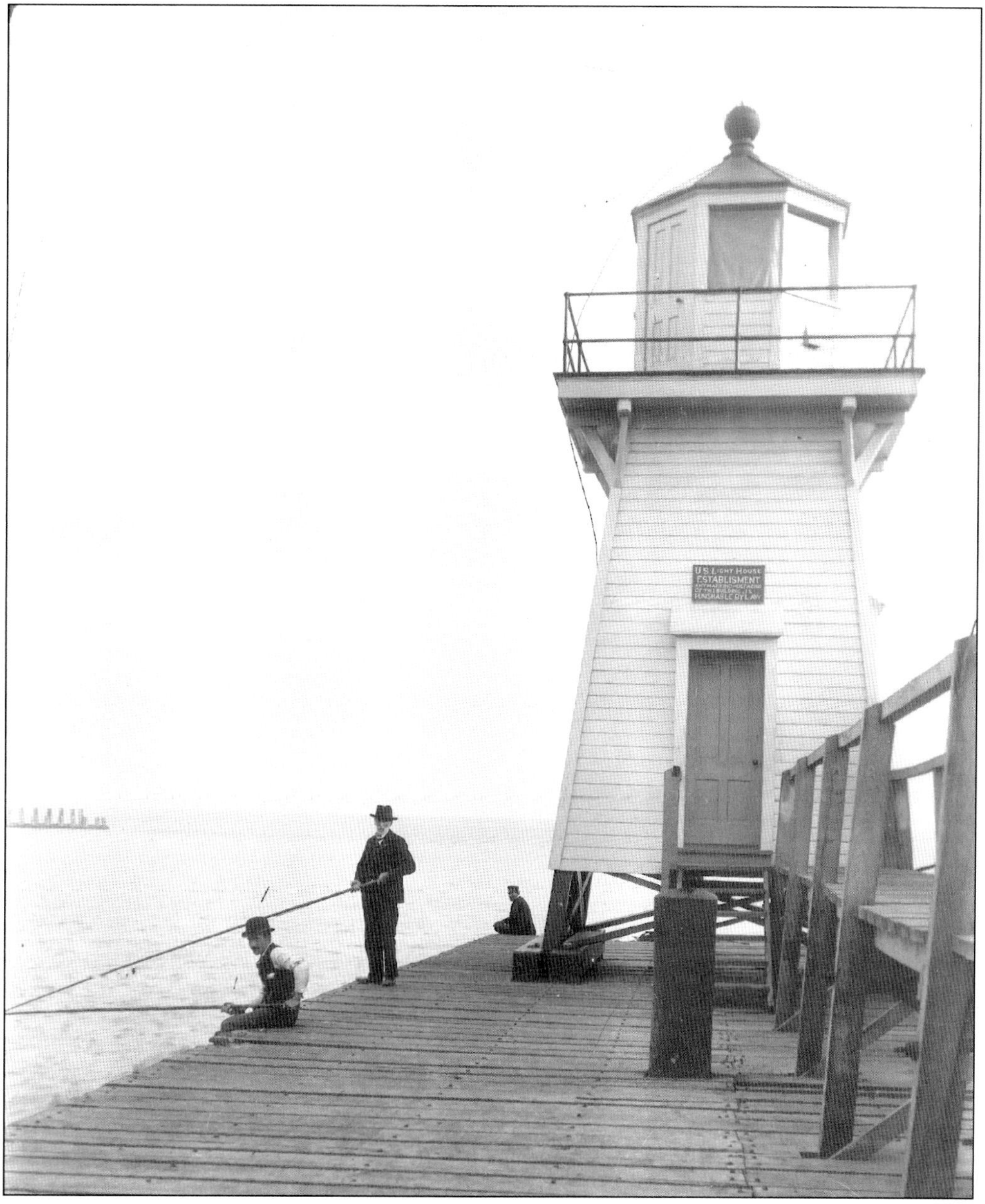

FISHERMEN ON EAST PIER, 1900. At this time, fish were still plentiful in the harbor. Today, fishing is still popular upstream along Conneaut Creek. (Courtesy of Conneaut Area Historical Society.)

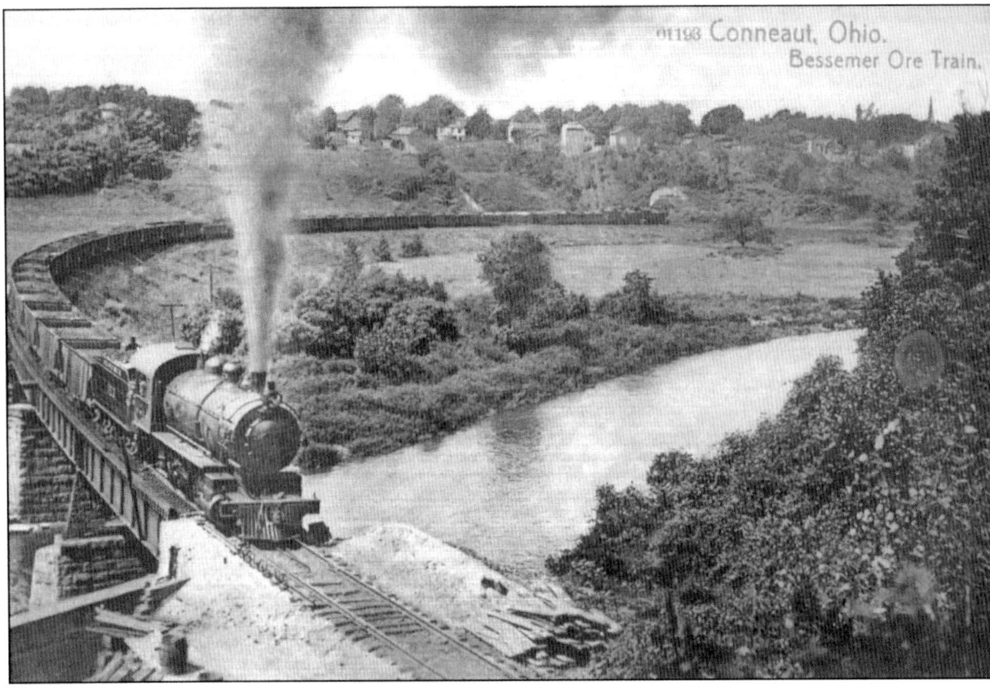

(Courtesy of Conneaut Area Historical Society.)

TWO GENERATIONS OF BESSEMER & LAKE ERIE ORE DRAG TRAINS. Above is the heavy-duty C3A-class Consolidation No. 153 built in 1902. Below is the No. 621, a 2-10-4 Texas type (equipped with a special cinder collector) built by Alco in 1937 and photographed on September 25, 1949.

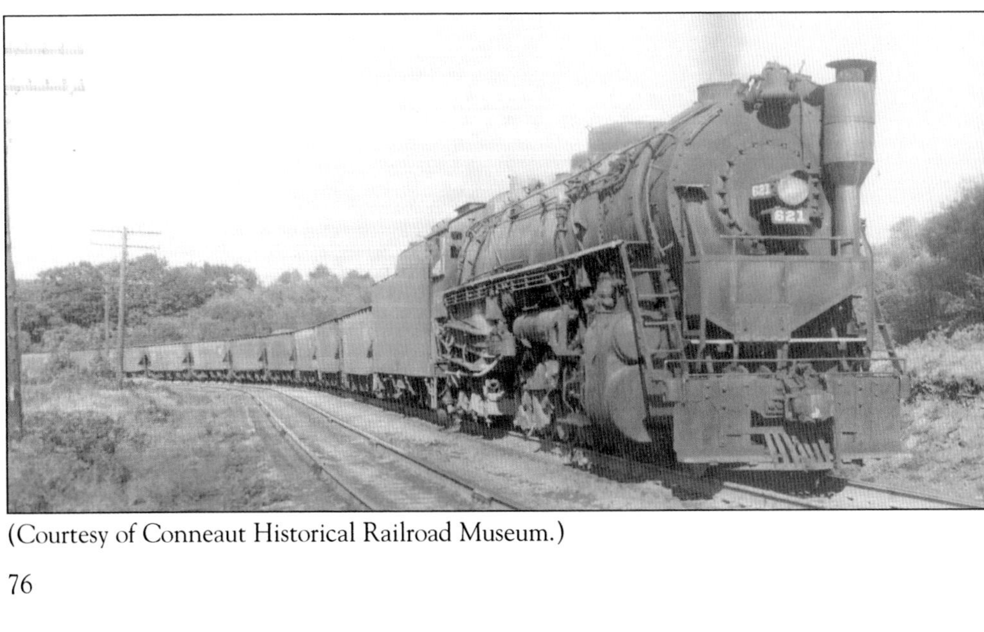

(Courtesy of Conneaut Historical Railroad Museum.)

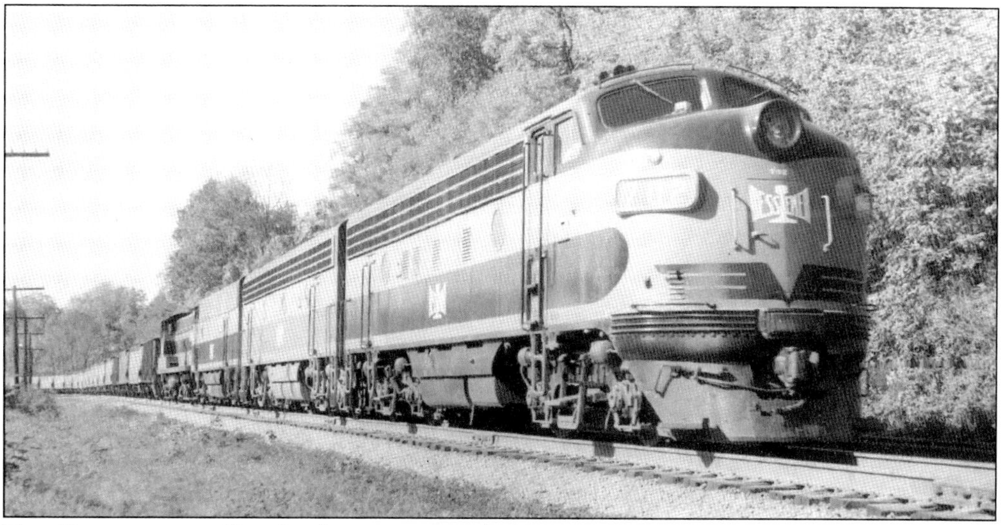

The Diesels that Did It. Bessemer & Lake Erie F7 "covered wagons" 702A/702B/703A, followed by SD7 No. 453, lead a northbound coal train into Conneaut on July 6, 1954. The "F" units were the hugely successful design from the Electro-Motive Division of General Motors that did more than any other diesels to force the retirement of steam across the country. Four demonstrators of EMD's earliest F unit, the FT, made a head-turning coast-to-coast tour in 1939-40, which covered more than 83,000 miles over 20 railroads. The "bulldog" nose quickly became synonymous with streamlining in the public's mind, but what convinced the railroads to begin dieselizing their fleets was the lower cost of maintenance and the fact that one crew could run as many units as needed. Of the 1500 hp F7s, 3,849—including 2,366 cab units and 1,483 cableless B units—were sold to American railroads from 1949–53. The last F units in U.S. revenue freight service, running on the B&LE's Western Allegheny subsidiary, were retired on October 13, 1992. (Courtesy of Conneaut Historical Railroad Museum.)

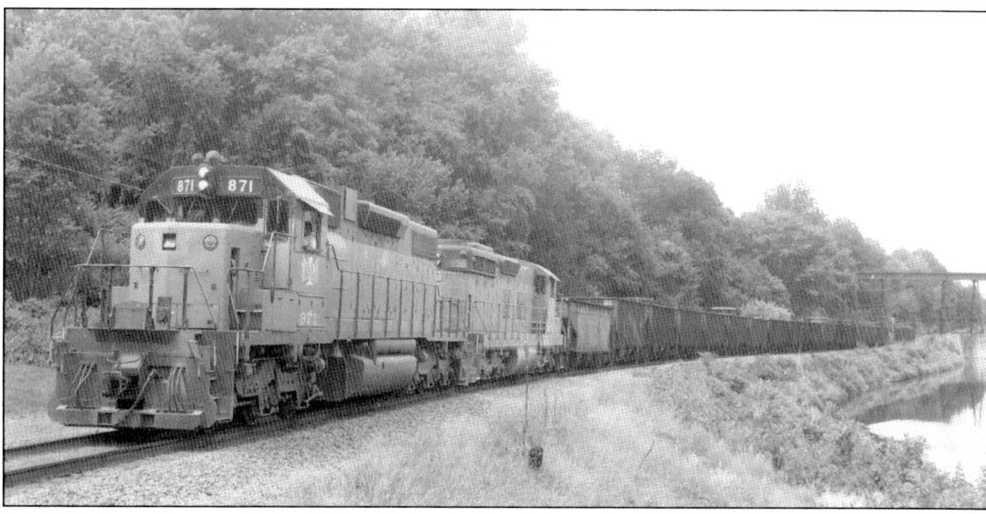

B&LE Hood Units. SD38-2 No. 871 and SD18 No. 856 just north of the Main Street grade crossing at Conneaut Creek. Road switchers of this style overtook the more attractive cab units in the 1950s. They allowed for much greater visibility in switching and could run in either direction if necessary, although, running long hood forward was (and is) avoided when possible for safety reasons. (Courtesy of Conneaut Historical Railroad Museum.)

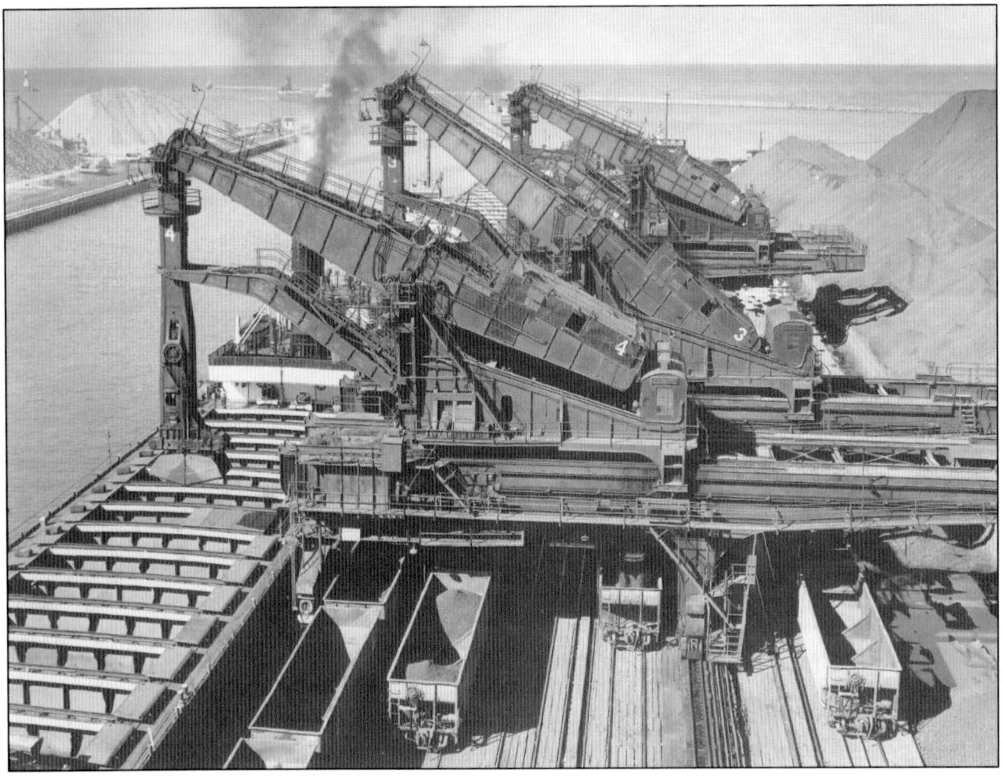

HULETT ORE UNLOADERS IN CONNEAUT HARBOR, C. 1960. (Courtesy of Conneaut Area Historical Society.)

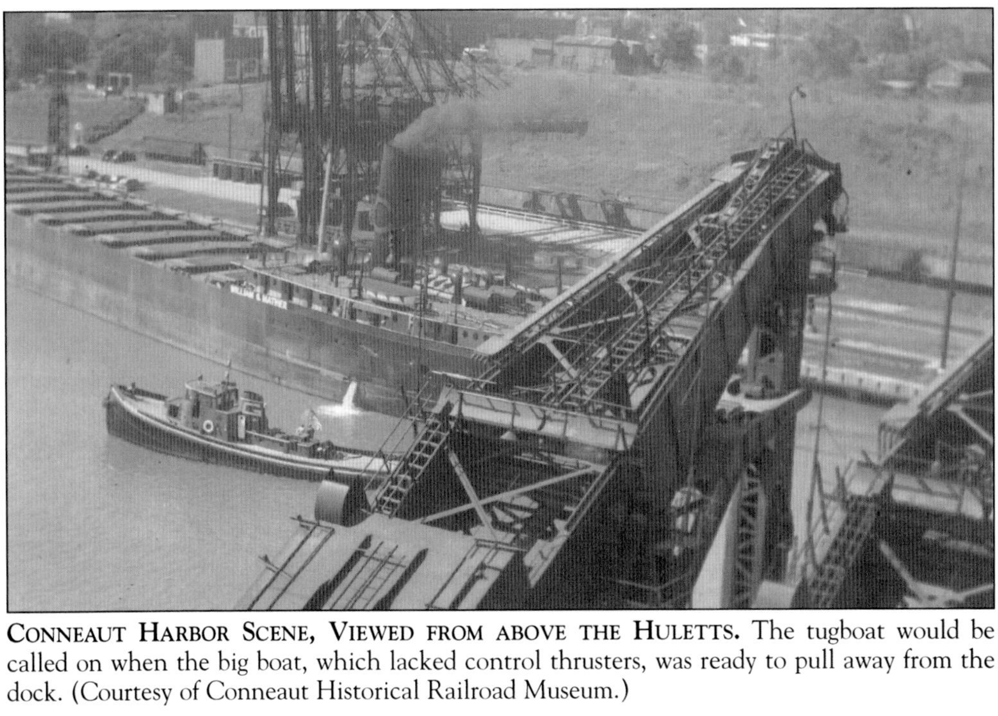

CONNEAUT HARBOR SCENE, VIEWED FROM ABOVE THE HULETTS. The tugboat would be called on when the big boat, which lacked control thrusters, was ready to pull away from the dock. (Courtesy of Conneaut Historical Railroad Museum.)

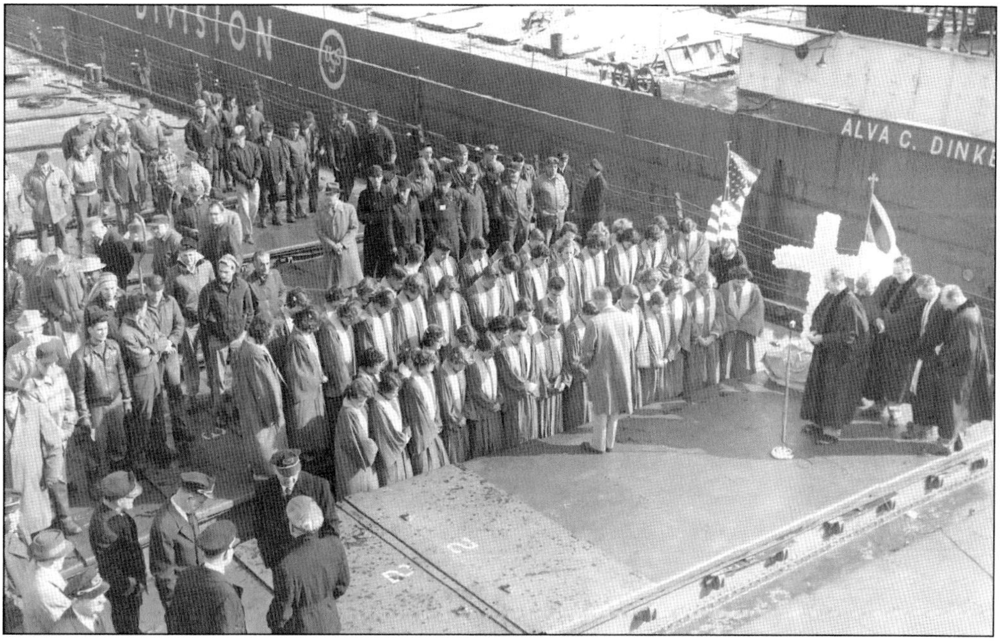

THE BLESSING OF THE FLEET IN CONNEAUT HARBOR, APRIL 2, 1956. The annual Blessing, practiced in harbors around the world, is an ancient tradition with origins in the Mediterranean fishing industry. The presiding clergyman offers a prayer for the safety of the sailors at the beginning of the shipping season. (*Cleveland Press*, courtesy of Special Collections, Cleveland State University Library.)

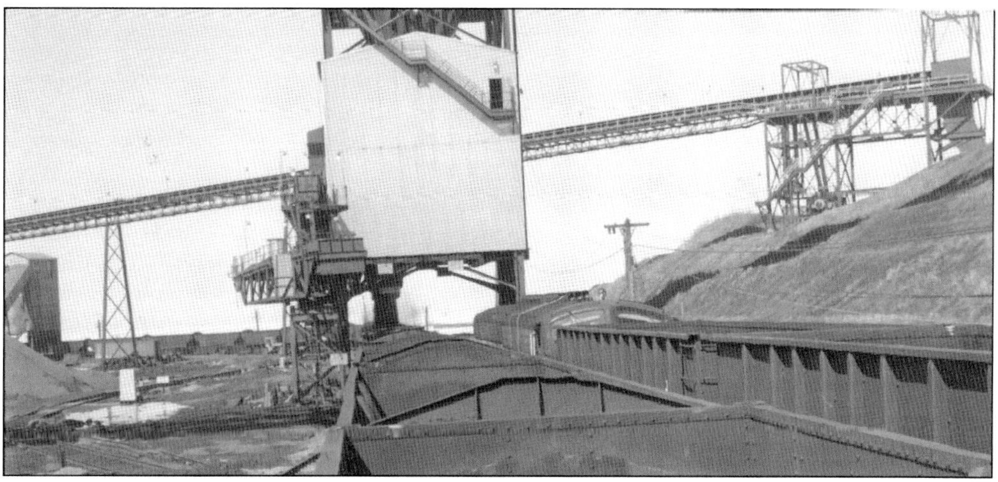

DIESELS AT THE PITTSBURGH & CONNEAUT DOCK COMPANY, 1974. At this ore/limestone loadout station, EMD F7s could move 400 cars through in 12 hours. These diesels are similar to those seen on the top of page 77, but are restricted to the docks and are radio controlled with no crew onboard. Painted yellow and black, they were among a total of eight leased to P&C Dock Company by the B&LE. The last remaining units, Nos. 715A, 715B, 719A, and 722A, were finally retired and sold in late 2000. The 722A, built in 1952, was rescued from a scrap yard in Youngstown by the Potomac Eagle Scenic Railroad, repainted, and put into excursion service. Several other B&LE cab units are in museums. (*Cleveland Press*, courtesy of Special Collections, Cleveland State University Library.)

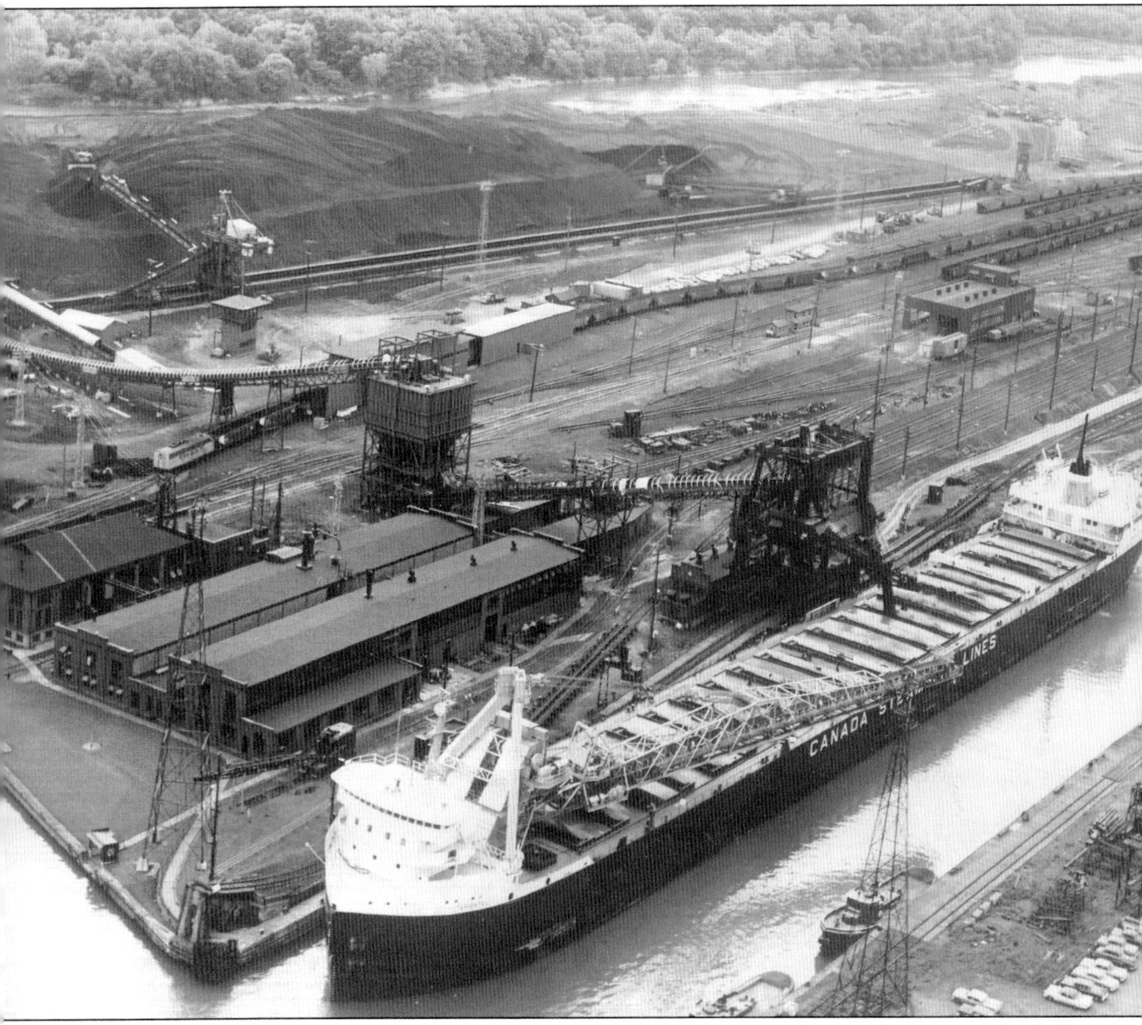

COAL STORAGE AND TRANSFER TERMINAL, JUNE 1965. At rear is the car dumper in which the hoppers had to be emptied by opening their bottom chutes, unlike many modern dumpers that tip the cars upside down by rotating them. At left center, a remote-controlled F7 moves a string of hoppers. (*Cleveland Press*, courtesy of Special Collections, Cleveland State University Library.)

HULETT ORE UNLOADER NO. 3 AT PITTSBURGH & CONNEAUT DOCK. Seen from a distance, the 950-ton Hulett Ore Unloaders made a unique and unmistakable profile as they dipped down into the hold of an ore boat and scooped out up to 17 tons of iron ore in just 50 seconds. Conneaut Harbor had five units. (Courtesy of Dale Olin.)

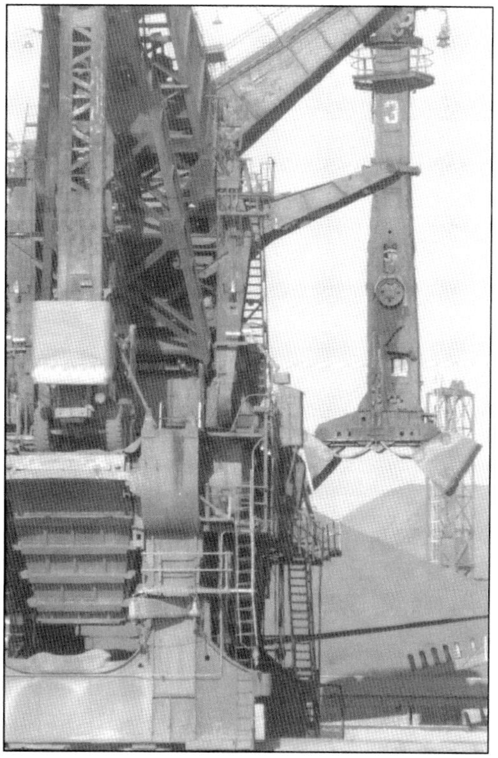

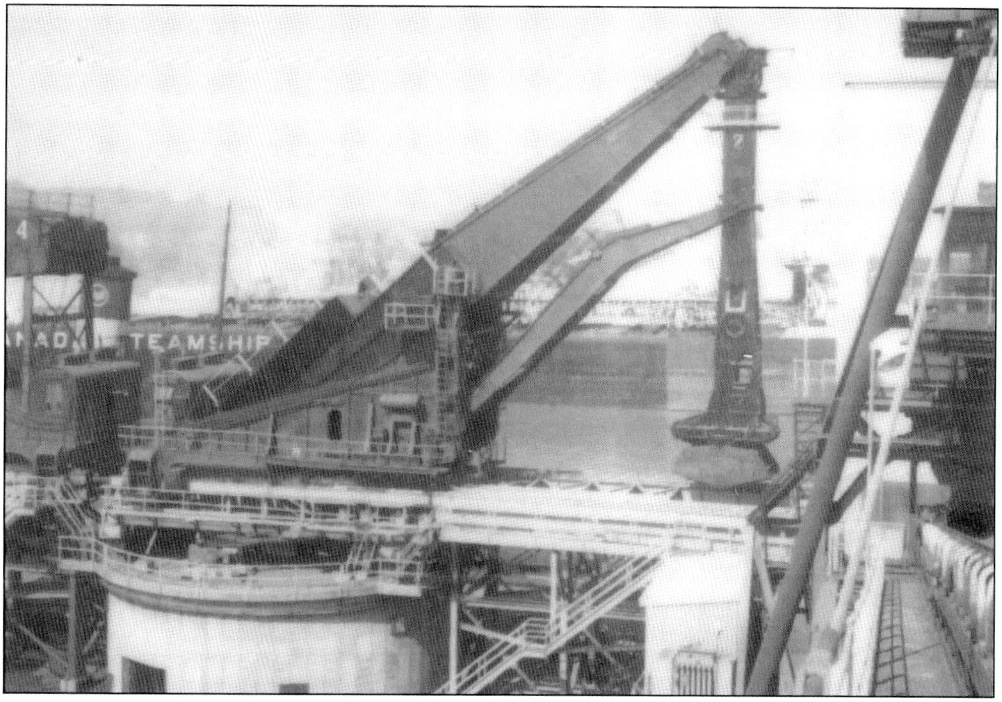

HULETT ORE UNLOADER NO. 2 ON THE TURNTABLE. The Huletts traveled on two sets of narrow-gauge rails. The turntable was used not only to turn the machines around, but as a place to perform some types of repairs. (Courtesy of Dale Olin.)

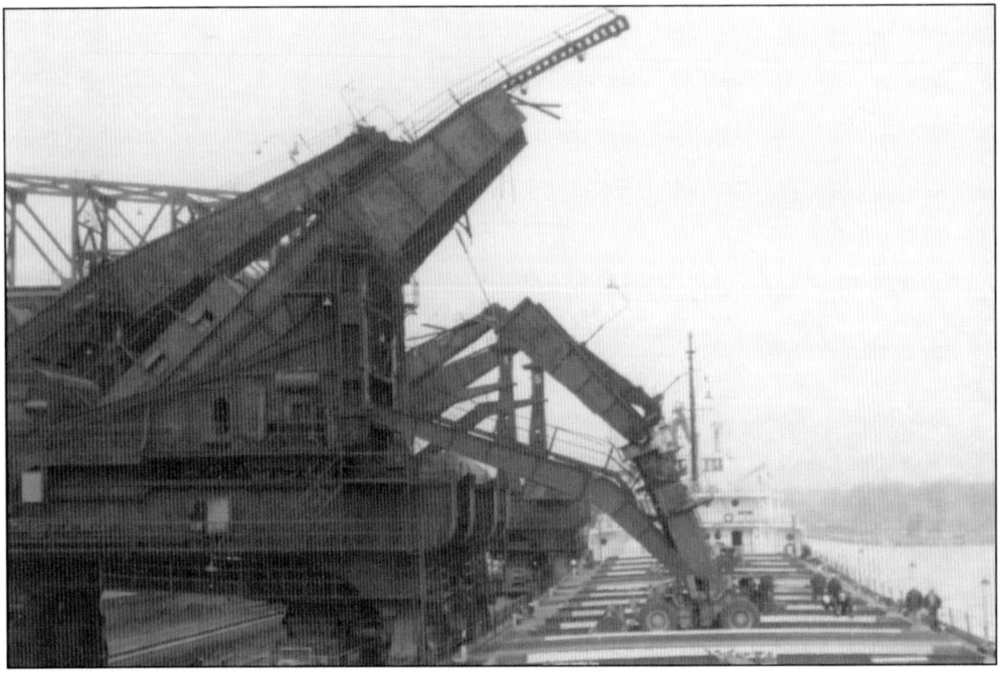

ACCIDENT ON A HULETT UNLOADER, LATE 1970S. The walking beam of Hulett No. 2 has broken due to the grab bucket being snared on the hatch coaming, which gives entrance to the boat's hold. (Courtesy of Dale Olin.)

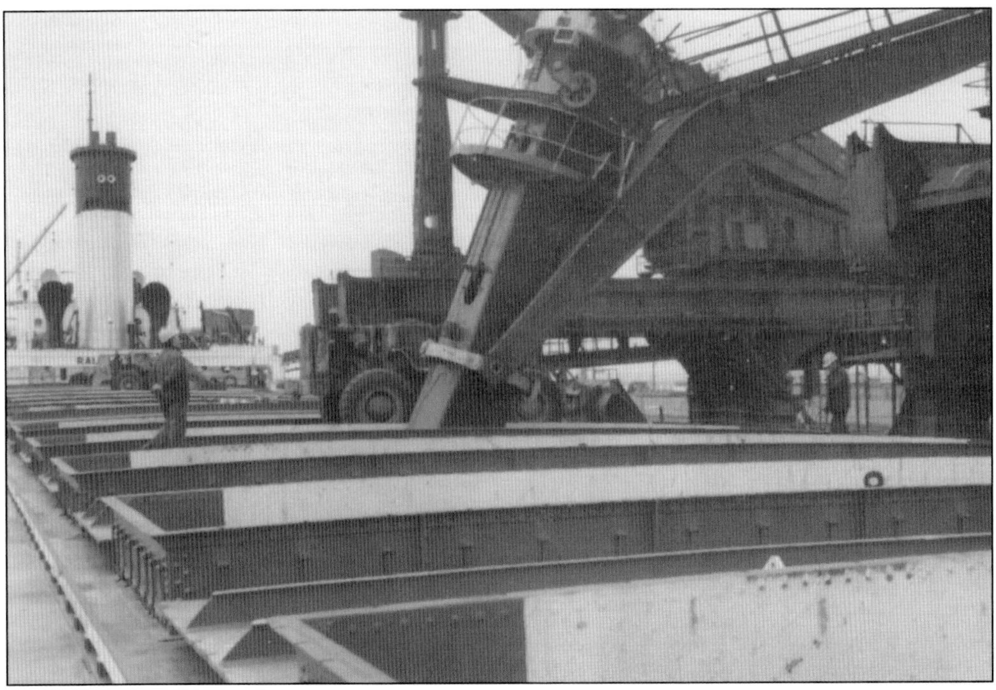

A CURIOUS WORKER EXAMINES THE BROKEN BEAM OF THE HULETT. The cause of the problem was later traced to the severing of a single electrical wire on the unloader. (Courtesy of Dale Olin.)

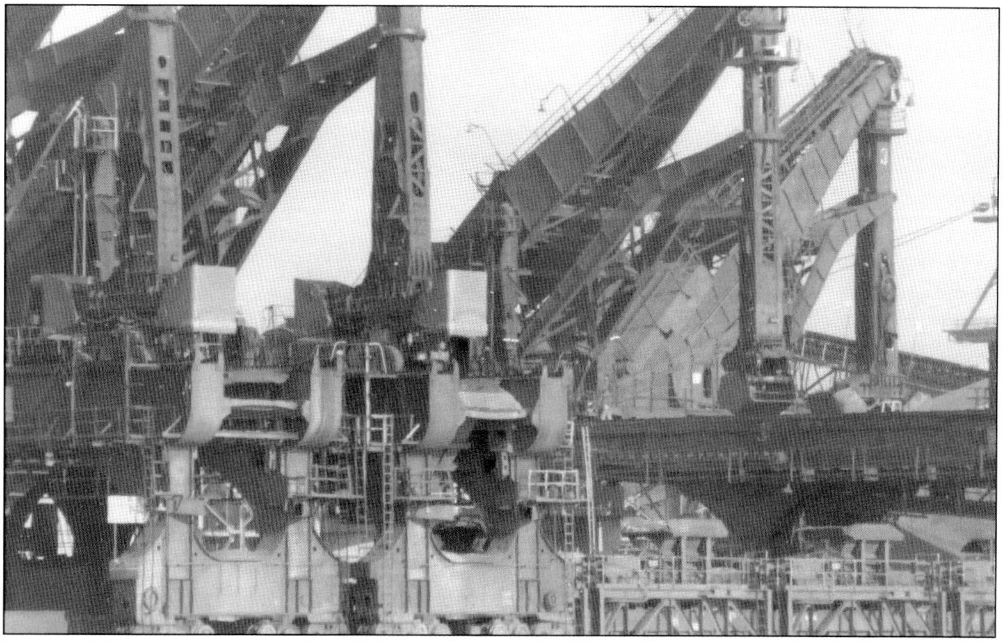

MAJOR HULETT REPAIRS. This photograph was taken from the west side of Conneaut Harbor in approximately 1979. The platform or "trolley" underneath Hulett No. 5, second from right, is being moved from its base in preparation for rebuilding. (Courtesy of Dale Olin.)

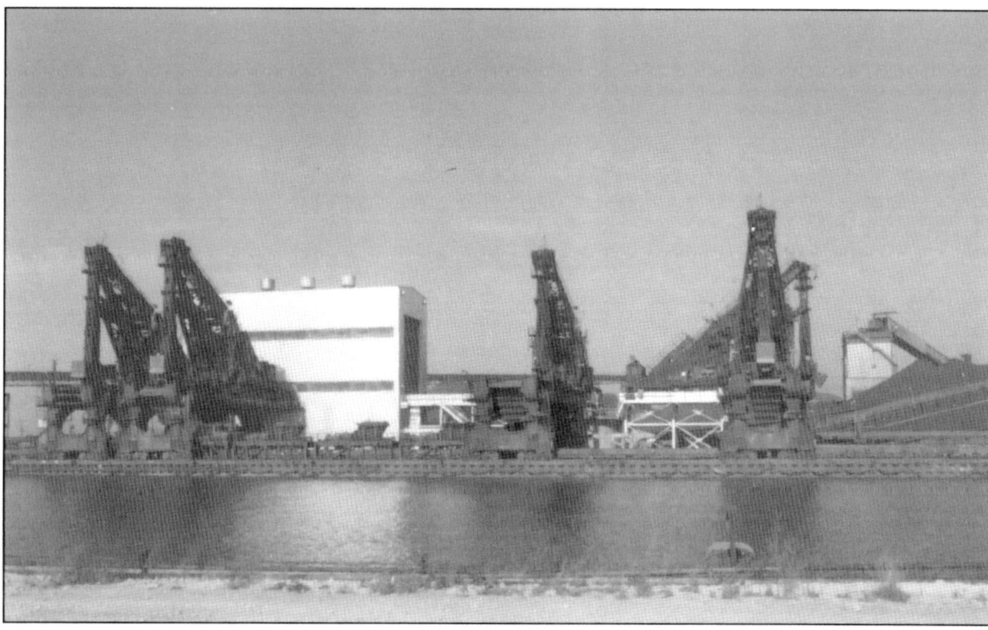

HULETT REPAIR BUILDING. This structure ended up a bit shorter than intended due to a Conneaut city regulation prohibiting the construction of buildings higher than nine stories. This was a major hindrance to maintenance crews. Structural maintenance could be done inside, but if the motor of a Hulett Ore Unloader needed to be removed, the work had to be done outside of the building. In general, major repairs would be done by the day shift, whereas at night the focus was merely upon keeping the machines running. (Courtesy of Dale Olin.)

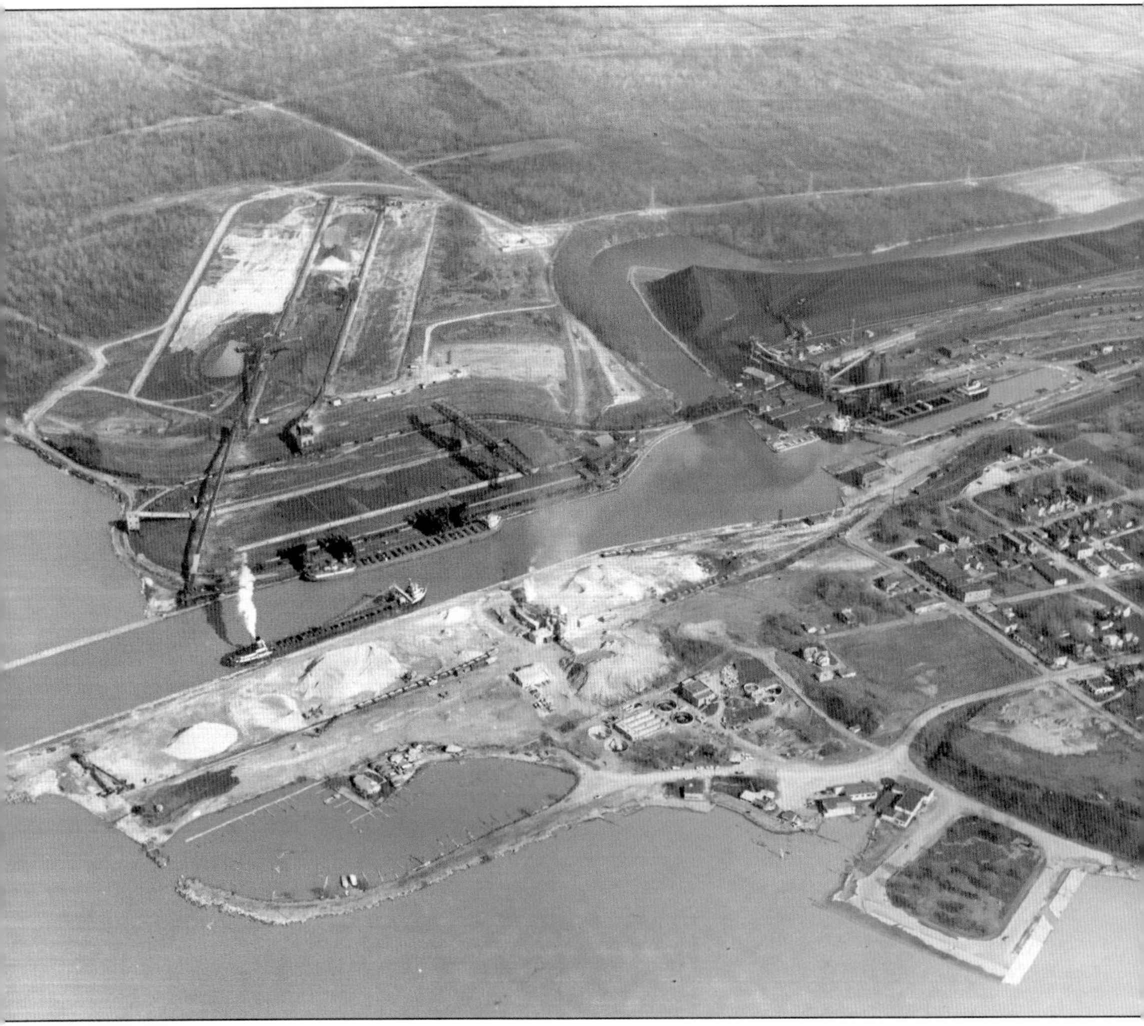

PITTSBURGH & CONNEAUT DOCK COMPANY, 1973. At the center of the photograph is the loop of track on which the set of radio-controlled locomotives move hopper cars to loading or unloading stations. The swing bridge spans the bend in the creek. (*Cleveland Press*, courtesy of Special Collections, Cleveland State University Library.)

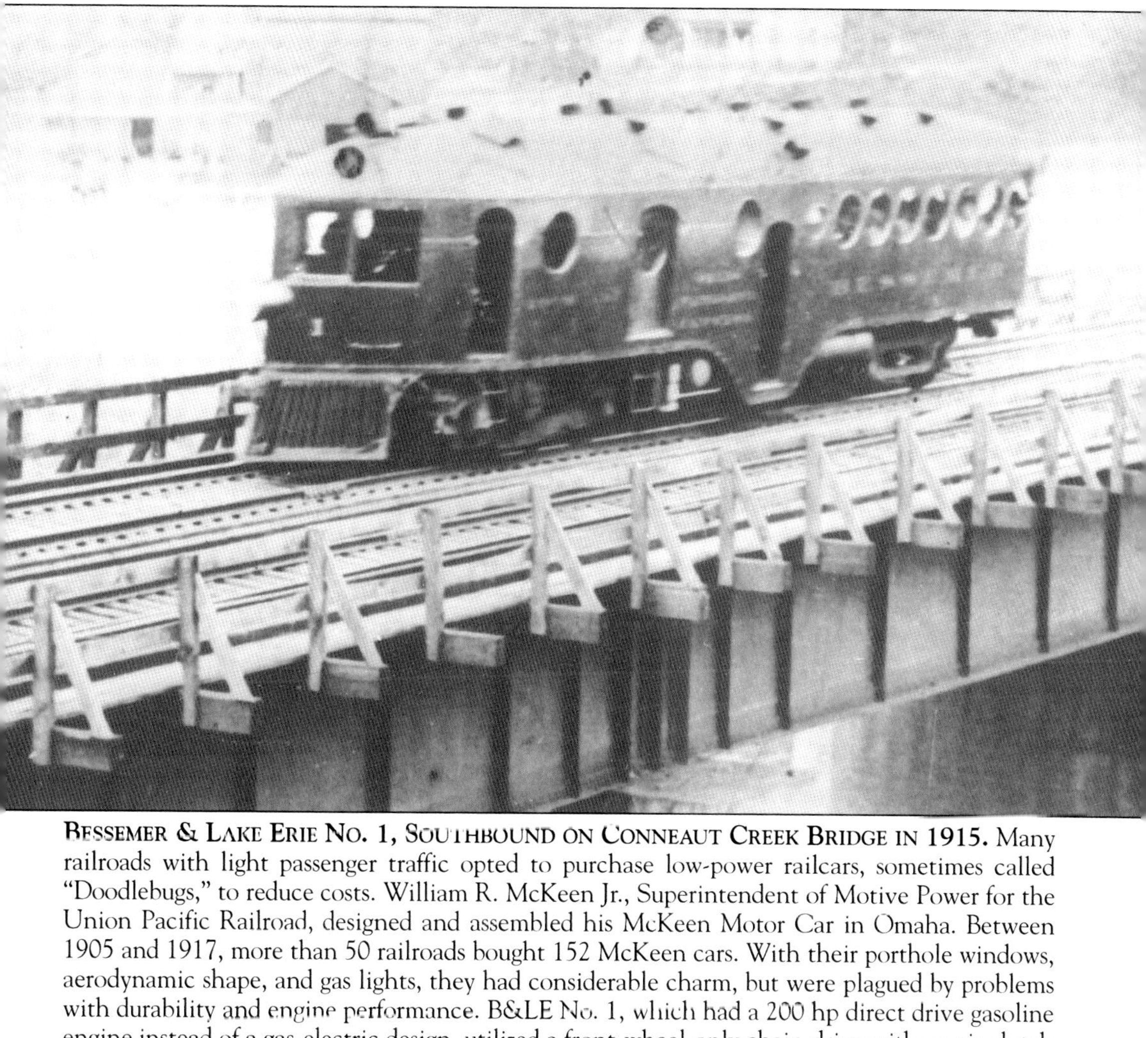

BESSEMER & LAKE ERIE NO. 1, SOUTHBOUND ON CONNEAUT CREEK BRIDGE IN 1915. Many railroads with light passenger traffic opted to purchase low-power railcars, sometimes called "Doodlebugs," to reduce costs. William R. McKeen Jr., Superintendent of Motive Power for the Union Pacific Railroad, designed and assembled his McKeen Motor Car in Omaha. Between 1905 and 1917, more than 50 railroads bought 152 McKeen cars. With their porthole windows, aerodynamic shape, and gas lights, they had considerable charm, but were plagued by problems with durability and engine performance. B&LE No. 1, which had a 200 hp direct drive gasoline engine instead of a gas-electric design, utilized a front-wheel-only chain drive with an air clutch and a two-speed transmission and lacked a reverse gear. It had a capacity of 66 passengers and a baggage compartment. One of two doodlebugs on the Bessemer roster, No. 1 was purchased in 1914 and ran all over the system, but it did not prove successful and was retired two years later, surviving on the scrap line until 1927. (Courtesy of Conneaut Historical Railroad Museum.)

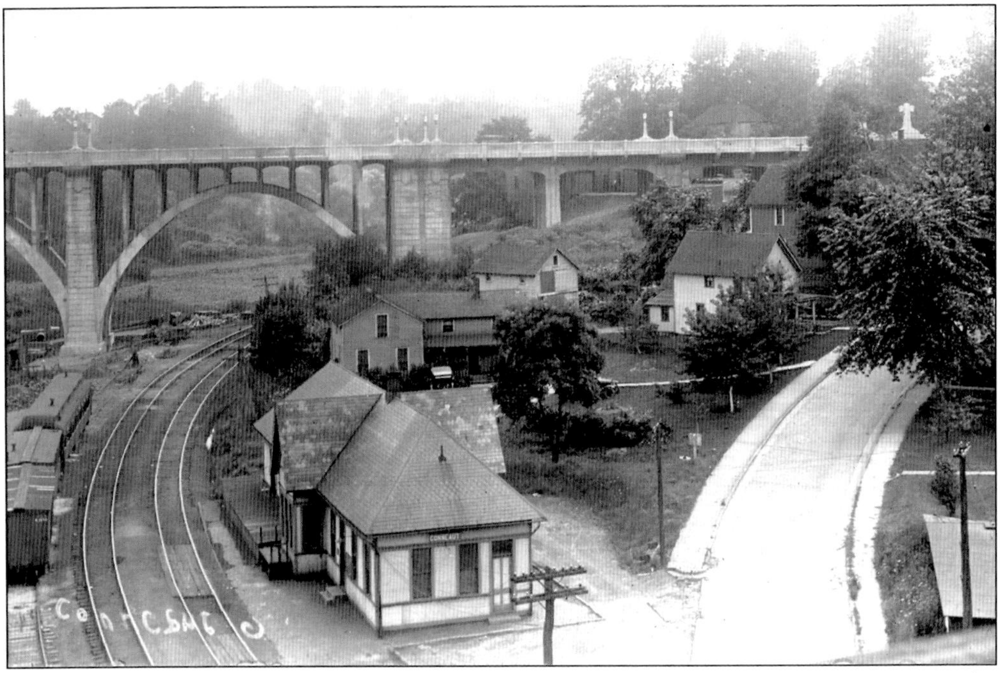

BESSEMER & LAKE ERIE DEPOT. The station was located at the bottom of Liberty Street under the viaduct. (Courtesy of Conneaut Area Historical Society.)

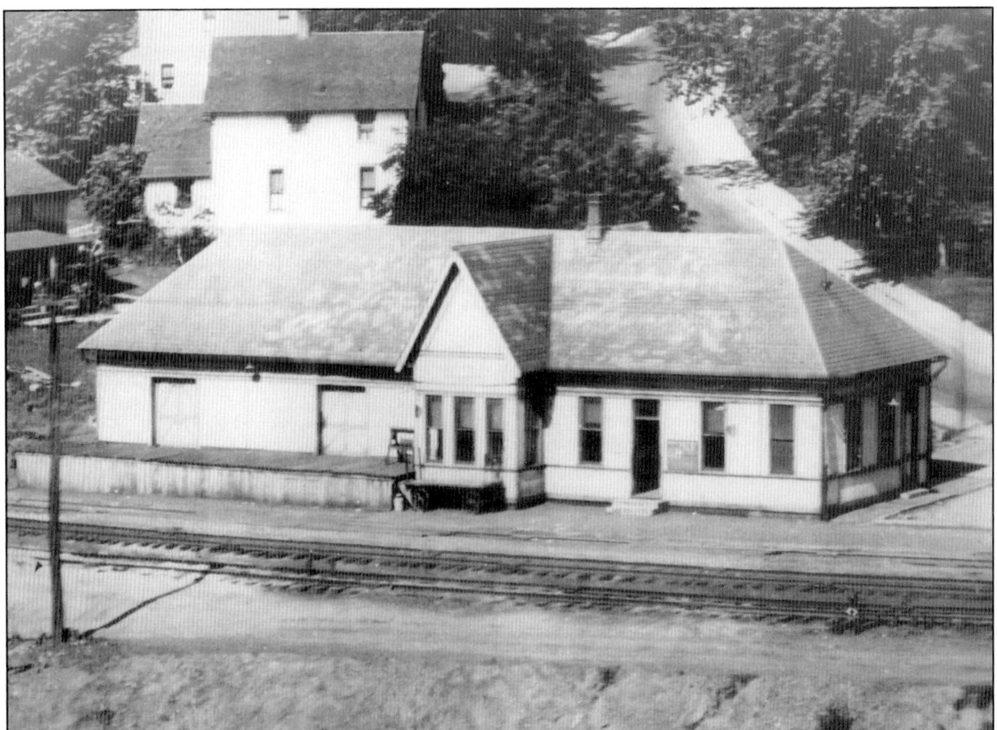

BESSEMER & LAKE ERIE DEPOT. The last passenger train on the Conneaut branch of the Bessemer ran May 31, 1932. (Courtesy of Conneaut Historical Railroad Museum.)

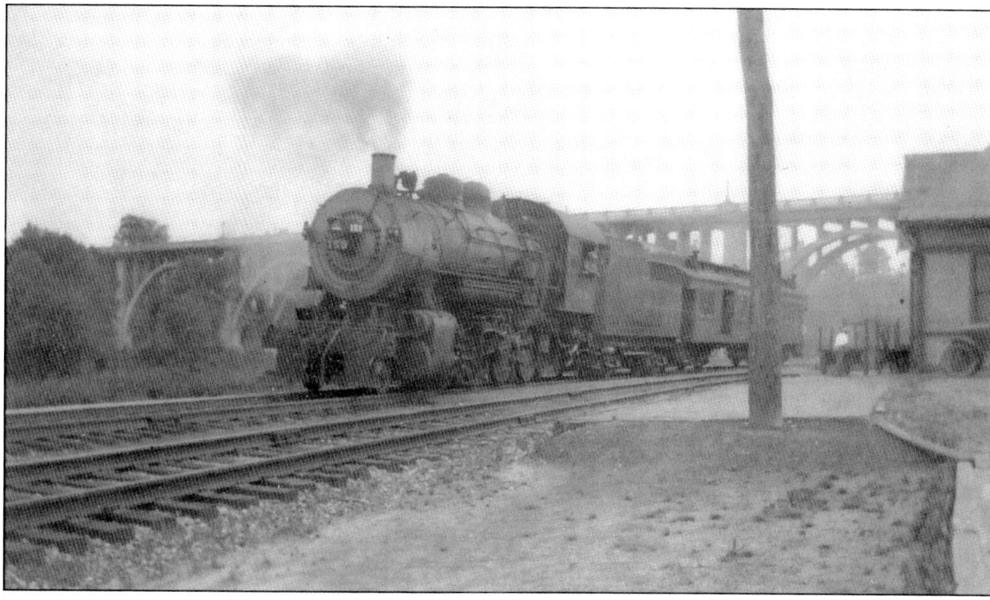

B&LE Passenger Train at the Depot. Business is light as evidenced by the single car. The locomotive, a 2-8-0 Consolidation of class C4a, was an interesting choice for a passenger assignment. Built by Baldwin in 1913, No. 159 was one of a group of 10 heavy 2-8-0s designed in 1900 by the Pittsburgh Locomotive Works specifically to haul slow "drag" freights over the steep grades between Conneaut and Albion (see p. 65). They were built purely for power with large cylinders and small drivers, and the small wheels inhibited high speeds even with a light passenger load. (Courtesy of Conneaut Historical Railroad Museum.)

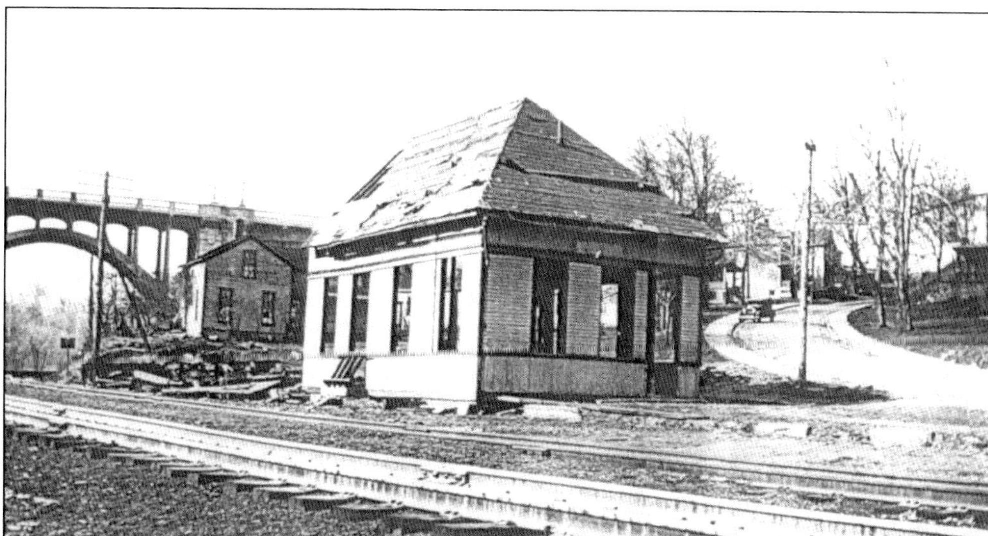

Demolition of the B&LE Depot. The structure was torn down on March 29, 1935. Passenger service over the system as a whole ceased on March 5, 1955, with the last runs of trains Nos. 12 and 13 between Greenville and Erie. (Courtesy of Conneaut Historical Railroad Museum.)

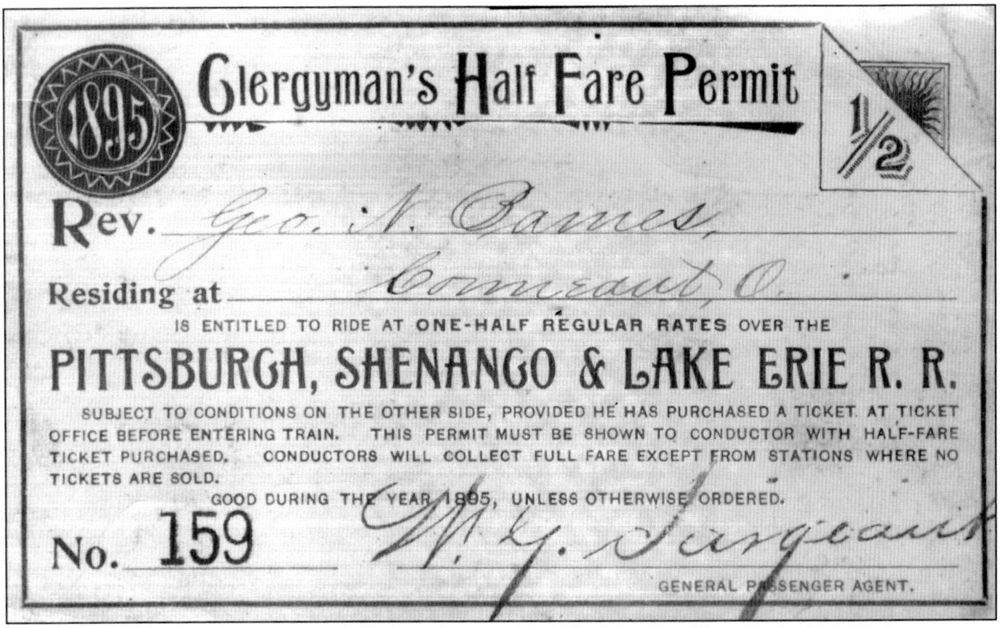
1895

Clergyman's Half Fare Permit

1/2

Rev. Geo. N. Barnes,

Residing at Conneaut, O.

IS ENTITLED TO RIDE AT ONE-HALF REGULAR RATES OVER THE

PITTSBURGH, SHENANGO & LAKE ERIE R. R.

SUBJECT TO CONDITIONS ON THE OTHER SIDE, PROVIDED HE HAS PURCHASED A TICKET AT TICKET OFFICE BEFORE ENTERING TRAIN. THIS PERMIT MUST BE SHOWN TO CONDUCTOR WITH HALF-FARE TICKET PURCHASED. CONDUCTORS WILL COLLECT FULL FARE EXCEPT FROM STATIONS WHERE NO TICKETS ARE SOLD.

GOOD DURING THE YEAR 1895, UNLESS OTHERWISE ORDERED.

No. 159

W. G. Sargeant

GENERAL PASSENGER AGENT.

CLERGYMAN'S PERMIT, 1895. (Courtesy of Conneaut Historical Railroad Museum.)

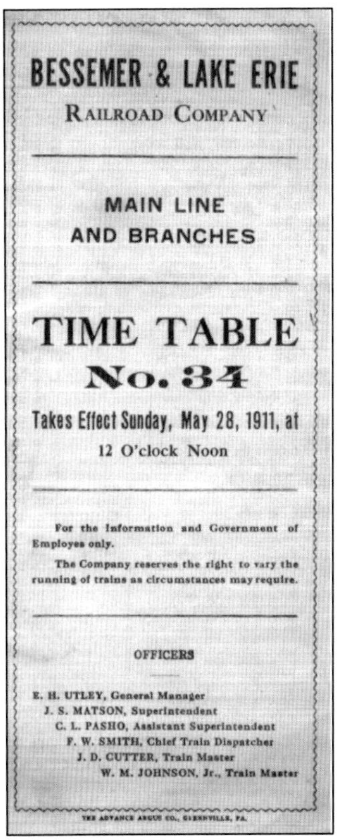
BESSEMER & LAKE ERIE

RAILROAD COMPANY

MAIN LINE
AND BRANCHES

TIME TABLE

No. 34

Takes Effect Sunday, May 28, 1911, at

12 O'clock Noon

For the Information and Government of Employes only.

The Company reserves the right to vary the running of trains as circumstances may require.

OFFICERS

E. H. UTLEY, General Manager
J. S. MATSON, Superintendent
C. L. PASHO, Assistant Superintendent
F. W. SMITH, Chief Train Dispatcher
J. D. CUTTER, Train Master
W. M. JOHNSON, Jr., Train Master

THE ADVANCE ARGUS CO., GREENVILLE, PA.

BESSEMER & LAKE ERIE TIMETABLE. Passenger business was never brisk on the Bessemer. (Courtesy of Conneaut Historical Railroad Museum.)

BESSEMER AND LAKE ERIE RAILROAD COMPANY

GREENVILLE, PENNSYLVANIA 16125

W. D. HELLYER
SUPERINTENDENT CAR DEPARTMENT

August 19, 1970

Mr. F. A. Betteys
1356 Lake Road
Conneaut, Ohio

Dear Floyd,

It has been brought to my attention that while performing your duties as a Carman at Conneaut, Ohio, you discovered two broken truck bolsters while repairing cars on August 7, 1970.

I want to take this opportunity to express my appreciation on a job well done. As you know, had you not detected the above-mentioned defects, they could have caused serious accidents. You are to be commended, and I will see that a copy of this letter is placed on your personal file. Also, Mr. Gariepy will give you a gift as a token of our appreciation.

Yours truly,

W D Hellyer
Superintendent Car Department

Bessemer & Lake Erie Correspondence. (Courtesy of Conneaut Historical Railroad Museum.)

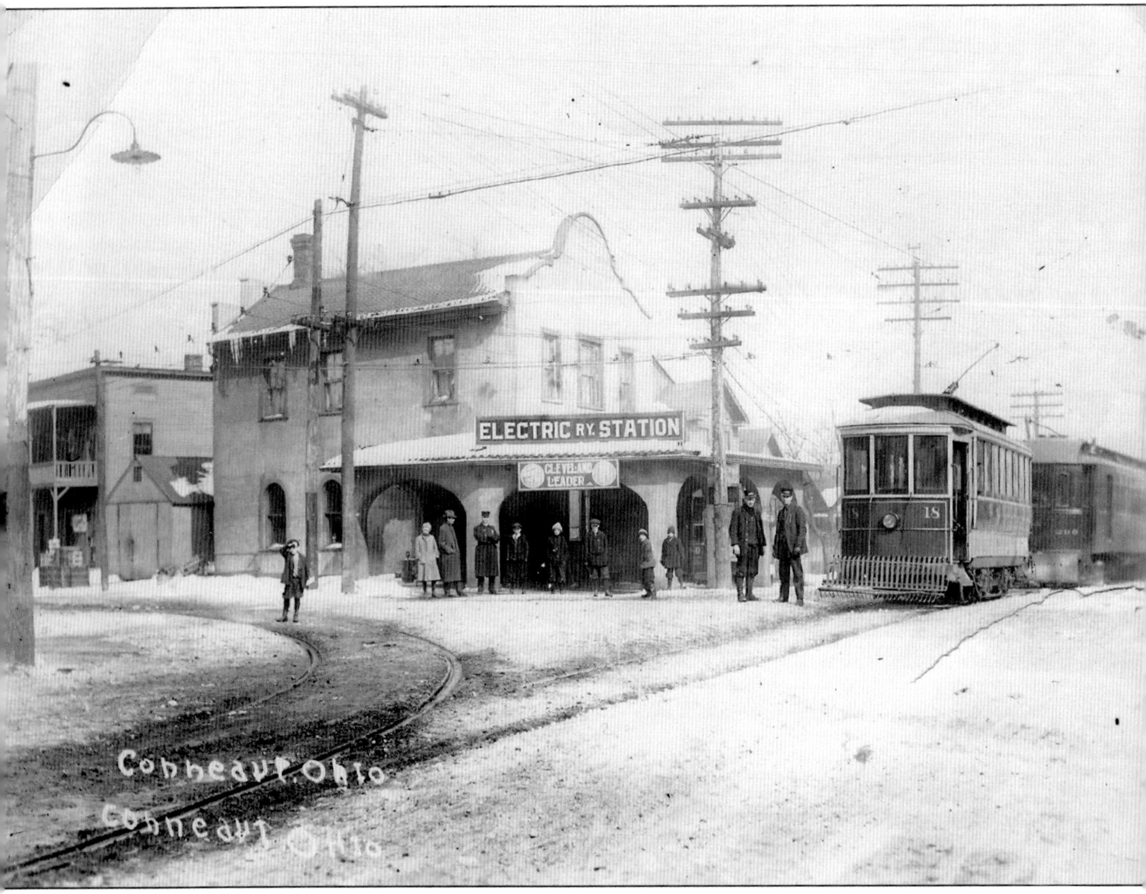

Electric Railway Station, Intersection of Main and Harbor Streets. (Courtesy of Conneaut Area Historical Society.)

Four

Traction
Trolleys and Interurbans

In 1902, with the expansion of Conneaut Village and its incorporation as a city, Main Street was paved with bricks. The following year, trolley tracks were laid in the street, branching off in spurs that connected to Park Place at the harbor and Lake View Park, as well as to the New York Central depot. At first, horses pulled the trolleys, but when the city built a municipal electric light plant soon afterward it became feasible to put up wires for electric traction.

City trolleys were not the only electrified railways to come to Conneaut. This was the heyday of the "interurbans," which connected adjacent cities and towns via a large network of rails with overhead electrification. Riding on the streetcar-type equipment of the interurbans was the easiest way to travel short and medium distances before the upgrading of roads and the increasing popularity of automobiles lessened Americans' appetite for public transit. On November 11, 1901, an interurban line called the Pennsylvania & Ohio Electric Railway opened for business between Ashtabula and Conneaut; westbound passengers could now connect to other Ohio interurbans. The P&O was expanded in 1902 with a line from Ashtabula southward to Jefferson. The complete run from Conneaut to Jefferson, with stops at Amboy, Kingsville, and Ashtabula, took 90 minutes and cost 60¢.

Concurrent with the creation of the P&O, developers moved to connect the extensive Pennsylvania and New York interurban networks with that of Ohio. Bridging of the gap between Erie and Conneaut, a distance of 35 miles, was begun in 1902 by the Lake Construction Company of Philadelphia. The physical plant for the route of the Conneaut & Erie Traction Company was completed in 1903. One hour and fifty minutes (and, again, 60¢) was required to ride the entire line, which had 12 intermediate stops.

The Electric Railway Station on the northwest corner of Main and Harbor (opposite page) was the focal point at which passengers could transfer to and from the P&O, the C&E, and Conneaut Union Station city trolleys. The end points of each interurban were not regarded as absolute barriers. The companies leased cars from each other as needed, and longer runs (such as C&E baseball specials that went all the way to Cleveland) were sometimes undertaken. Interurban freight cars also ventured into "foreign" railway territory. Milk and meat were among the commodities that were transported every morning on the electrified lines.

Financial trouble always loomed for America's interurbans, which were in decline by the 1920s. The C&E ran afoul of high costs and went bankrupt in 1907 even though ridership was high. Reorganized as Cleveland & Erie Railway Company, it emerged from bankruptcy in 1909, but the reprieve was temporary. After contending with rising costs and the failure of its eastern neighbor the Buffalo & Lake Erie Traction Company, the C&E entered bankruptcy again in 1920 and ceased operations on September 16, 1922. The Conneaut city trolleys had stopped running the year before, and the P&O would fare no better. In the wake of reorganization in 1919 as the Pennsylvania & Ohio Traction Company, the railway folded on February 24, 1924.

Various bus lines picked up the interurbans' business, but a charming mode of travel was lost. Today, in an era when pollution, gridlock, and high gasoline prices make the concept of a nationwide network of electric railways seem more relevant than ever, the prohibitive costs of creating the infrastructure confine the implementation of light rail systems to a few very large urban areas.

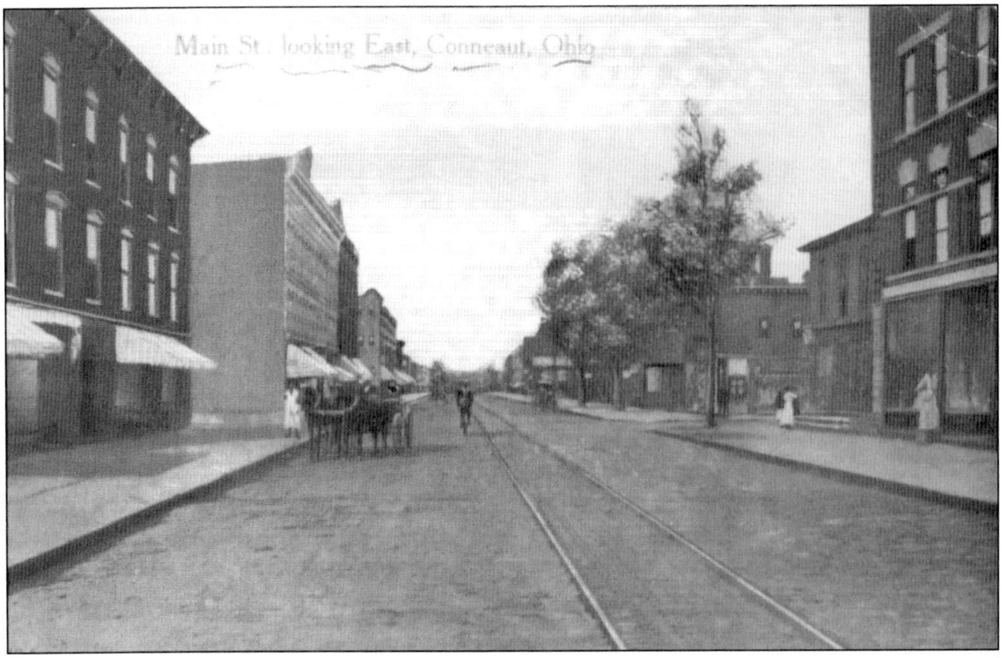

HORSE CAR LINE ON MAIN STREET, BEFORE ELECTRIFICATION. The street has been bricked and tracks laid, but trolley wires will not be hung until the municipal electric plant has been built. Horses were also required in the first six weeks of the Conneaut & Erie interurban line to pull cars across the high-level bridge over Conneaut Creek seen on the opposite page. (Courtesy of Conneaut Area Historical Society.)

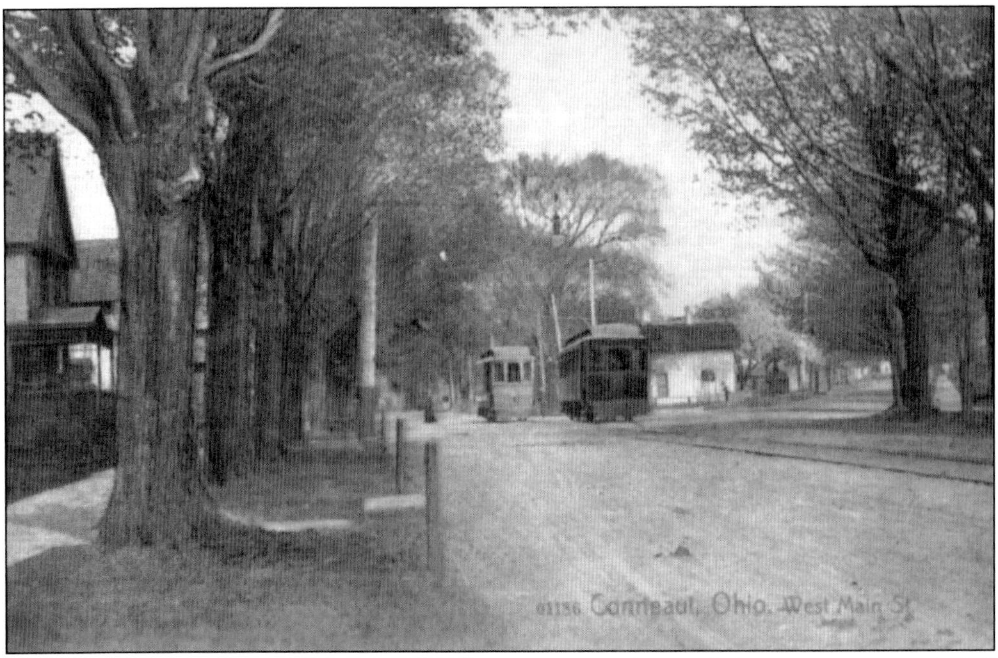

TROLLEYS ON WEST MAIN STREET. Electrification is complete and the streetcar era is in full swing. Unfortunately, it would be a brief one. (Courtesy of Conneaut Area Historical Society.)

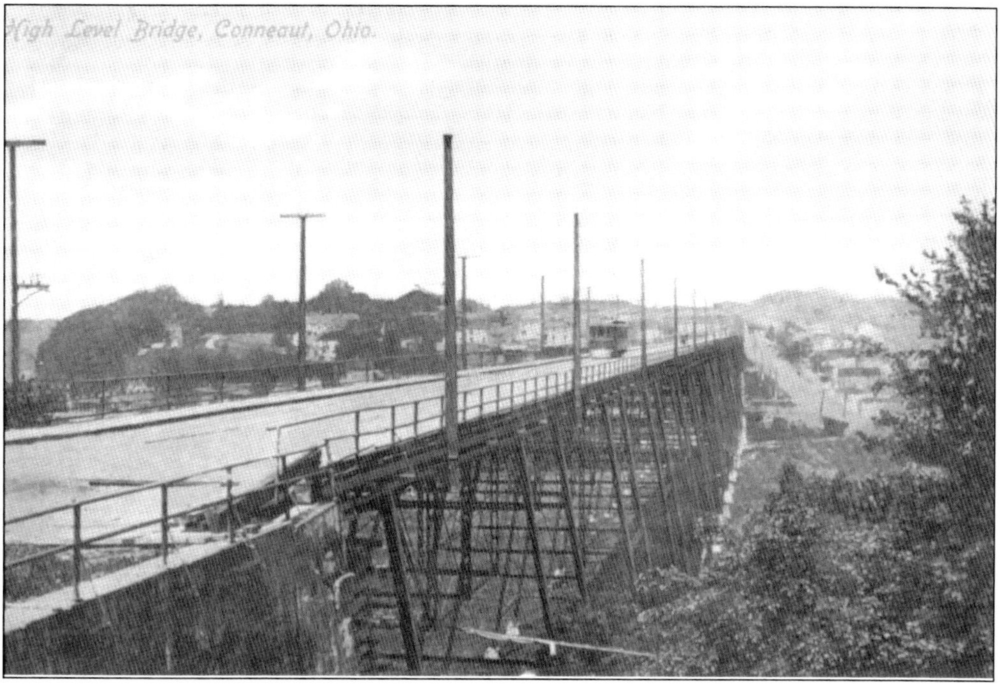

CONNEAUT & ERIE INTERURBAN CAR ON CONNEAUT CREEK BRIDGE. This 1860-foot bridge, formerly used by the Nickel Plate, was modified for the inclusion of East Main Street auto traffic with the interurban cars running along an external frame attached to the north edge of the bridge. Its conversion was the last engineering task required to complete the building of the C&E's route. A borrowed Pennsylvania & Ohio car made the first run over the line on September 25, 1903, although construction and electrification on the bridge were not completed until November 7 (requiring the use of horses on the bridge).

A near-disaster occurred on the bridge in March 1906, when a brace popped loose as an eastbound C&E car went across. The crew alertly gunned the motor and whisked the passengers to safety in East Conneaut, but the bridge had to be closed for some time so that the attached framework could be removed and the tracks could be safely repositioned in the middle of the roadway. This photograph was taken after the completion of those repairs. (Courtesy of Conneaut Area Historical Society.)

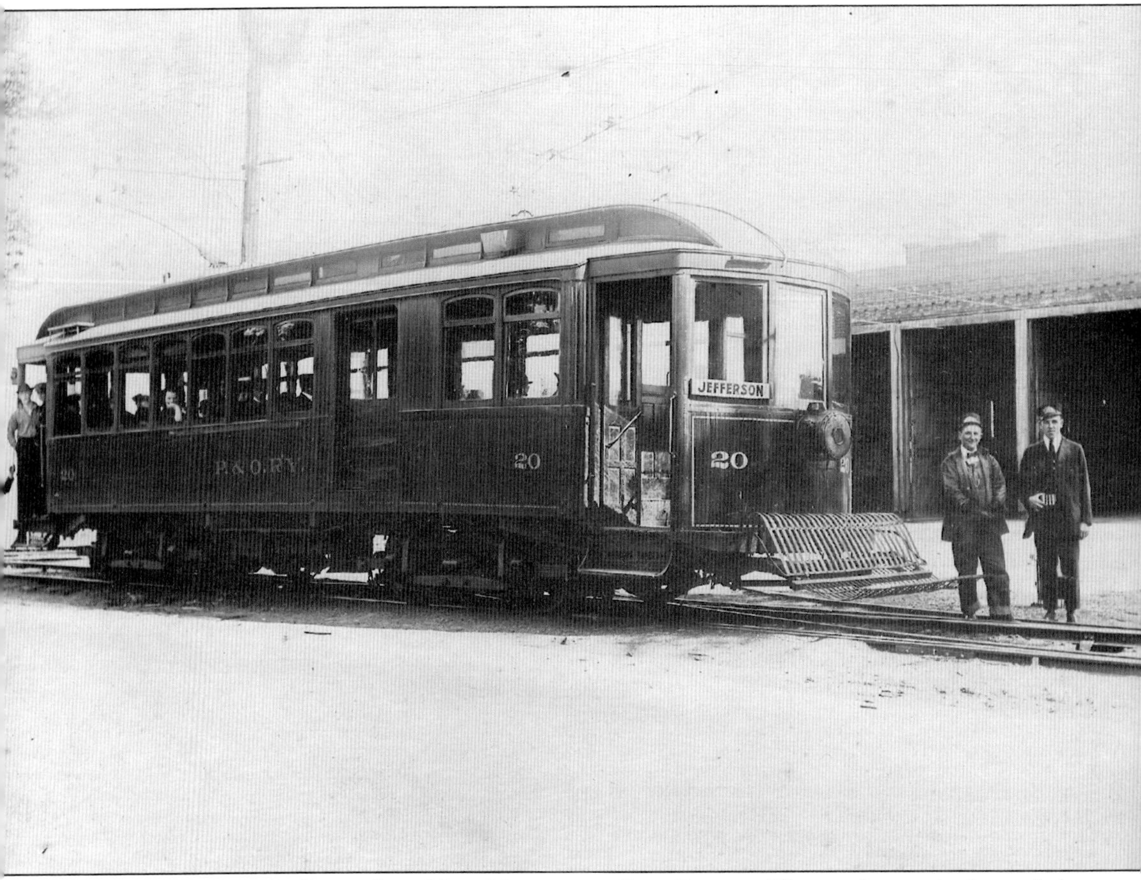

PENNSYLVANIA & OHIO CAR NO. 20 AT THE CAR BARNS. This is the equivalent of the roundhouse or backshop on a conventional railroad. (Courtesy of Conneaut Historical Railroad Museum.)

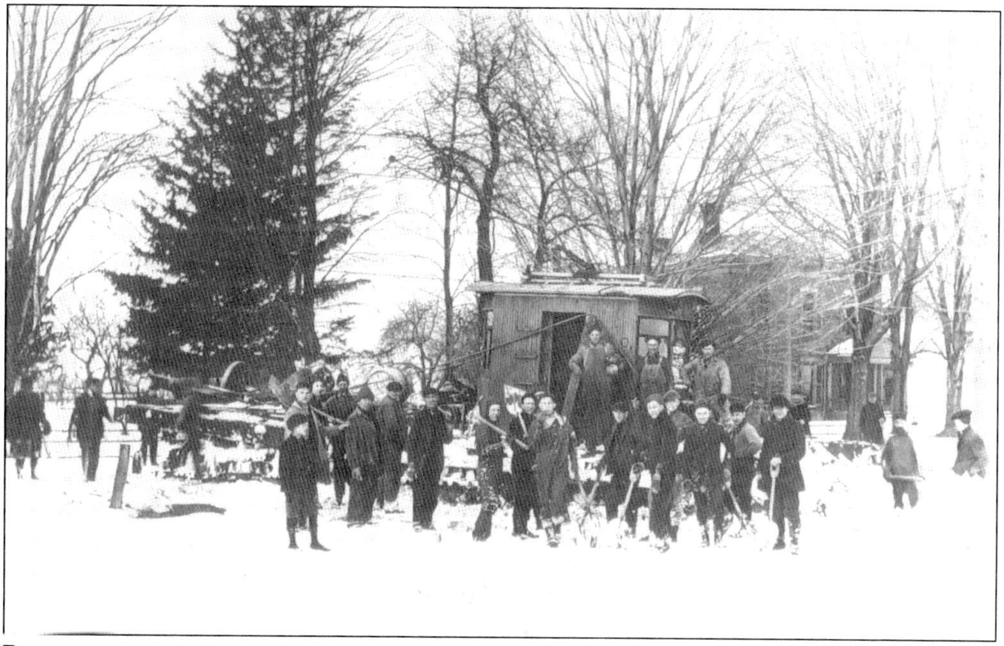

PENNSYLVANIA & OHIO WORK CAR. The house is the G.M. Brown Homestead, later converted into the Brown Memorial Hospital. (Courtesy of Conneaut Area Historical Society.)

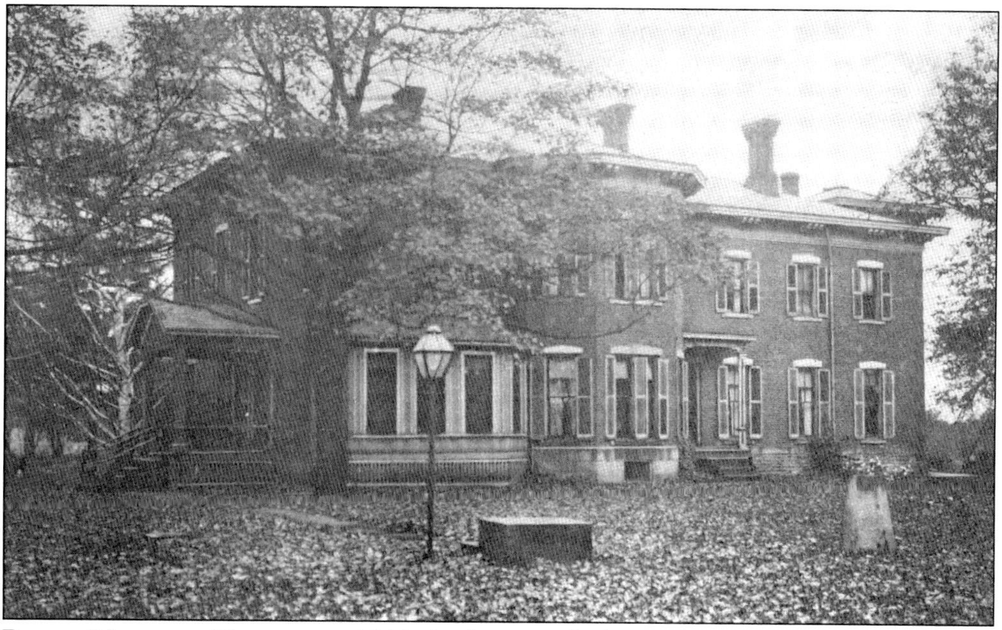

BROWN MEMORIAL HOSPITAL IN 1919. At this time, the hospital was not yet open for business. Donated by the Brown family in 1919, the building was refurbished and refitted as a hospital after an $80,000 community-wide fundraising effort. It opened with 25 beds on April 11, 1922. Its capacity was more than doubled with the addition of a new wing in 1951. Many more additions and upgrades were carried out to Brown Memorial over the following decades, but the original house had to be demolished in 1977. (Courtesy of Conneaut Area Historical Society.)

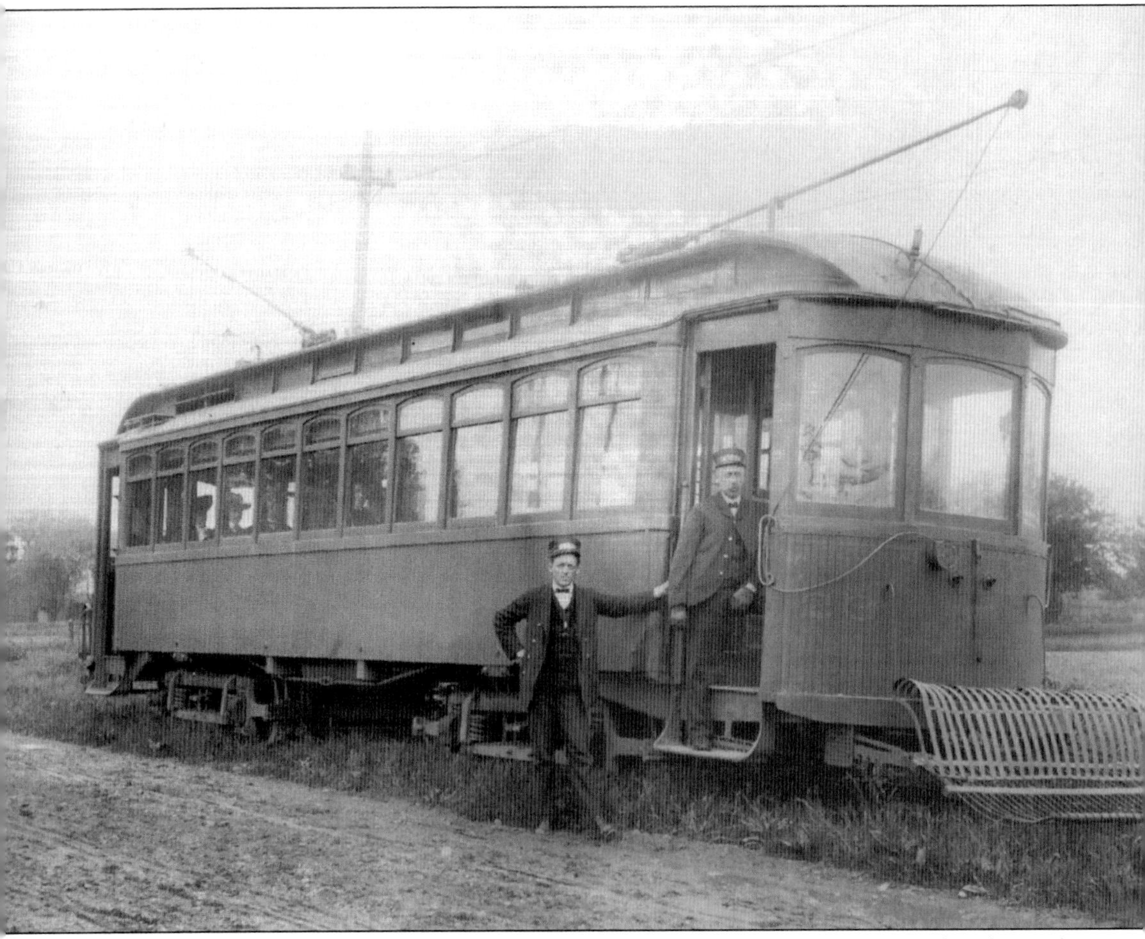

P&O INTERURBAN PASSENGER CAR. To stay financially solvent, most interurban lines also carried mail and freight in baggage cars. This was particularly advantageous for towns along the electric route that were not located near a large freight railroad. (Courtesy of Conneaut Area Historical Society.)

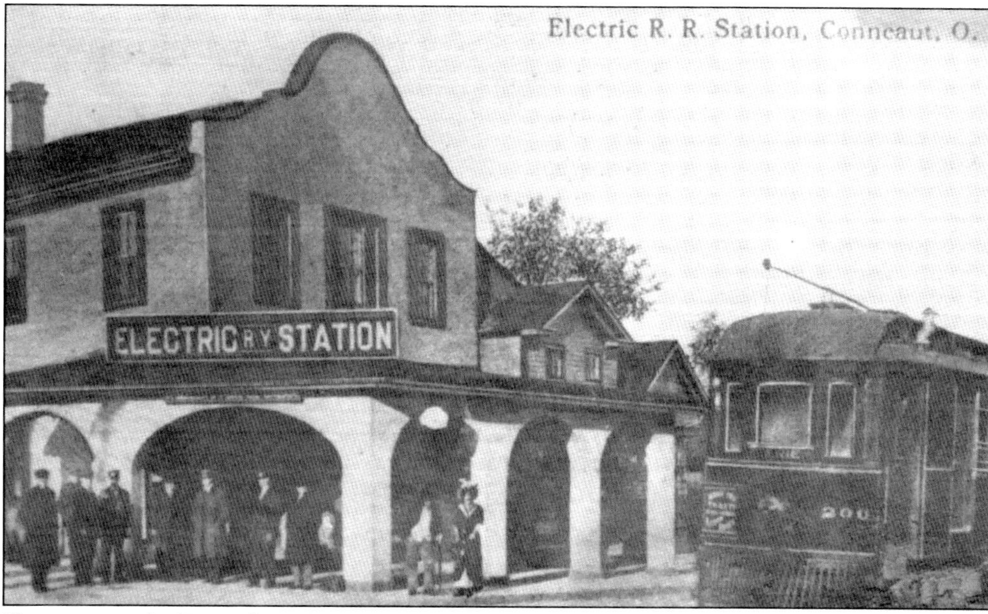

CONNEAUT & ERIE CAR NO. 206 AT THE CONNEAUT ELECTRIC RAILWAY STATION. Unfortunately this very interesting building was not preserved. (Courtesy of Conneaut Area Historical Society.)

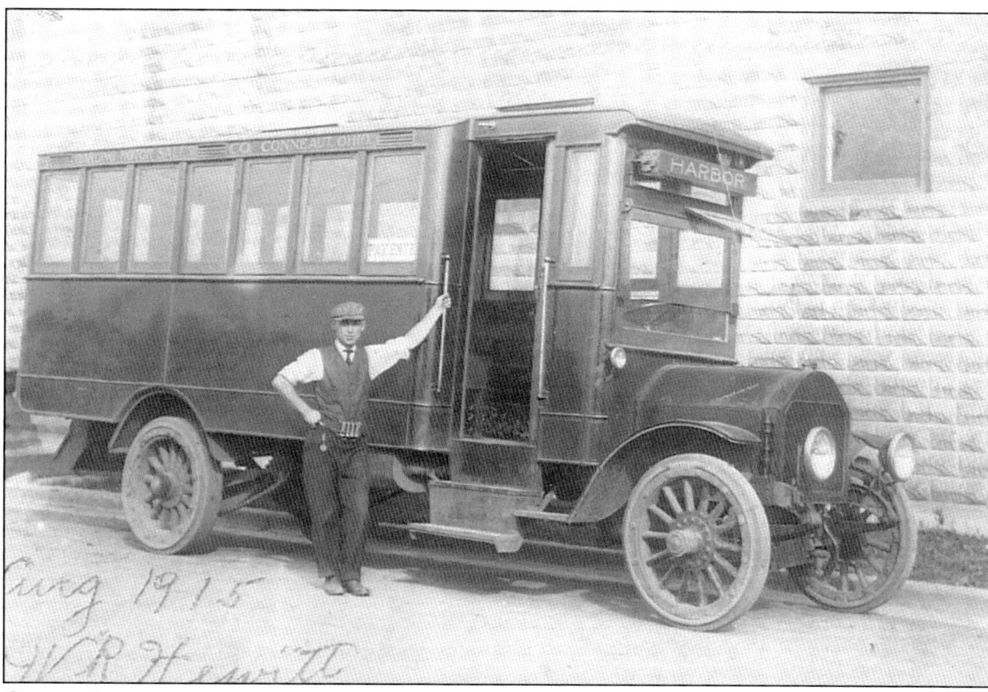

ONE OF FIRST BUSES IN CONNEAUT, 1915. As the popularity of the automobile began to rise, jitney buses began running in 1914. Within a decade, buses would force the electric railways out of the transportation picture. (Courtesy of Conneaut Area Historical Society.)

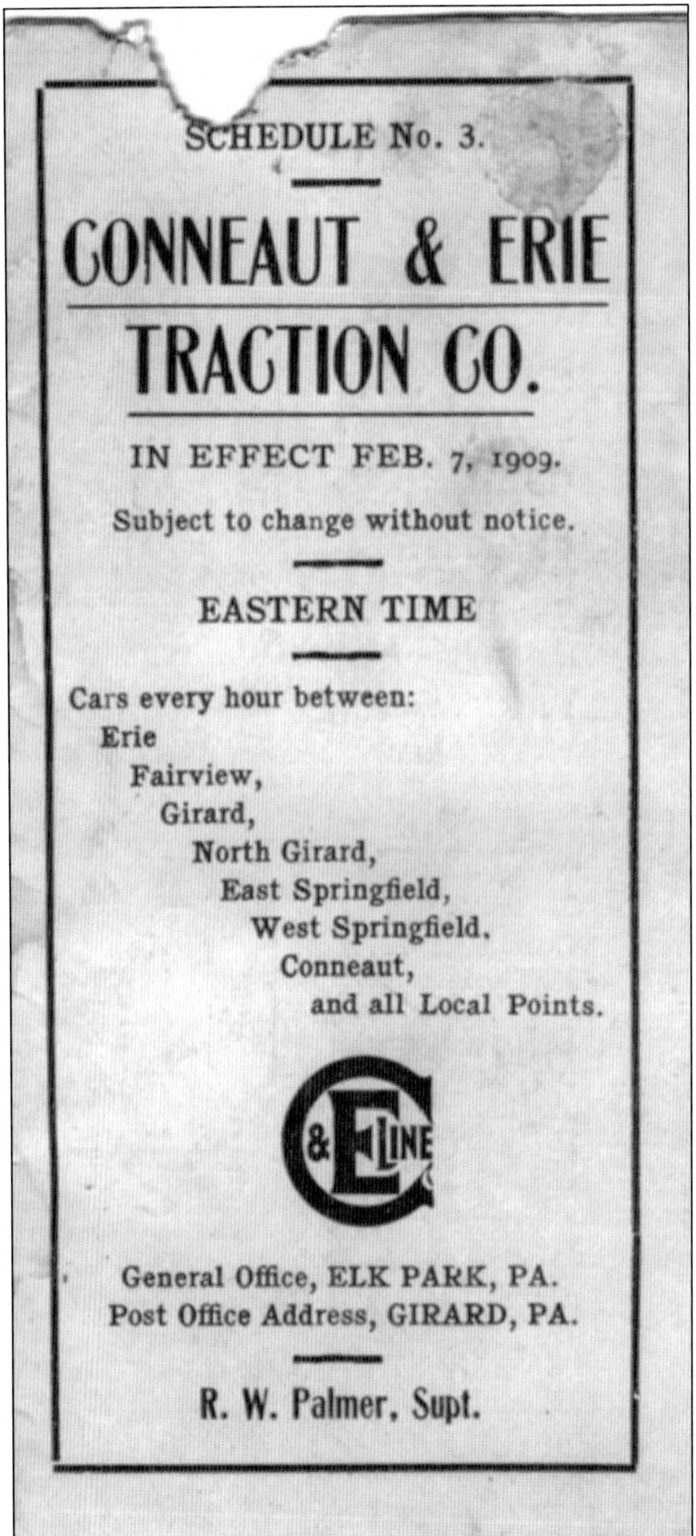
SCHEDULE No. 3.

CONNEAUT & ERIE TRACTION CO.

IN EFFECT FEB. 7, 1909.

Subject to change without notice.

EASTERN TIME

Cars every hour between:
Erie
Fairview,
Girard,
North Girard,
East Springfield,
West Springfield.
Conneaut,
and all Local Points.

General Office, ELK PARK, PA.
Post Office Address, GIRARD, PA.

R. W. Palmer, Supt.

CONNEAUT & ERIE TRACTION COMPANY TIMETABLE. The main stops on the 35-mile route are shown here, but the cars also served half a dozen points in between them. (Courtesy of Conneaut Historical Railroad Museum.)

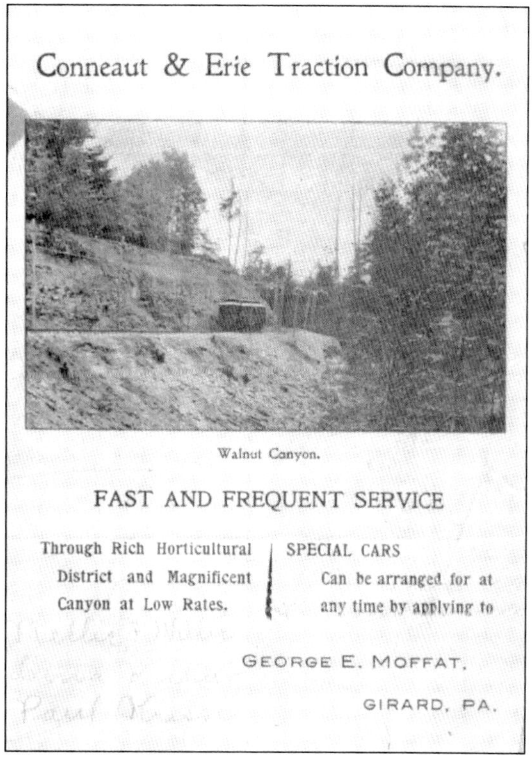

Conneaut & Erie Traction Company.

Walnut Canyon.

FAST AND FREQUENT SERVICE

Through Rich Horticultural District and Magnificent Canyon at Low Rates.	SPECIAL CARS Can be arranged for at any time by applying to

GEORGE E. MOFFAT,
GIRARD, PA.

CONNEAUT & ERIE TRACTION COMPANY BROCHURE. The C&E cars ran hourly from 7 a.m.–11 p.m. in the road's heyday. (Courtesy of Conneaut Historical Railroad Museum.)

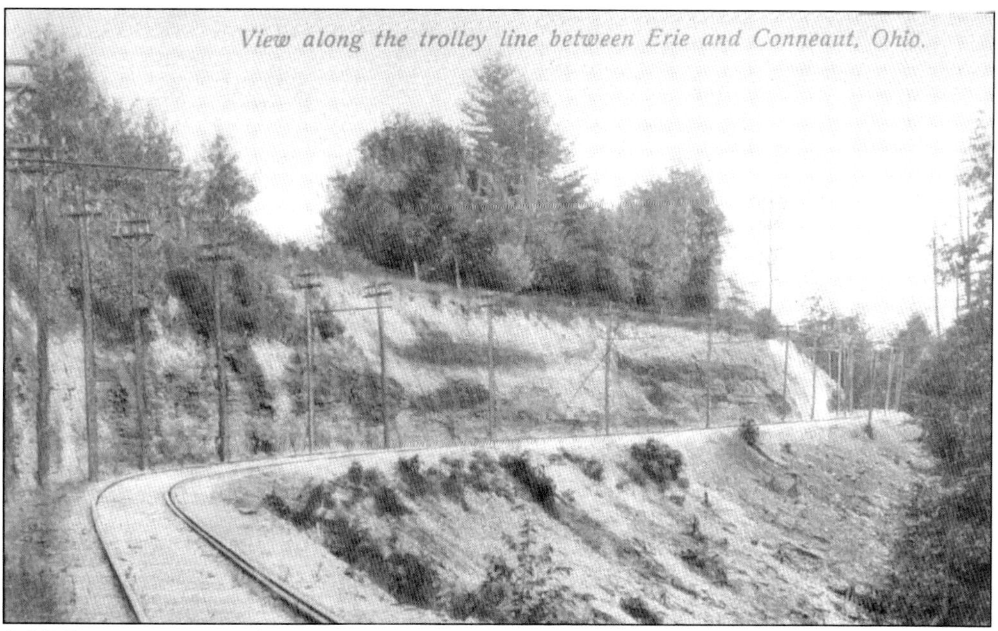

C&E ROUTE BETWEEN CONNEAUT AND ERIE. The line ran on 740 volts DC, generated by steam engines at the coal-burning main power station in Elk Creek, Pennsylvania. At the Conneaut end of the line, which lacked a substation, the power levels dipped so far that at night the car lights would dim almost completely. (Courtesy of Conneaut Area Historical Society.)

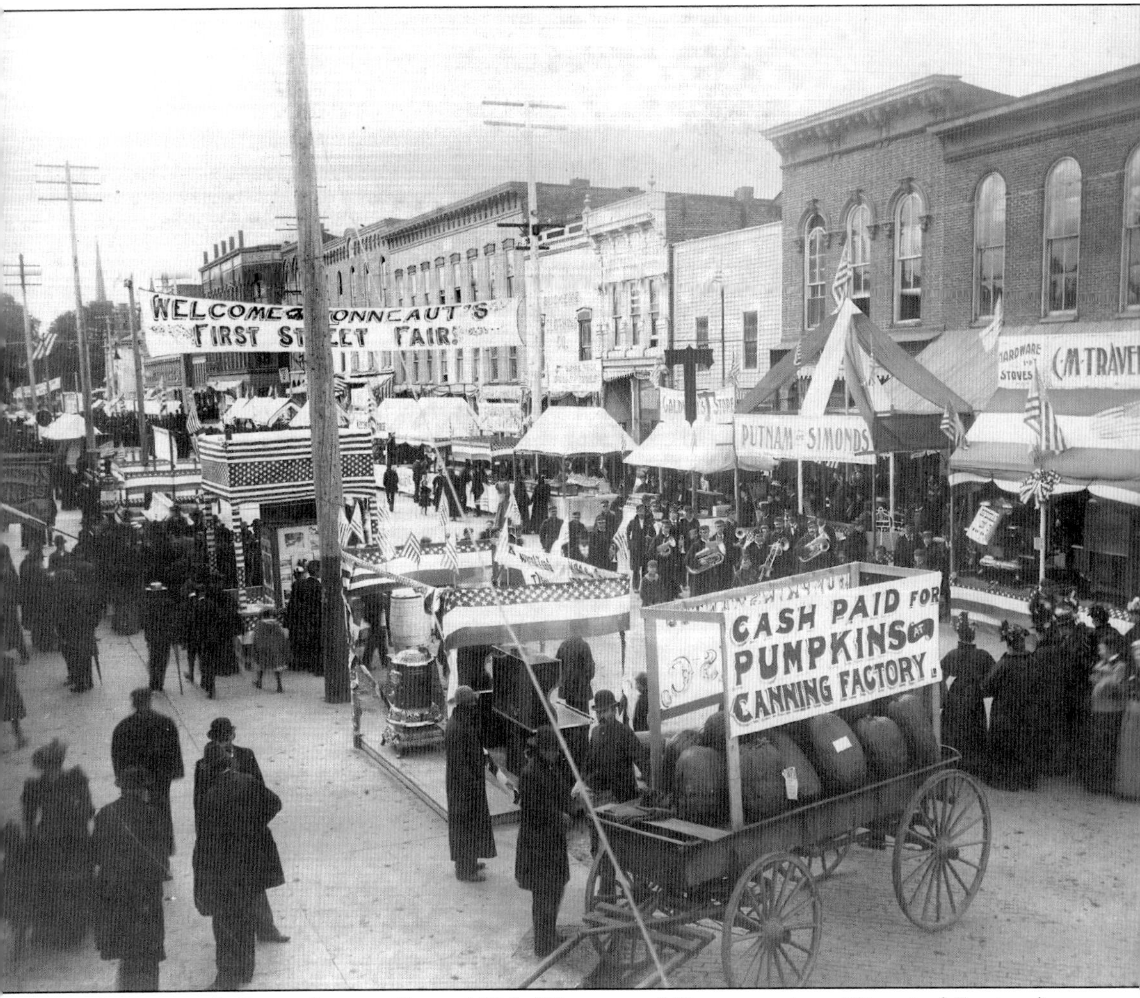

CONNEAUT'S FIRST STREET FAIR, 1896. (Courtesy of Conneaut Area Historical Society.)

Five

HISTORICAL IMAGES OF CONNEAUT

Conneaut has many summer attractions. Visitors from a wide region come to visit the area's beaches and lakefront parks, marinas and restaurants, golf courses and campgrounds, wineries and bed-and-breakfasts, and the Railroad Museum and Conneaut Creek, where the fishing and the scenery are first class.

In winter, it is a different story. Conneaut's name is generally thought to derive from a Seneca Indian word that means "where snows remain later." Life in winter was hard not only for Native Americans, but for the white settlers who began arriving around 1800. General Moses Cleaveland (after whom the city of Cleveland is named) surveyed the mouth of Conneaut Creek from Lake Erie in 1796, and soon roads were being cut through the dense forests of the area: the Old Girdled Road, the roads along the North and South Ridges, and the Old Salt Road, which ran to the south. Early settlers grouped around the harbor and spread southwards from there. In Salem, as the town was then called, postal service began in 1808, the first school opened in 1816, and local shipbuilding commenced two years later. The Village of Conneaut was incorporated in 1834, and firefighters were assembled in 1841. Local forestry and a brick plant by Conneaut Creek provided ample materials for building. The first east–west railroad arrived in 1852, and the town's commerce grew as the harbor developed, but the first real shot in the arm for the local economy was the Nickel Plate Road's decision to make Conneaut its division point in 1881. The local population in 1880 was 1,256, and by 1890, with the new employment generated by the NKP, the town had swelled to 3,214 people. The north –south railroad connection to the Harbor in 1892 further built up the local workforce, and the 1900 census showed 7,133 residents.

A small but vital downtown was developing with attractive architecture and plentiful shopping to serve citizens' needs. There is not space here to make a comprehensive account of life in Conneaut during its developing decades and its industrial peak, but the photographs here do give a sense of the times as a small, struggling village was transformed into a railroading powerhouse.

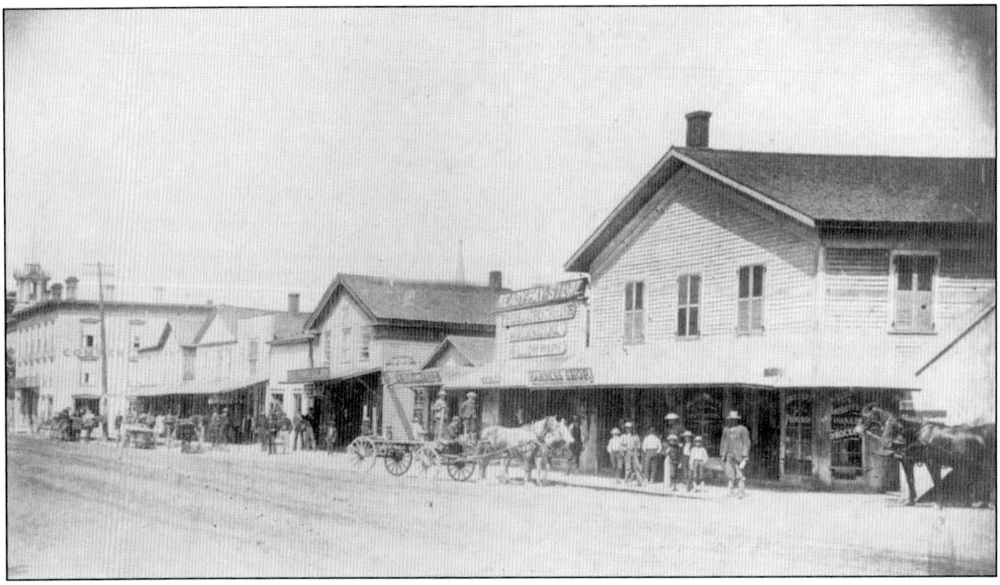

CONNEAUT IN 1882. The tower of the City Hall, built in 1876, is seen at far left. The theatre inside the City Hall hosted stage productions, concerts, and dances. (Courtesy of Conneaut Area Historical Society.)

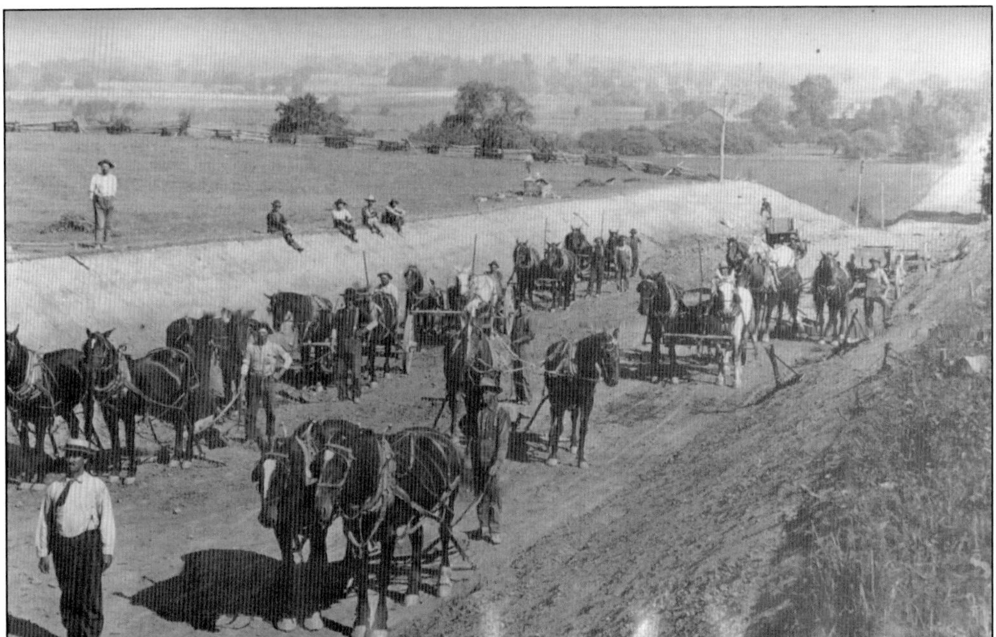

GRADING OF ROUTE 7 AT FARNHAM HILL. William J. Hallett II and his men are looking north toward Conneaut. These horses hauled the road bricks from a brick plant located under the LS&MS bridge. (Courtesy of Conneaut Public Library.)

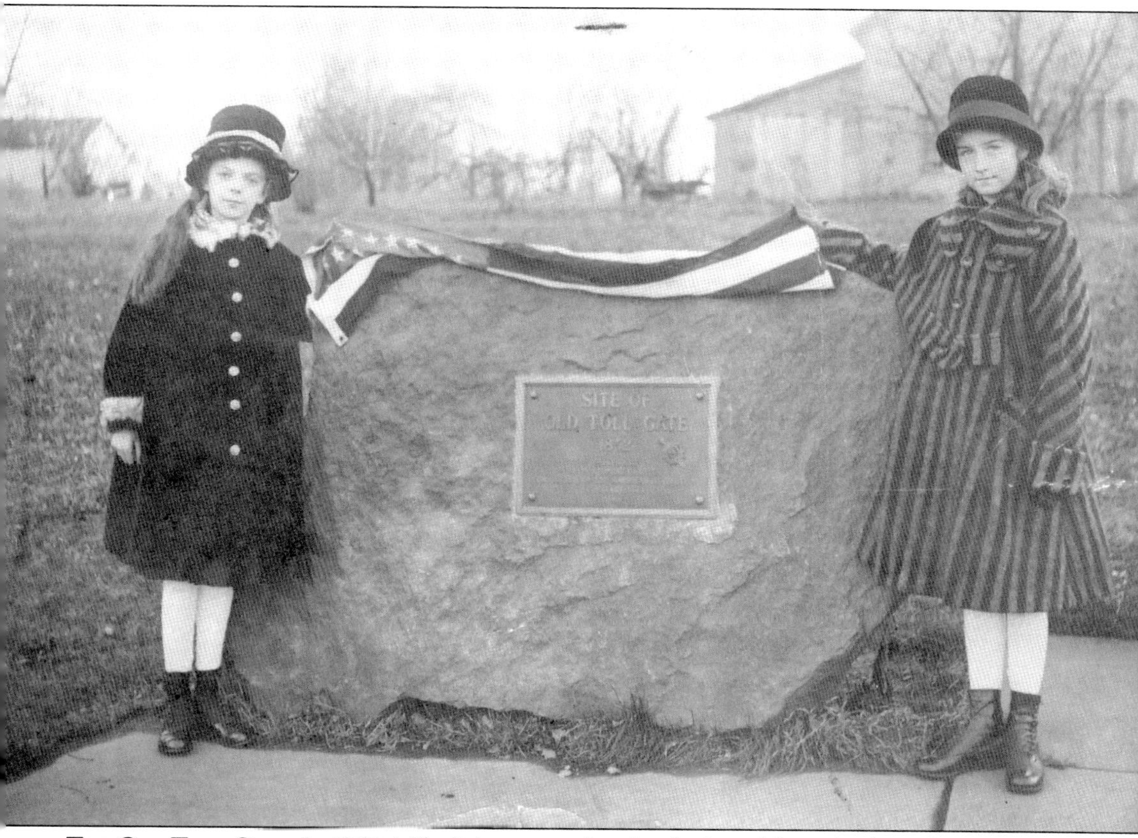

THE OLD TOLL GATE. In 1852, Milo Osborn completed a plank road from the foot of Main Street to Amboy, for which a toll was charged. The Mary Redmond Chapter of the Daughters of the American Revolution erected this monument in 1919. (Courtesy of Conneaut Public Library.)

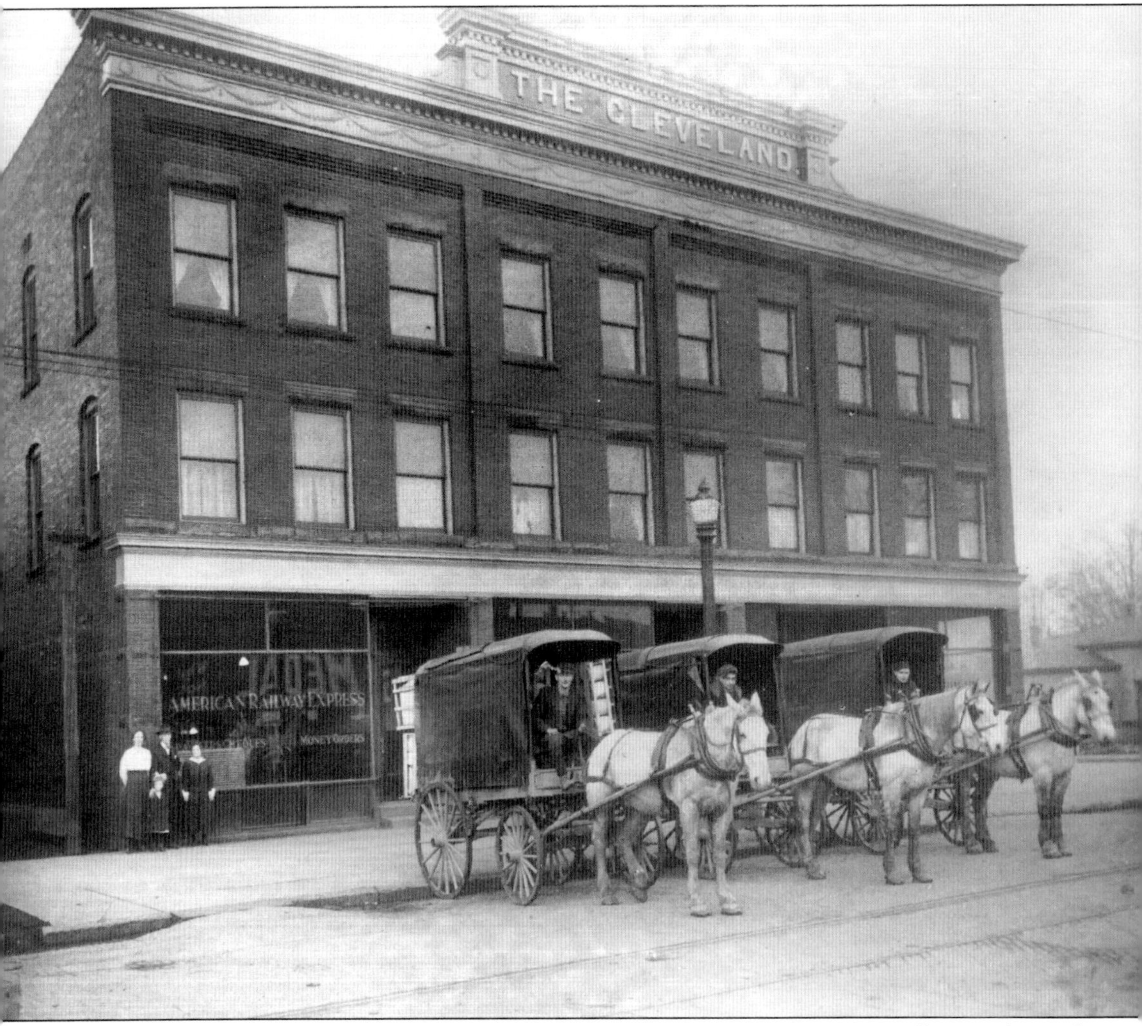

THE CLEVELAND HOTEL, 234 STATE STREET. The Railway Express Agency office was located inside the hotel from 1915-20. At left are REA agent Roy Peases and his family. Drivers are, from left to right, Roy Joslin, George Marvin, and Bubbles Merrick. (Courtesy of Conneaut Area Historical Society.)

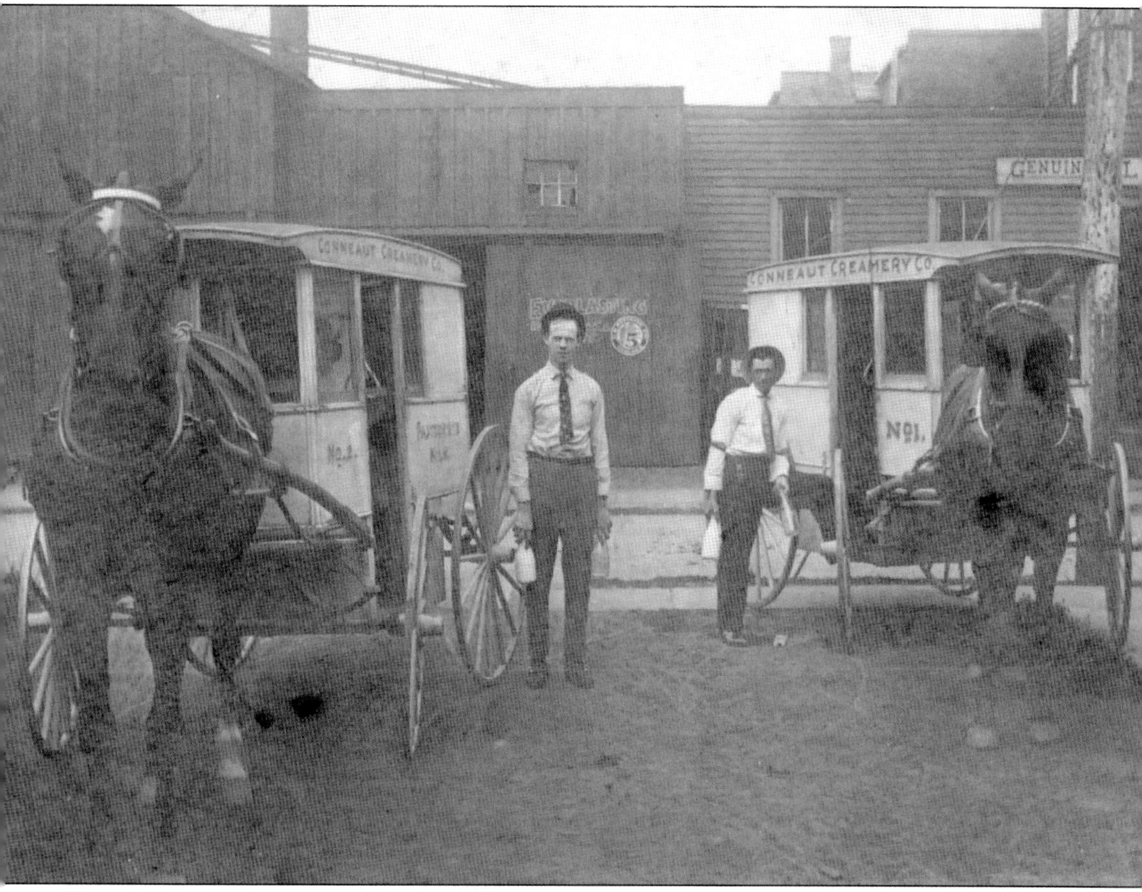

CONNEAUT CREAMERY, A LOCAL ICON. In 1908, Fred Wolcott and Frank Watson opened this creamery at the intersection of Underridge Road and old Route 7. They were soon bought out by two local doctors who sensed the promise of such an investment and formed a corporation called Conneaut Creamery, Inc. in 1909. The business was moved twice in four years, ending up at 234 Harbor. The company added a butter and ice factory and began producing the town's first artificial ice in 1924. The creamery's soda fountain was very popular, and its dairy business boomed. In the 1960s, the creamery was purchased by Lockie Lee Dairy of Painesville, which presided over its gradual decline and fall. The building at 234 Harbor was razed in 1975. (Courtesy of Studio Antiques.)

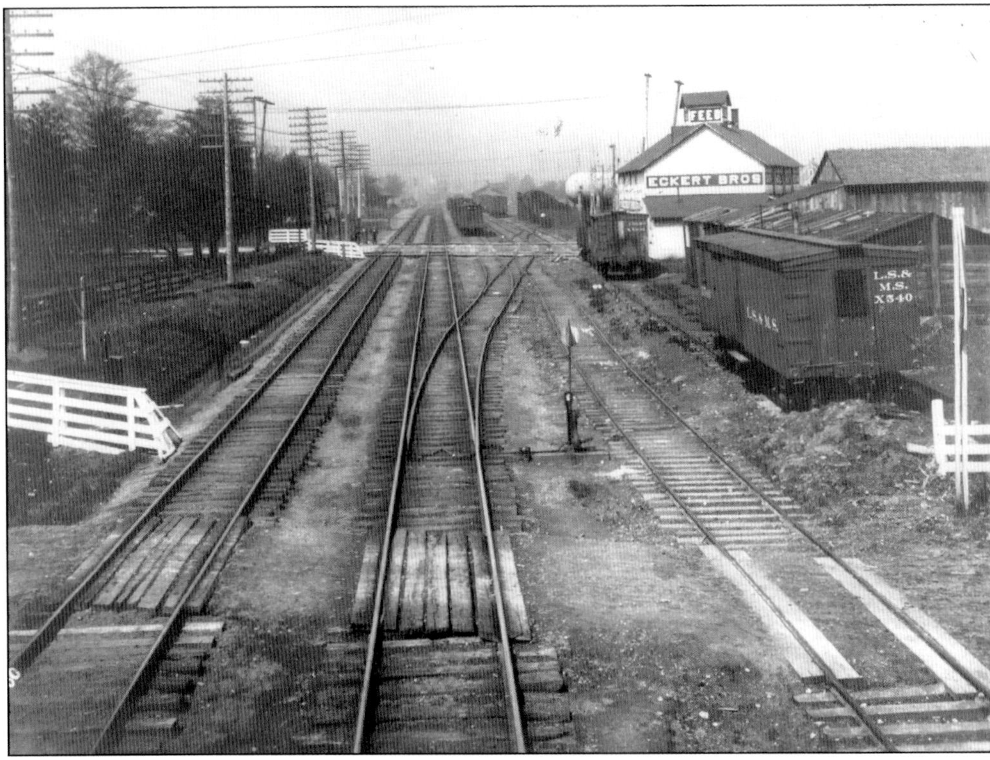

TRACKSIDE INDUSTRIES IN CONNEAUT, MAY 1906. The Eckert Brothers feed store was one of several local businesses served by the New York Central. In addition to the Central's high-speed freight and passenger trains, way freights would amble through town each day to pick up and set out cars on the spurs. (Courtesy of Bruce Hearn.)

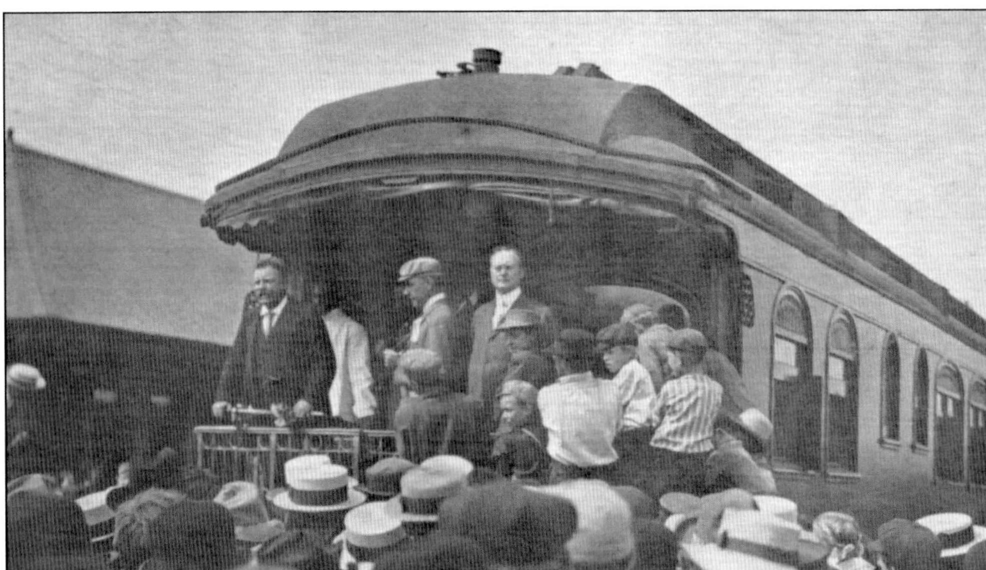

THEODORE ROOSEVELT CAMPAIGNS DURING A WHISTLE STOP IN CONNEAUT. The New York Central depot looms in the background. (Courtesy of Conneaut Area Historical Society.)

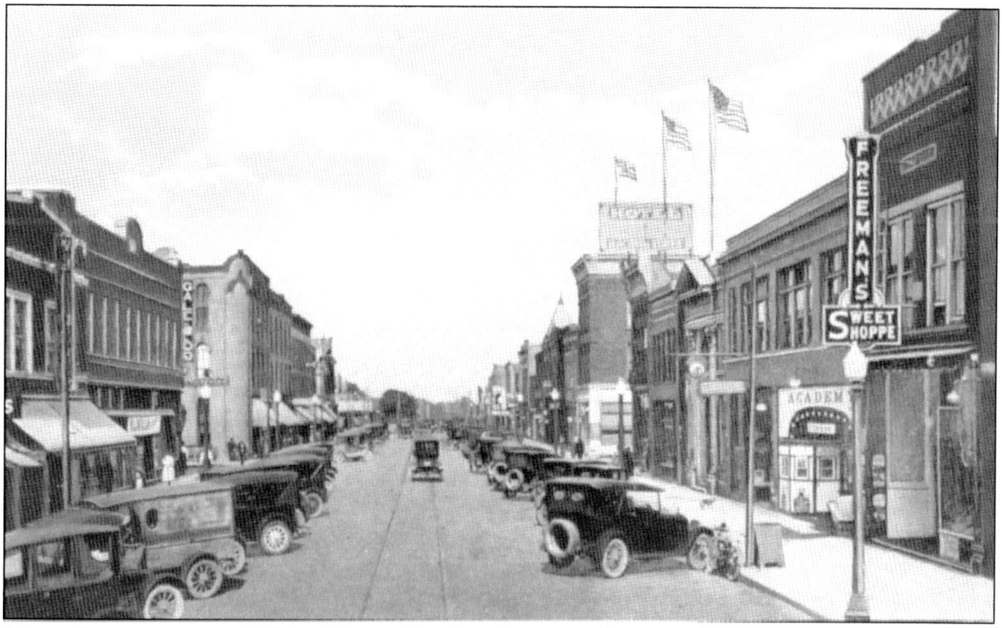

MAIN STREET IN THE 1920S. The trolley line has ceased to operate, and the wires have been taken down, but the tracks remain. (Courtesy of Conneaut Area Historical Society.)

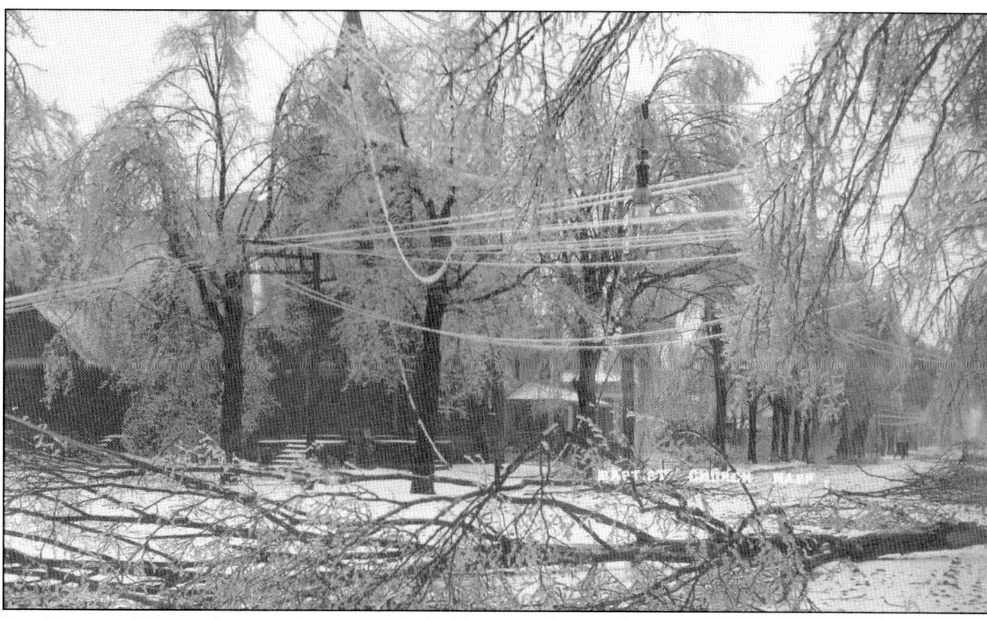

ICE STORM. Downed power lines, raw Lake Erie winds, and heavy snow are all hazards of winter in Ohio's northernmost city. (Courtesy of Conneaut Area Historical Society.)

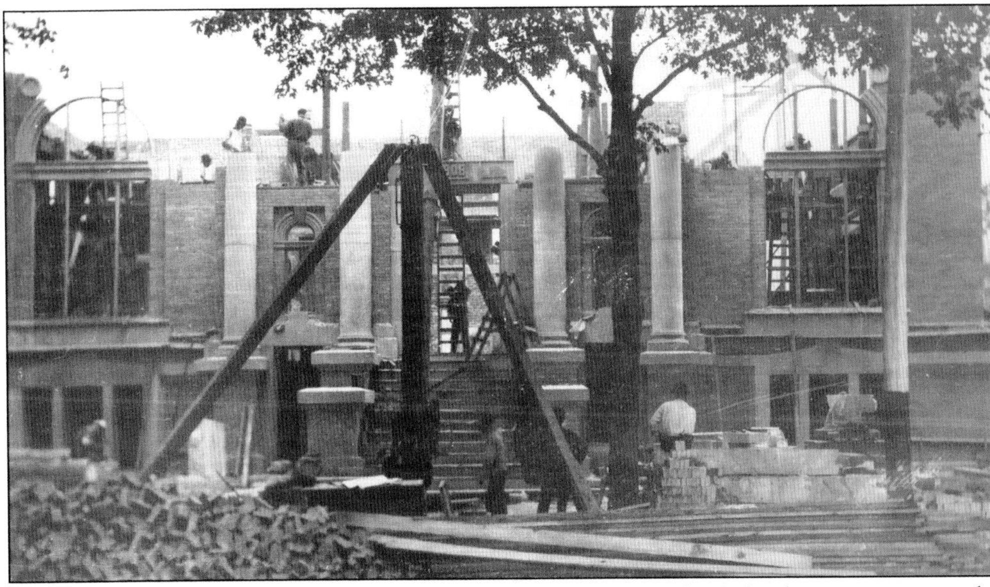

BUILDING THE CARNEGIE LIBRARY, 1908. Conneaut's first book-lending system was the Peoples Free Library Association, available via subscription. Books were lent at the storefront of local bookseller H.H. Timby. A library tax levy was passed in 1905, and after additional fundraisers, a new board of trustees oversaw the purchase of a $4,000 parcel of land at Buffalo and State Streets. In 1907, steel baron Andrew Carnegie donated $25,000 for the construction of the Conneaut library, one of many that he funded around the country. (Courtesy of Conneaut Public Library.)

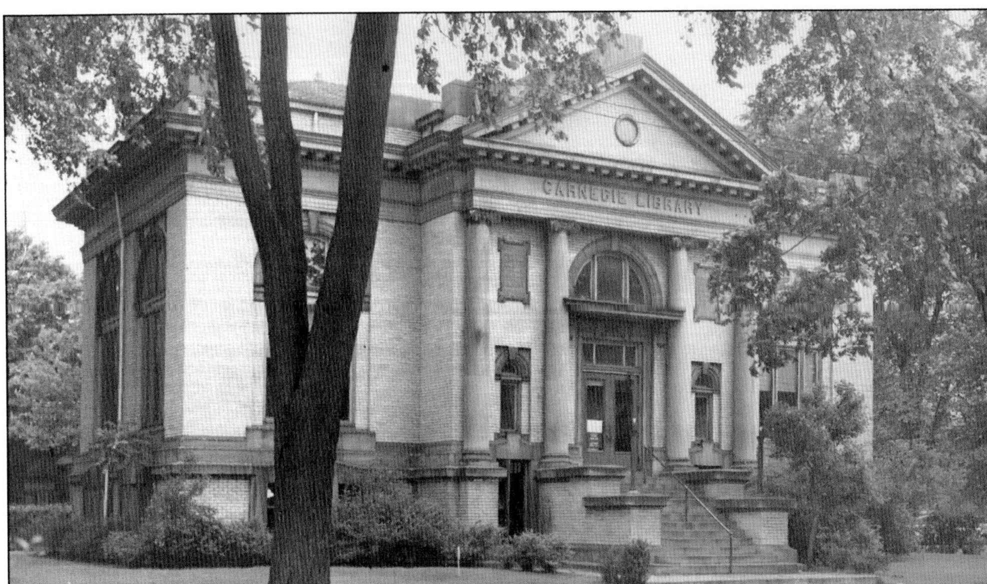

CARNEGIE LIBRARY. The Library opened on May 3, 1909 with a collection of 12,000 books and served the community well for decades. In 1996, a tax levy was passed for the creation of a new library just to the north of the old one on Buffalo Street. The new Conneaut Public Library opened on May 17, 1998. The beautiful old Carnegie Library building still stands today. (Courtesy of Conneaut Historical Railroad Museum.)

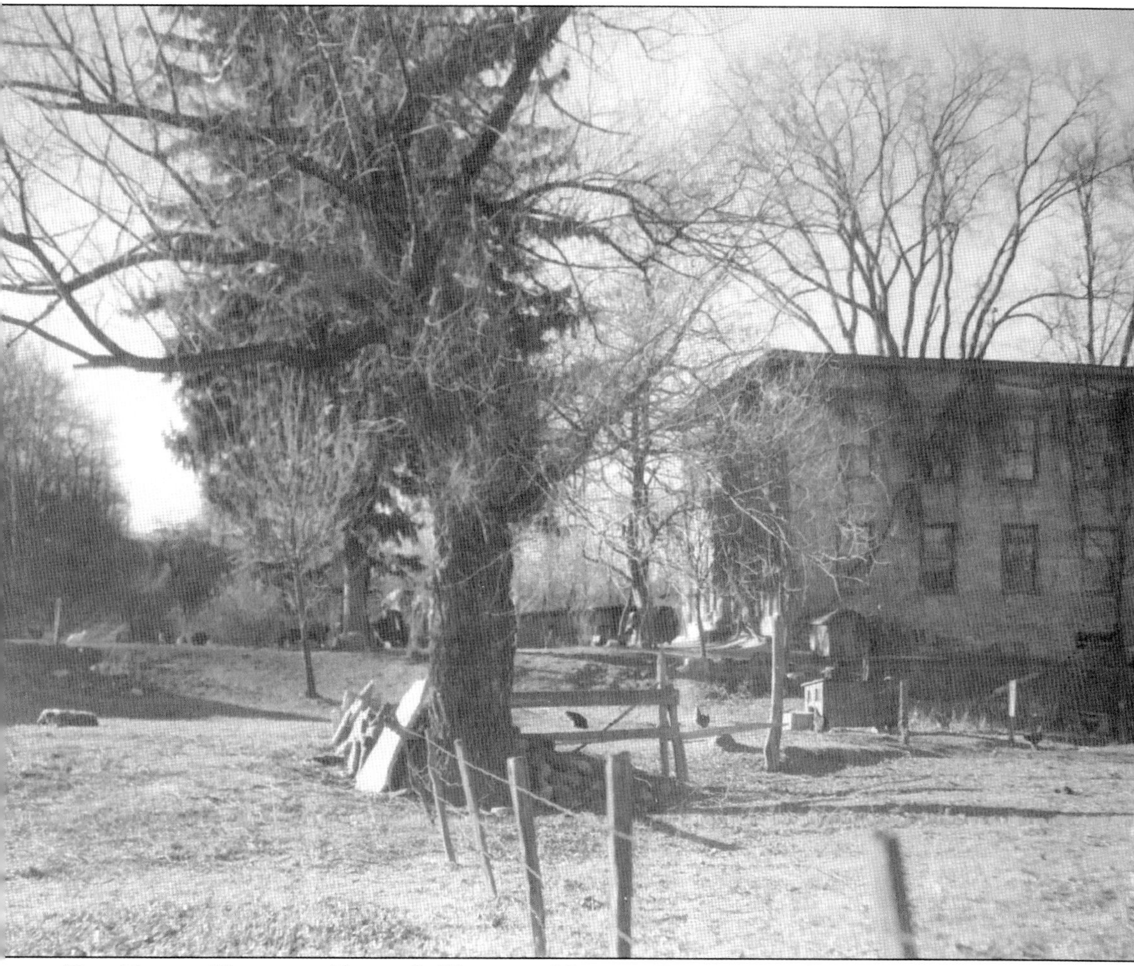

The Tinker House at Tinker's Hollow, Monroe Township. The Tinker family built a small iron foundry where they created an early mowing machine that was unveiled in July 1853. (Courtesy of Conneaut Public Library.)

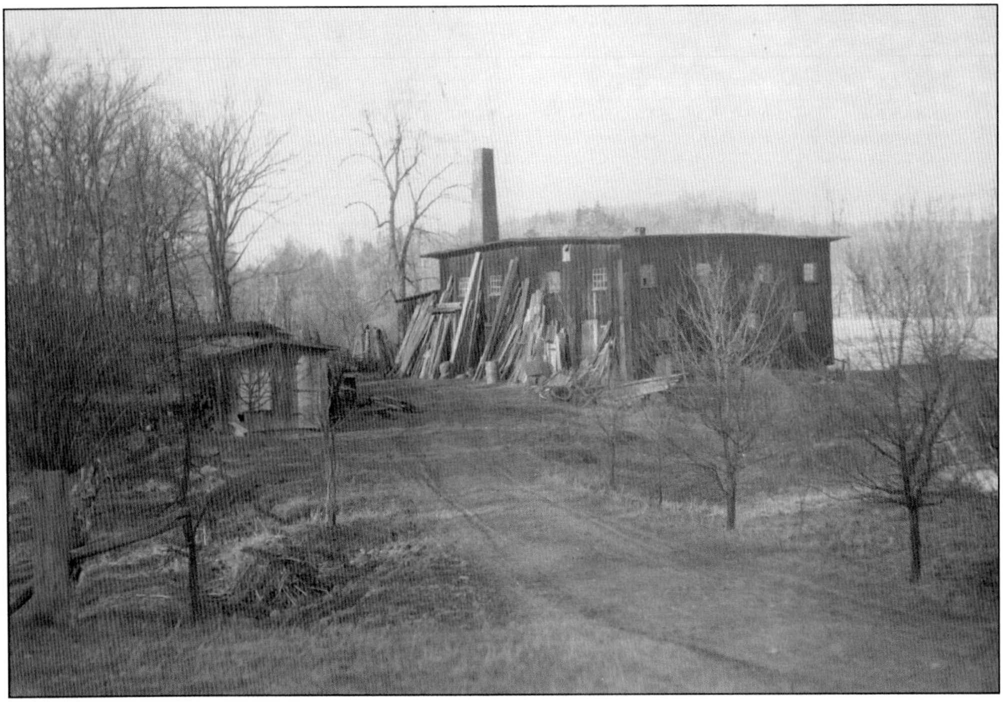

Two Views of the Foundry at Tinker's Hollow. These undated photographs show the venerable structure, which was built in 1835. (Both courtesy of Conneaut Public Library.)

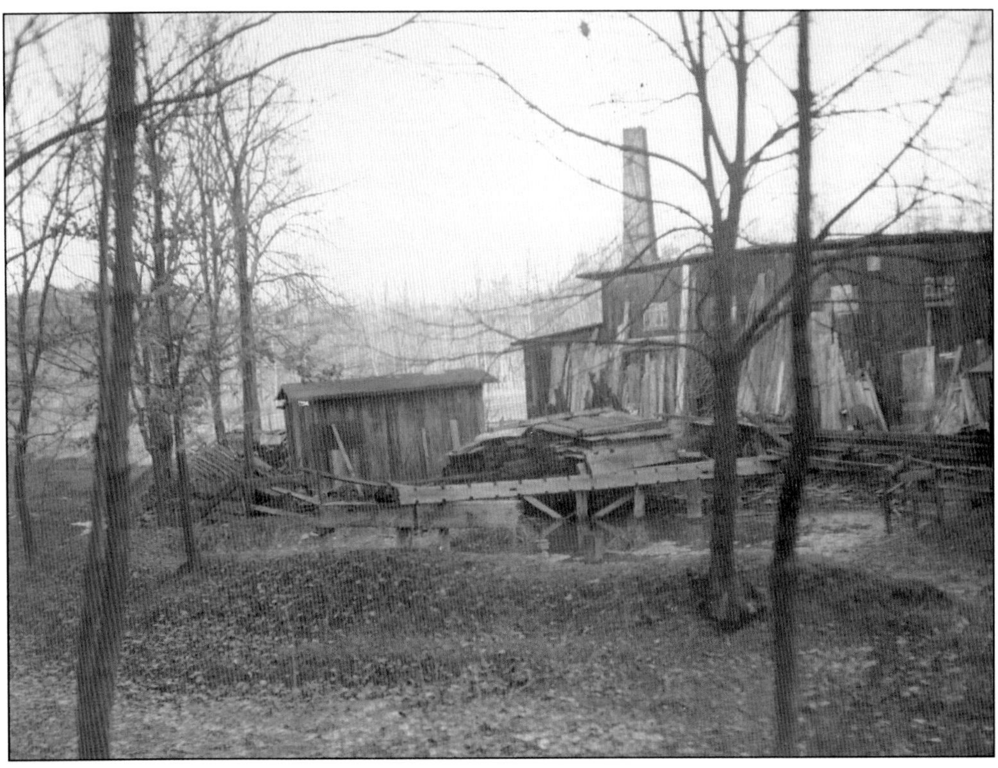

Interior of the Foundry. The family had a reputation for manufacturing tools of exceptional hardness. (Courtesy of Conneaut Public Library.)

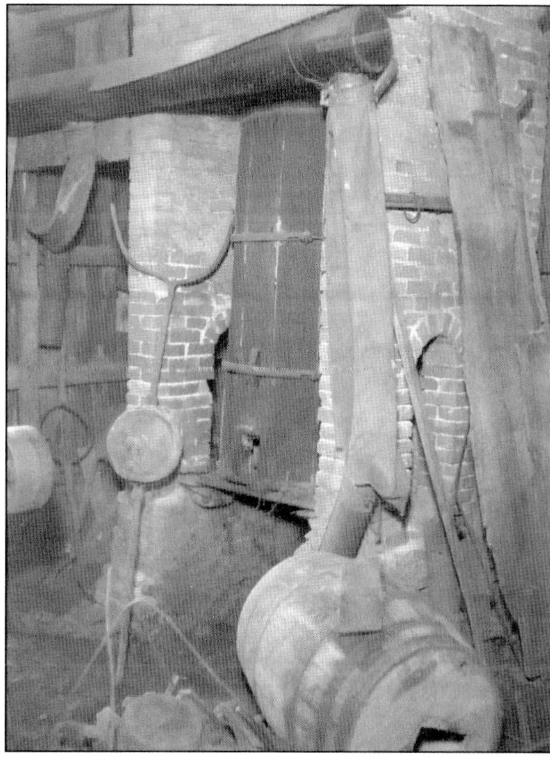

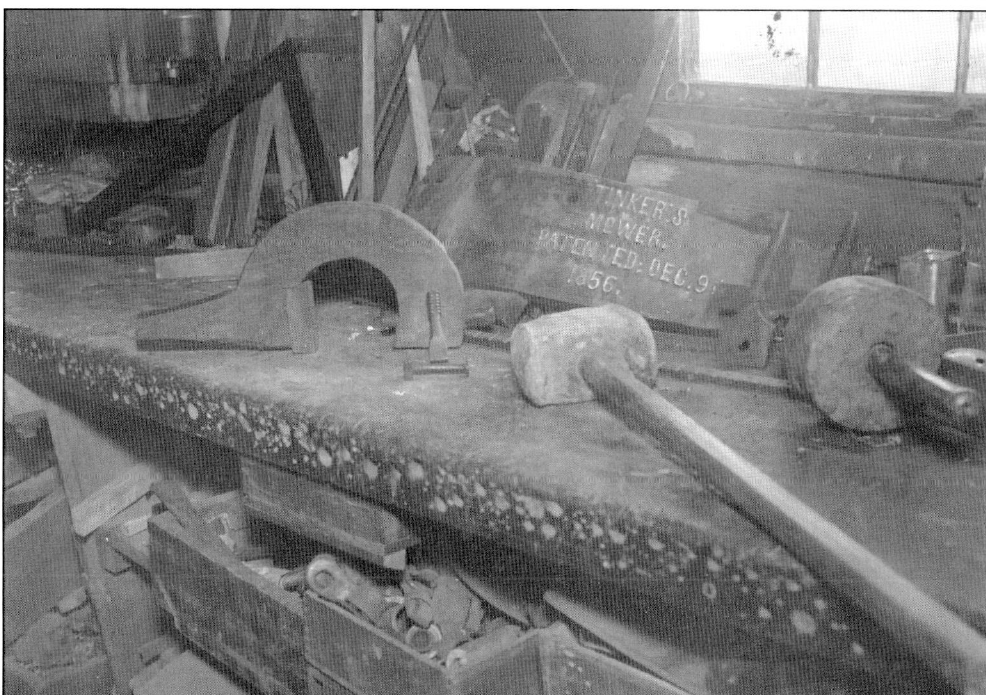

Iron Tools Made at the Tinker Foundry. Such antique tools are extremely valuable today. (Courtesy of Conneaut Public Library.)

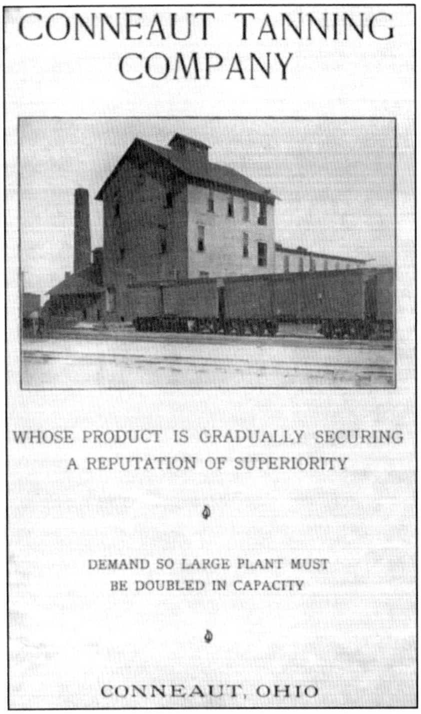

CONNEAUT TANNING COMPANY ADVERTISEMENT IN *CONNEAUT DAILY POST-HERALD*, NOVEMBER 11, 1905. The newspaper was founded in 1895. At the beginning of 1907, the *Daily Post-Herald* and the rival *Conneaut Evening News* merged to become the *Conneaut News-Herald*. (Courtesy of Conneaut Public Library.)

BOOSTERISM IN *CONNEAUT DAILY POST-HERALD*, 1905. With two new railroads (the NKP of 1882 and the PB&LE of 1892) pumping dollars into the local economy, optimism was high indeed. (Courtesy of Conneaut Public Library.)

PROSPECTS
OF
THE FUTURE

The location of Conneaut is one which renders it impossible for any combination of circumstances to arrest its growth, either as a place of business or residence.

It has no lack of men with business sagacity equal to any improvement of every opportunity, and it is safe to predict that the historian of the industries of the future will be able to point back to those of to-day as the auspicious beginnings of a greater and brighter destiny.

POSTCARD POETRY, 1933. This nostalgic piece comes from a boom time in the city's history. (Courtesy of Conneaut Area Historical Society.)

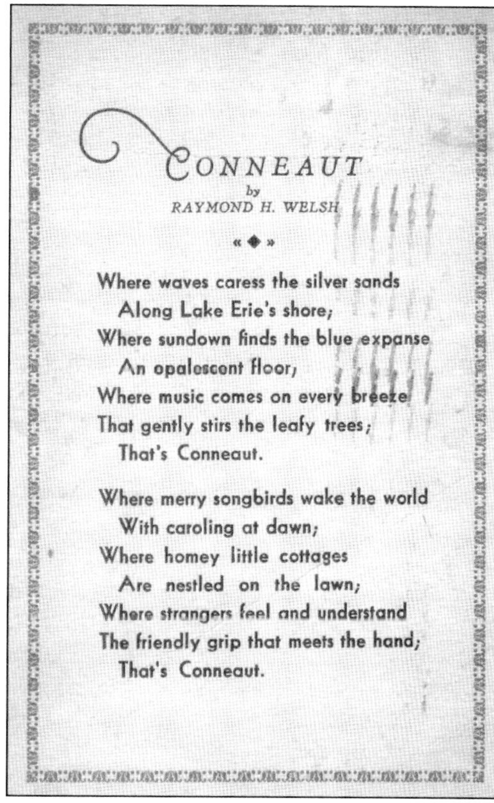
CONNEAUT

by

RAYMOND H. WELSH

Where waves caress the silver sands
Along Lake Erie's shore;
Where sundown finds the blue expanse
An opalescent floor;
Where music comes on every breeze
That gently stirs the leafy trees;
That's Conneaut.

Where merry songbirds wake the world
With caroling at dawn;
Where homey little cottages
Are nestled on the lawn;
Where strangers feel and understand
The friendly grip that meets the hand;
That's Conneaut.

FORD OF CONNEAUT CREEK AT TINKER'S HOLLOW. The foundry is long gone now, except for fragments of its foundation. (Courtesy of Conneaut Public Library.)

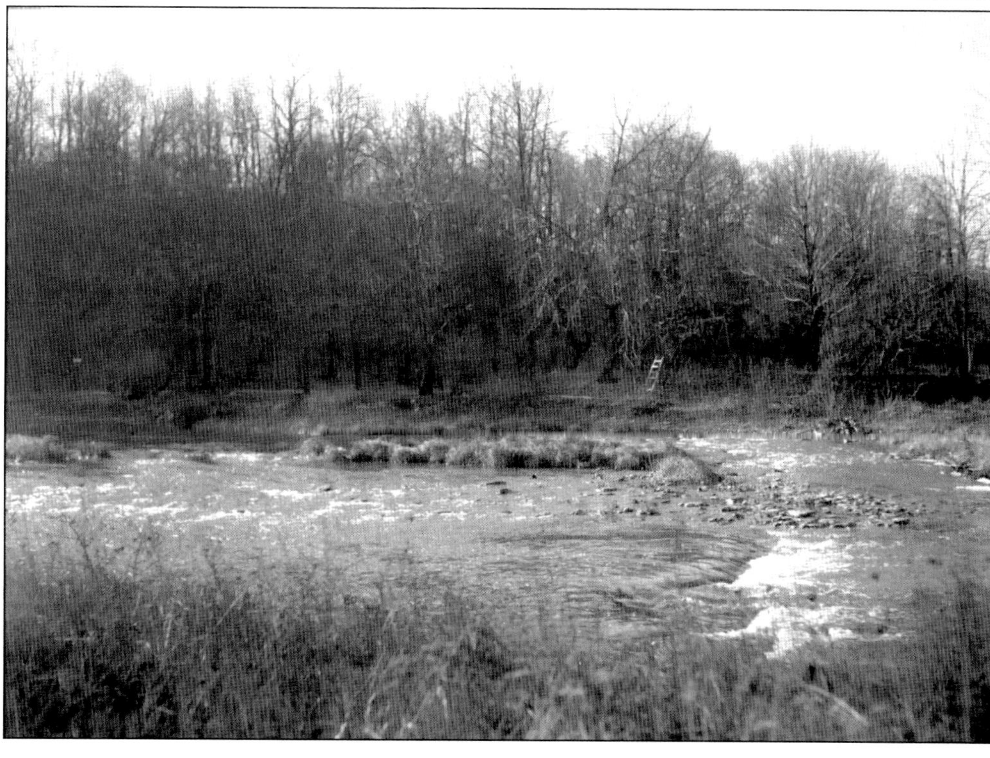

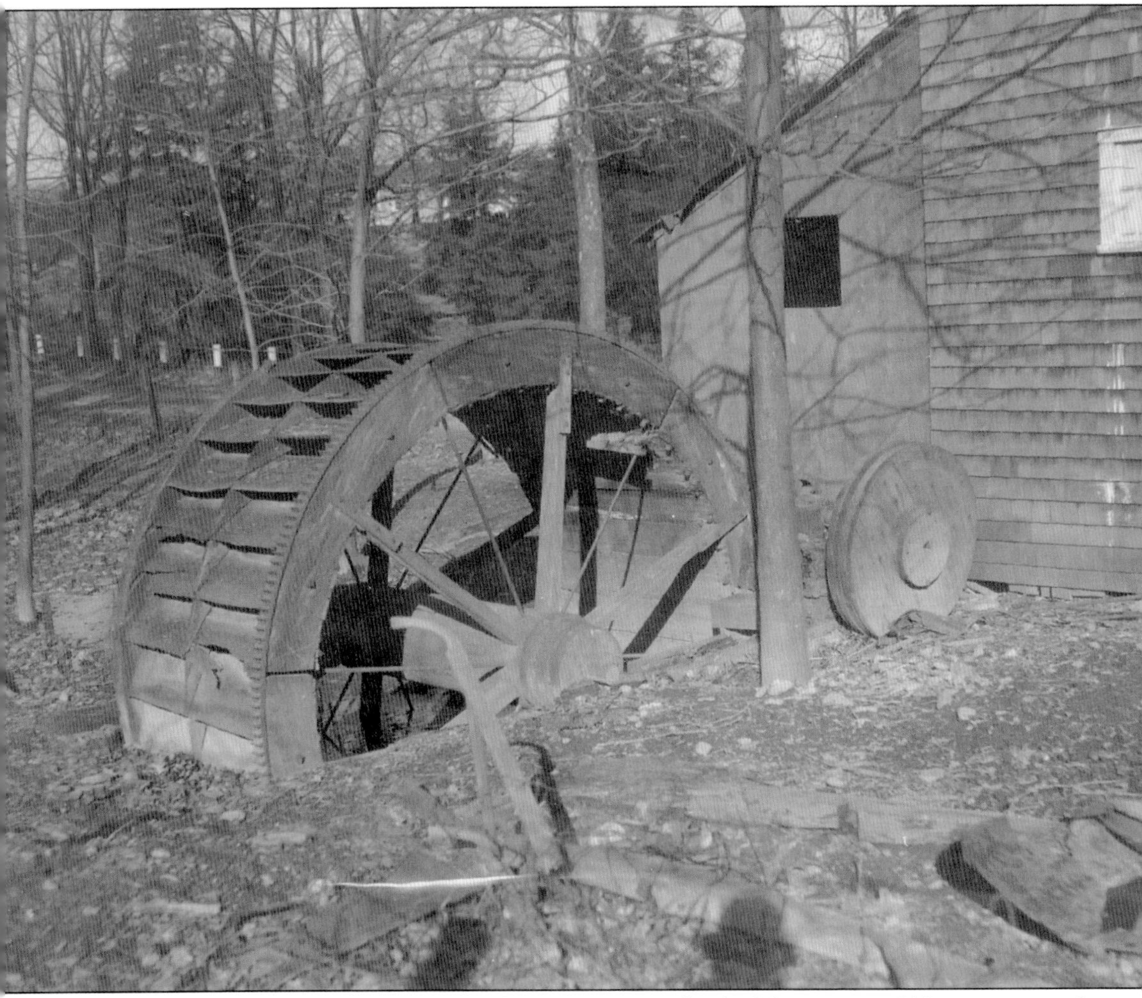

PECK'S VALLEY FARM FORD, AT BIG CREEK. A waterwheel of this size would have generated ample hydroelectric power to run the farm. (Courtesy of Conneaut Public Library.)

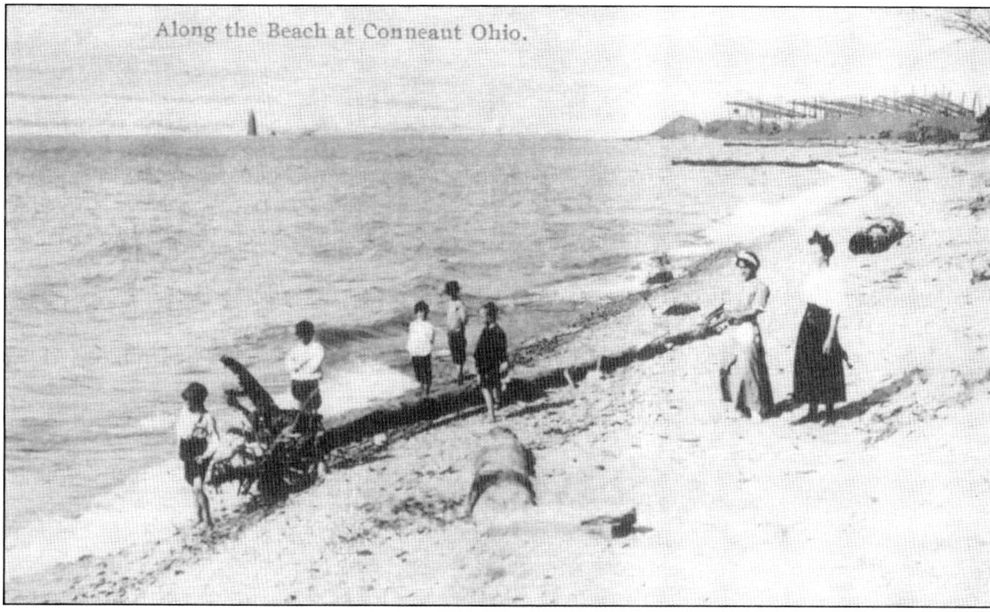

The Beach and the Harbor. Children wade on the shore of Lake Erie with the industrial skyline of Conneaut Harbor in the background. (Courtesy of Conneaut Area Historical Society.)

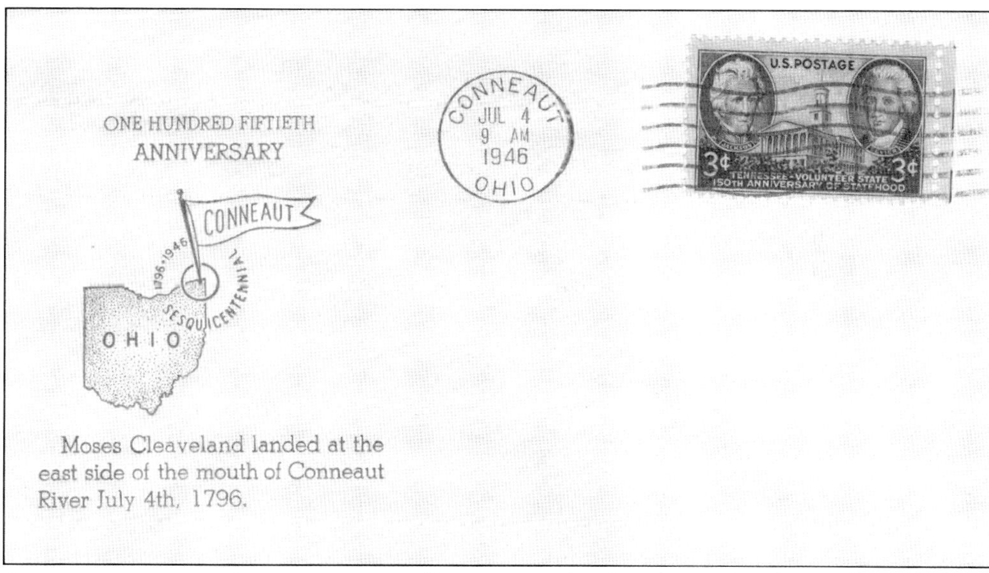

Sesquicentennial Commemorative Envelope. On July 4, 1796, Moses Cleaveland, an agent for the Connecticut Land Company, landed with a surveying party of 50 men at the sandbar-clogged mouth of Conneaut Creek, where dense woods came down to the sandy beach. Cleaveland wrote, "The day memorable as the birthday of American Independence… and memorable as the day on which the settlement of this new country was commenced, and in time may raise her head amongst the most enlightened and improved states… The men under Captain Tinker, ranged themselves on the beach and fired a Federal salute of fifteen rounds and then the sixteenth in honor of New Connecticut. We gave three cheers and christened the place Fort Independence. Drank several toasts …." (Courtesy of Conneaut Area Historical Society.)

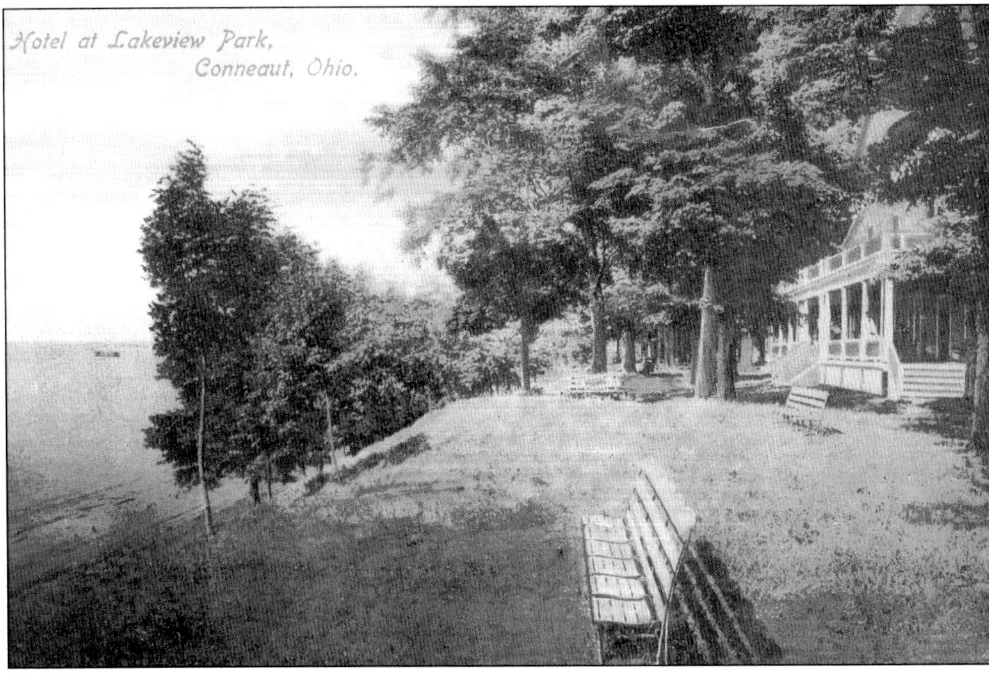

LAKEVIEW PARK HOTEL. The building was originally constructed as a summer resort, the Brunton Sanitarium, in the early 1890s. It was taken over by the city shortly thereafter, and it functioned as a tourist camp with horse racing, baseball games, dances, and band concerts. The hotel burned down in the late 1930s. (Courtesy of Conneaut Area Historical Society.)

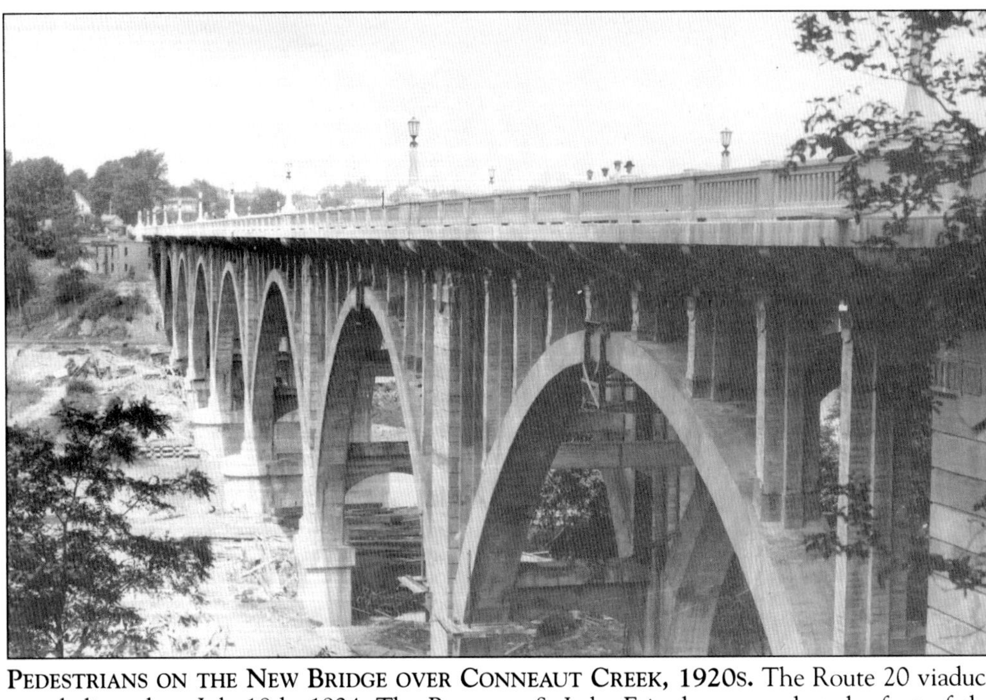

PEDESTRIANS ON THE NEW BRIDGE OVER CONNEAUT CREEK, 1920S. The Route 20 viaduct was dedicated on July 18th, 1924. The Bessemer & Lake Erie depot stood at the foot of the bridge. (Courtesy of Conneaut Public Library.)

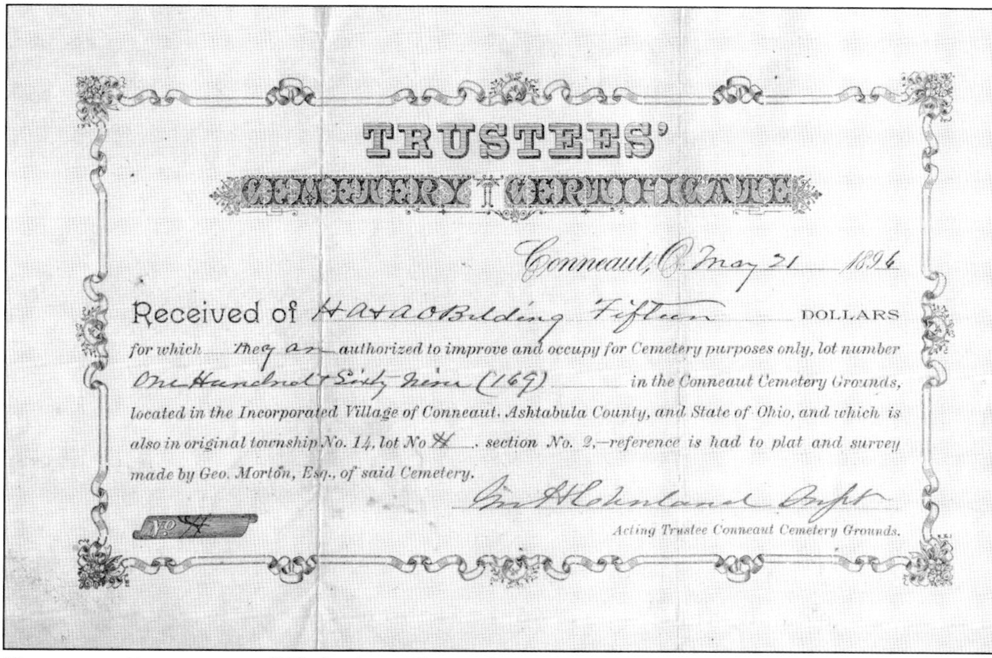

TRUSTEES'

CEMETERY CERTIFICATE

Conneaut, O. May 21 1896

Received of H A & A O Belding Fifteen DOLLARS for which they are authorized to improve and occupy for Cemetery purposes only, lot number One Hundred & Sixty nine (169) in the Conneaut Cemetery Grounds, located in the Incorporated Village of Conneaut, Ashtabula County, and State of Ohio, and which is also in original township No. 14, lot No 4, section No. 2,—reference is had to plat and survey made by Geo. Morton, Esq., of said Cemetery.

Acting Trustee Conneaut Cemetery Grounds.

No. 4

CEMETERY CERTIFICATE. While the Village of Conneaut was well-established by 1896, earlier in that century the town had been called Salem, and in a few maps, "Gore." (Courtesy of Conneaut Public Library.)

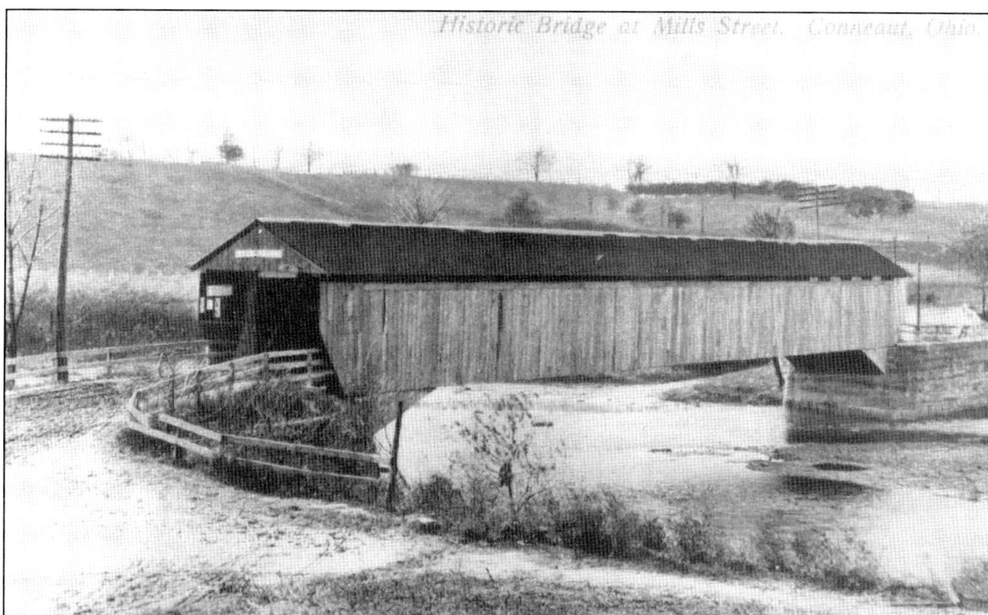

COVERED BRIDGE AT MILL STREET. The bridge was torn down decades ago, unlike many beautiful Ashtabula County covered bridges that still survive today. (Courtesy of Conneaut Public Library.)

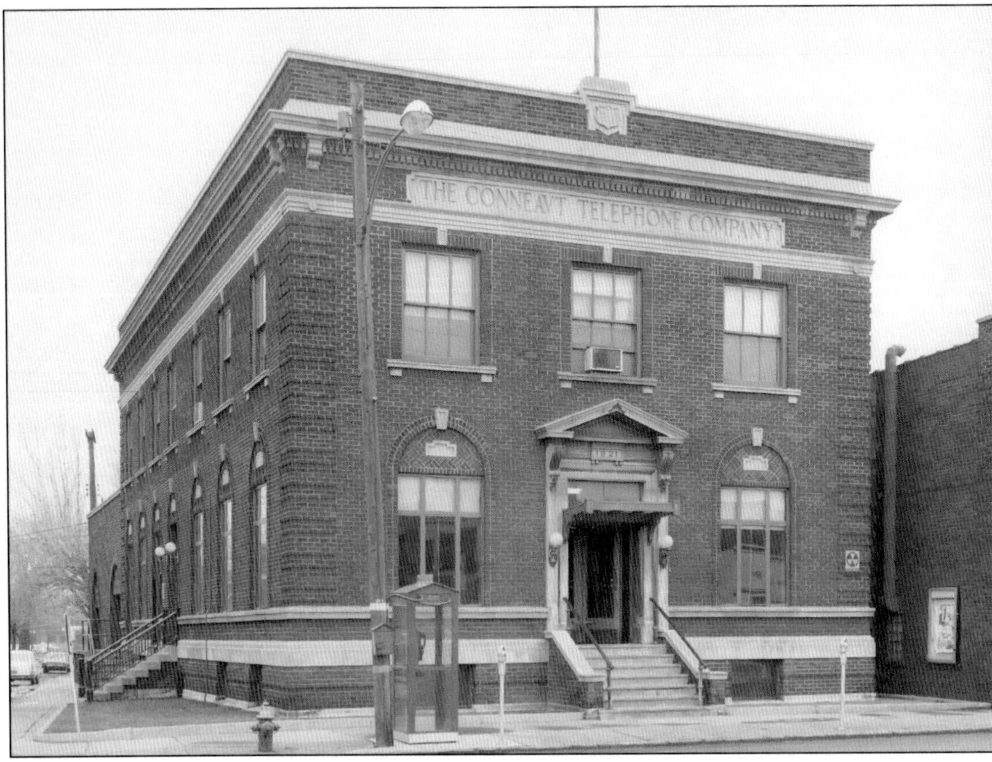

CONNEAUT TELEPHONE COMPANY BUILDING. The company, which began operations in 1897, is still in business today. (Courtesy of Conneaut Area Historical Society.)

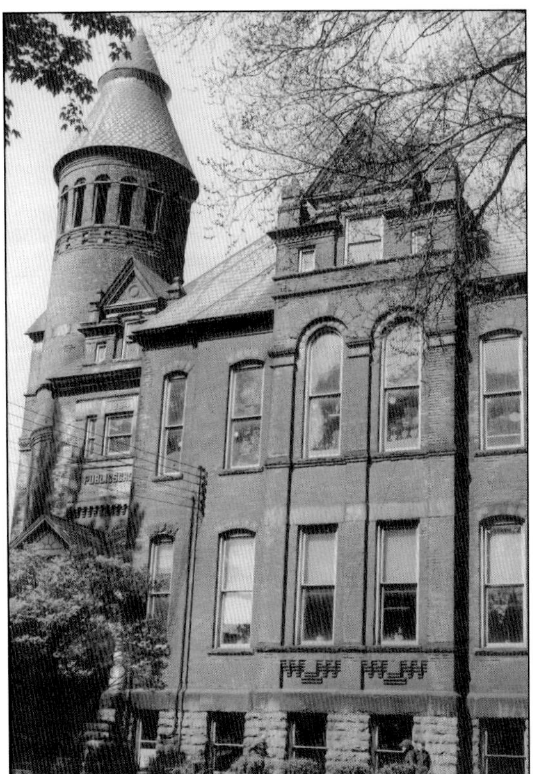

BROAD STREET HIGH SCHOOL. The school, built in 1894-96 north of Broad and Madison, was demolished in 1960. (*Cleveland Press*, courtesy of Special Collections, Cleveland State University Library.)

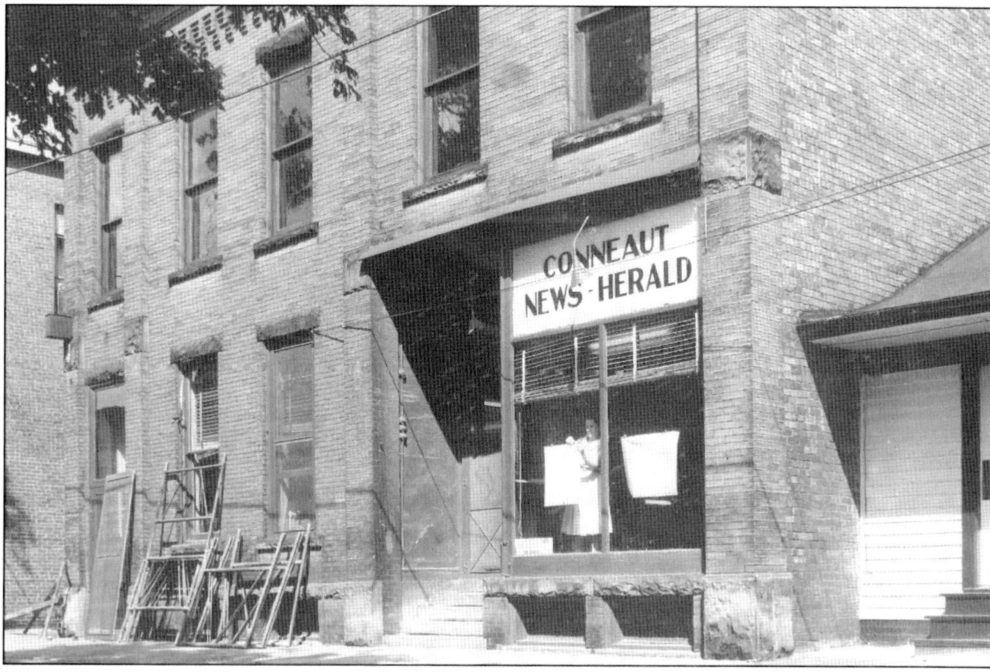

CONNEAUT NEWS-HERALD BUILDING. On January 1, 1907, the *Conneaut Daily Post-Herald* and *Conneaut Evening News* combined to become the *Conneaut News-Herald*. The paper went out of business in 1992. (Courtesy of Conneaut Area Historical Society.)

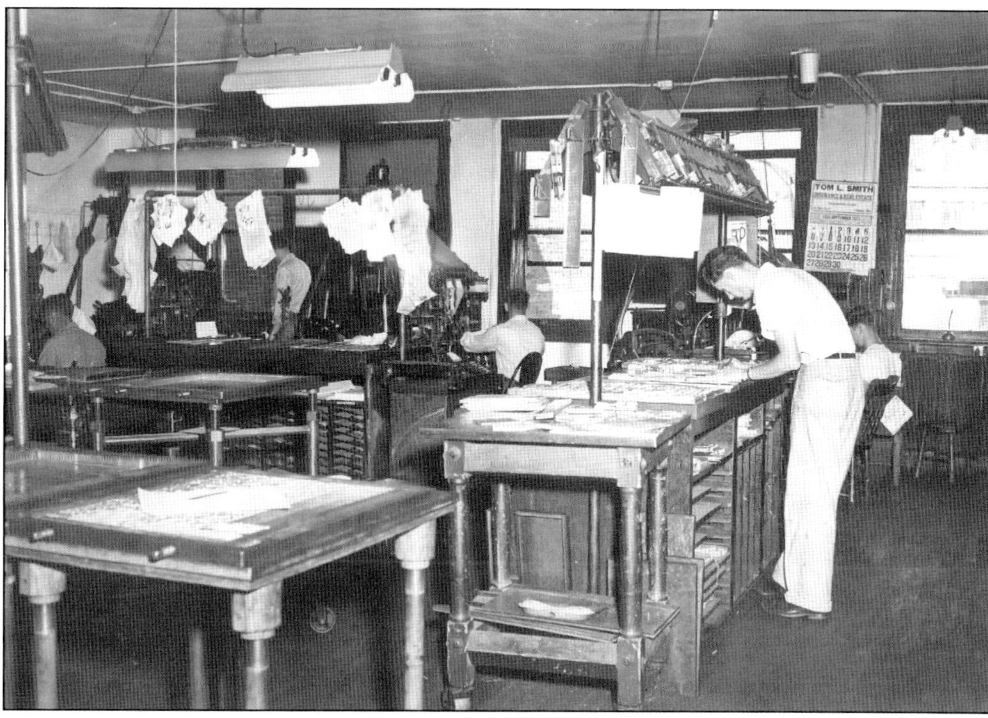

PUTTING TOGETHER THE *CONNEAUT NEWS-HERALD*. Today the city has only a weekly paper. (Courtesy of Conneaut Area Historical Society.)

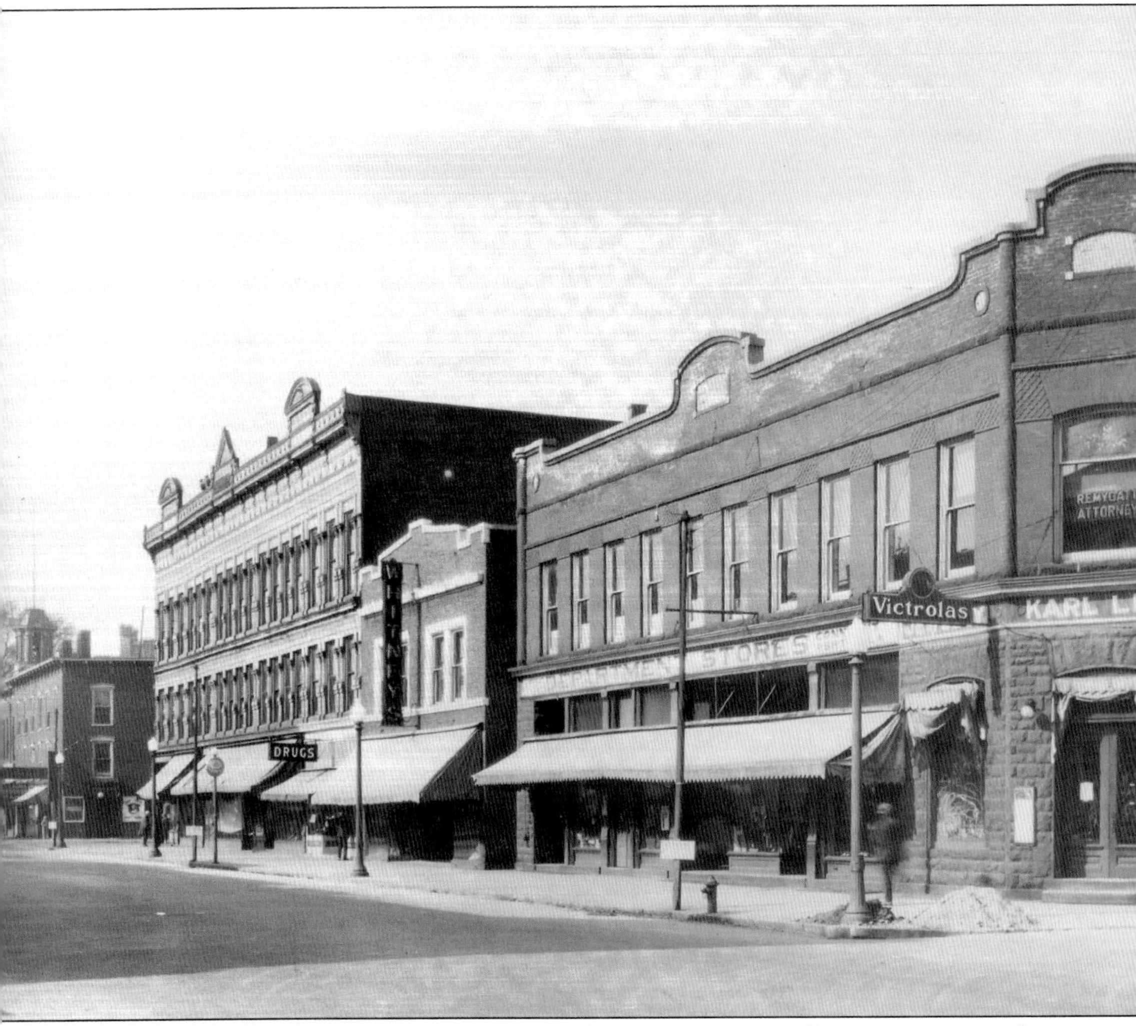

MAIN STREET, C. 1940S. Downtown was a vital, prosperous area in this era. Stores stayed open until 9:00 p.m. on Friday nights when townspeople would mingle in their finery. (Courtesy of Conneaut Area Historical Society.)

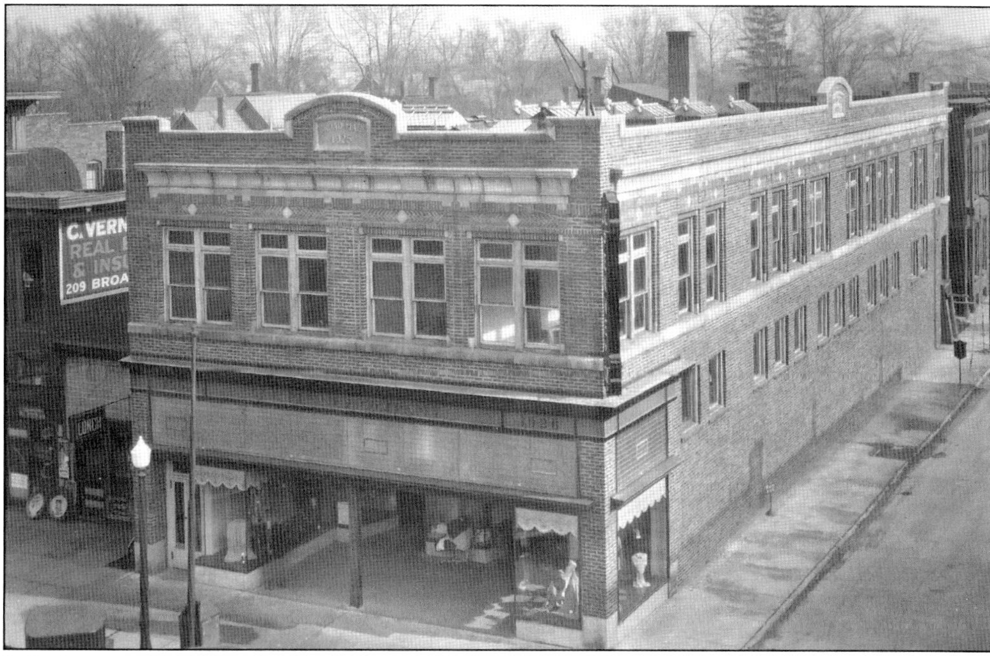

J.C. PENNEYS AT WASHINGTON AND MAIN IN CONNEAUT. The store closed in the 1960s. (Courtesy of Conneaut Area Historical Society.)

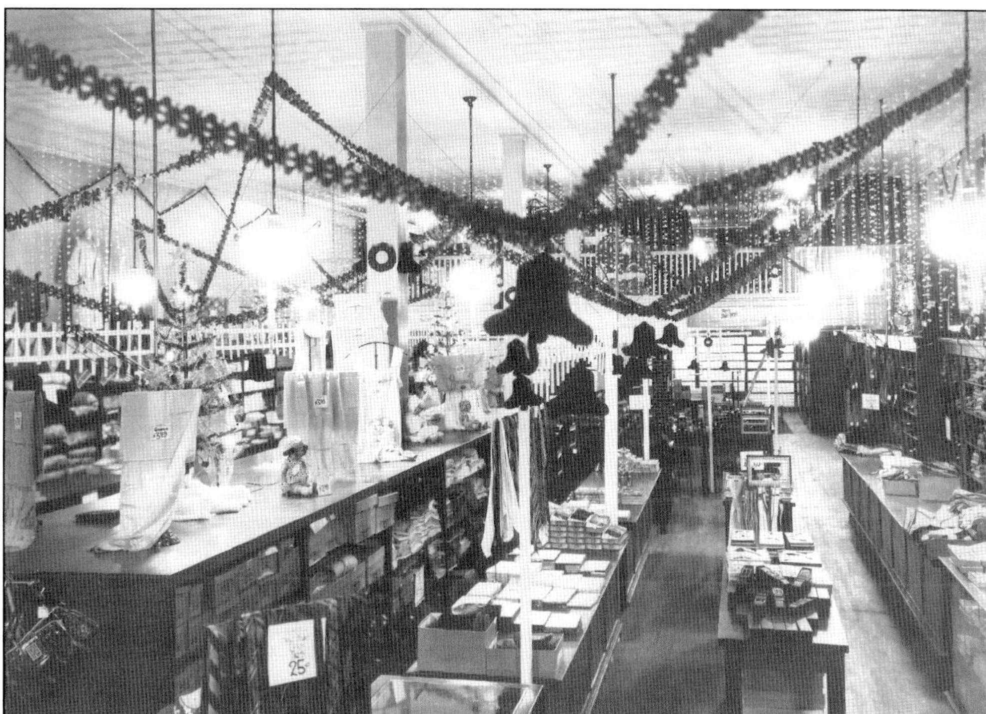

INTERIOR OF THE J.C. PENNEY STORE. Items that could not be stocked due to limited space would be ordered through the Penney's catalog. (Courtesy of Conneaut Area Historical Society.)

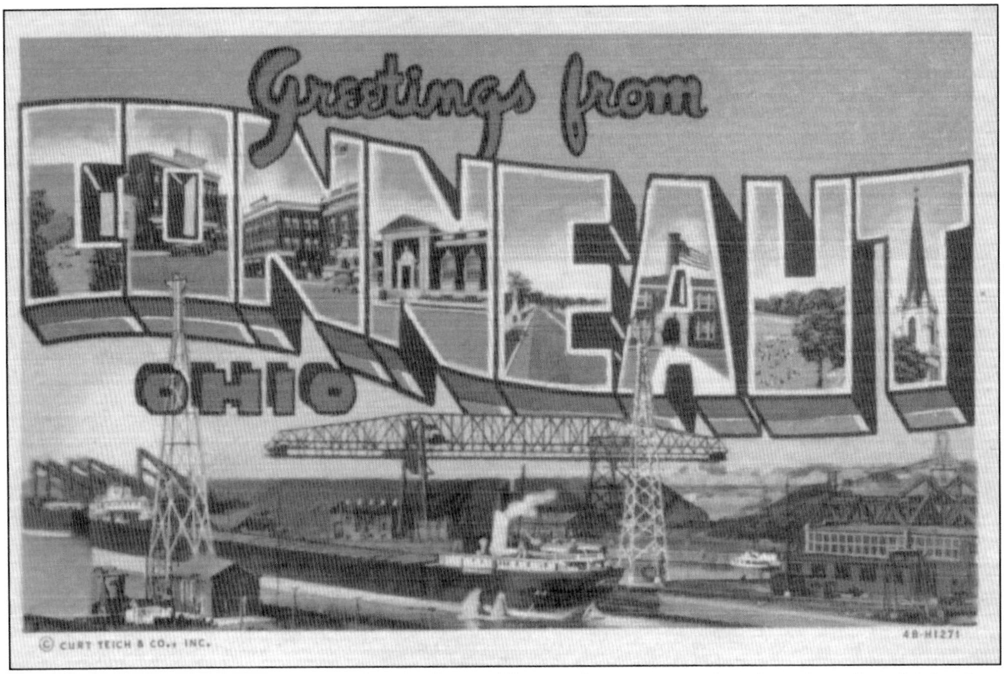

POSTCARD CELEBRATING THE CITY'S LAKE BOAT COMMERCE. In this decades-old harbor scene, Hulett Unloaders and a giant ore bridge tower over the lake boats. All are gone now. (Courtesy of Conneaut Area Historical Society.)

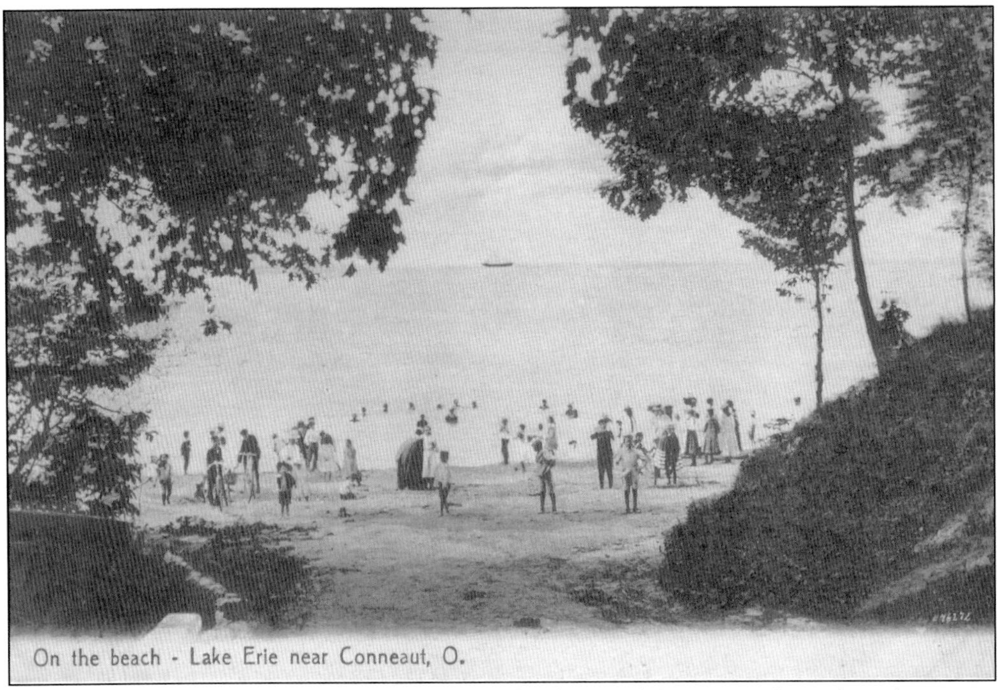

CONNEAUT'S BEAUTIFUL LAKE VIEW. Today, the future of Conneaut depends in large part upon developing the area for tourism. (Courtesy of Conneaut Area Historical Society.)

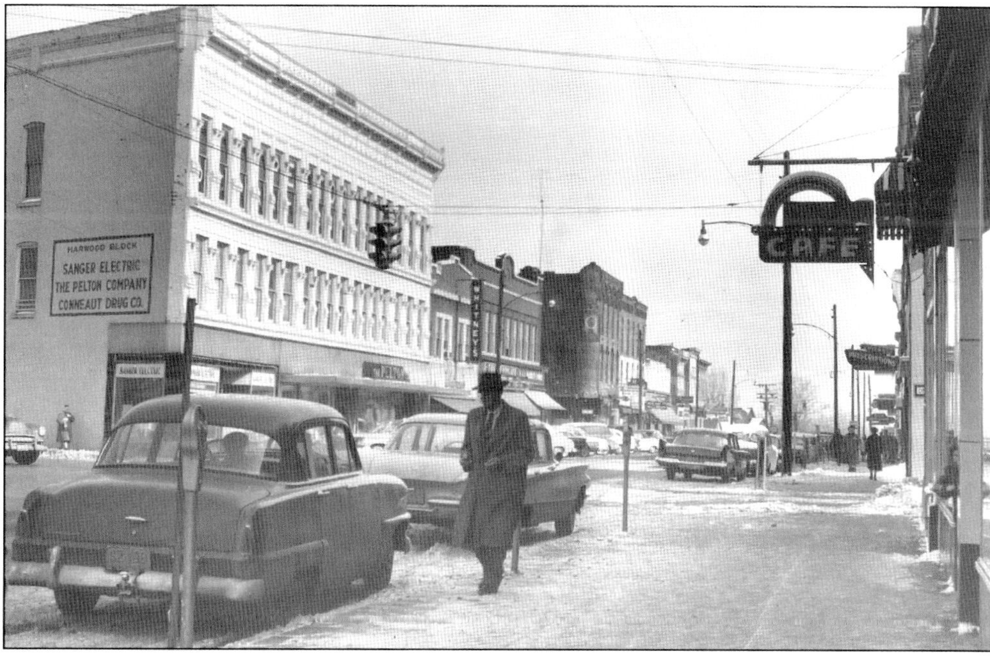

TWO VIEWS OF MAIN STREET, 1960. The historic Pelton building at left boasted a large cast iron facade sent from Chicago, which was assembled in the street and then hoisted into position. It is part of the Harwood block built in 1880-82. Cushman Pelton's grocery and his brother Arvine's dry goods store occupied parts of the first and second floors, while an opera house was built into the third floor. The A.W. Pelton Department Store that grew out of the earlier stores was a local institution until its closure in 1969. Offices, a smoke shop, and a dance academy took up parts of the building in various eras, and the opera auditorium was used to muster troops in World War I. (*Cleveland Press*, both courtesy of Special Collections, Cleveland State University Library.)

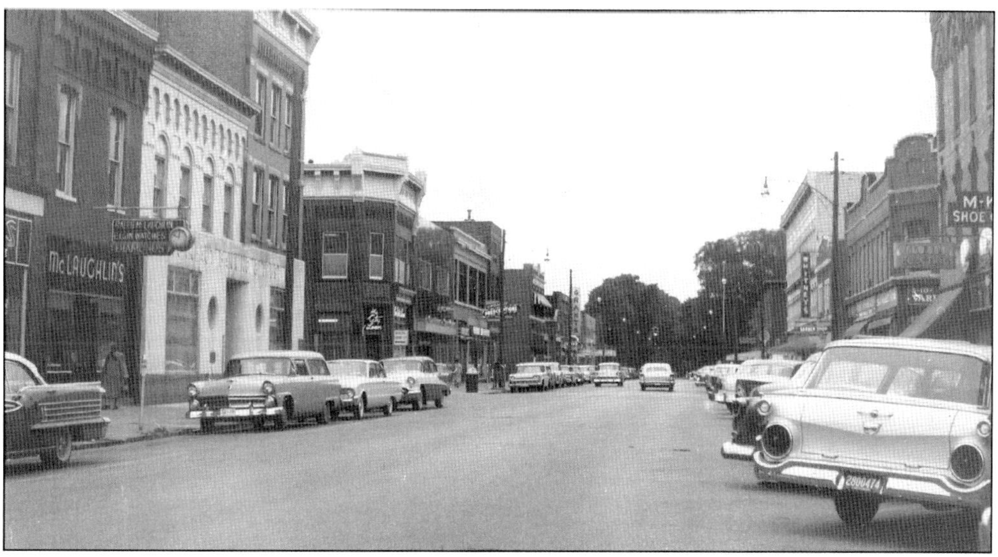

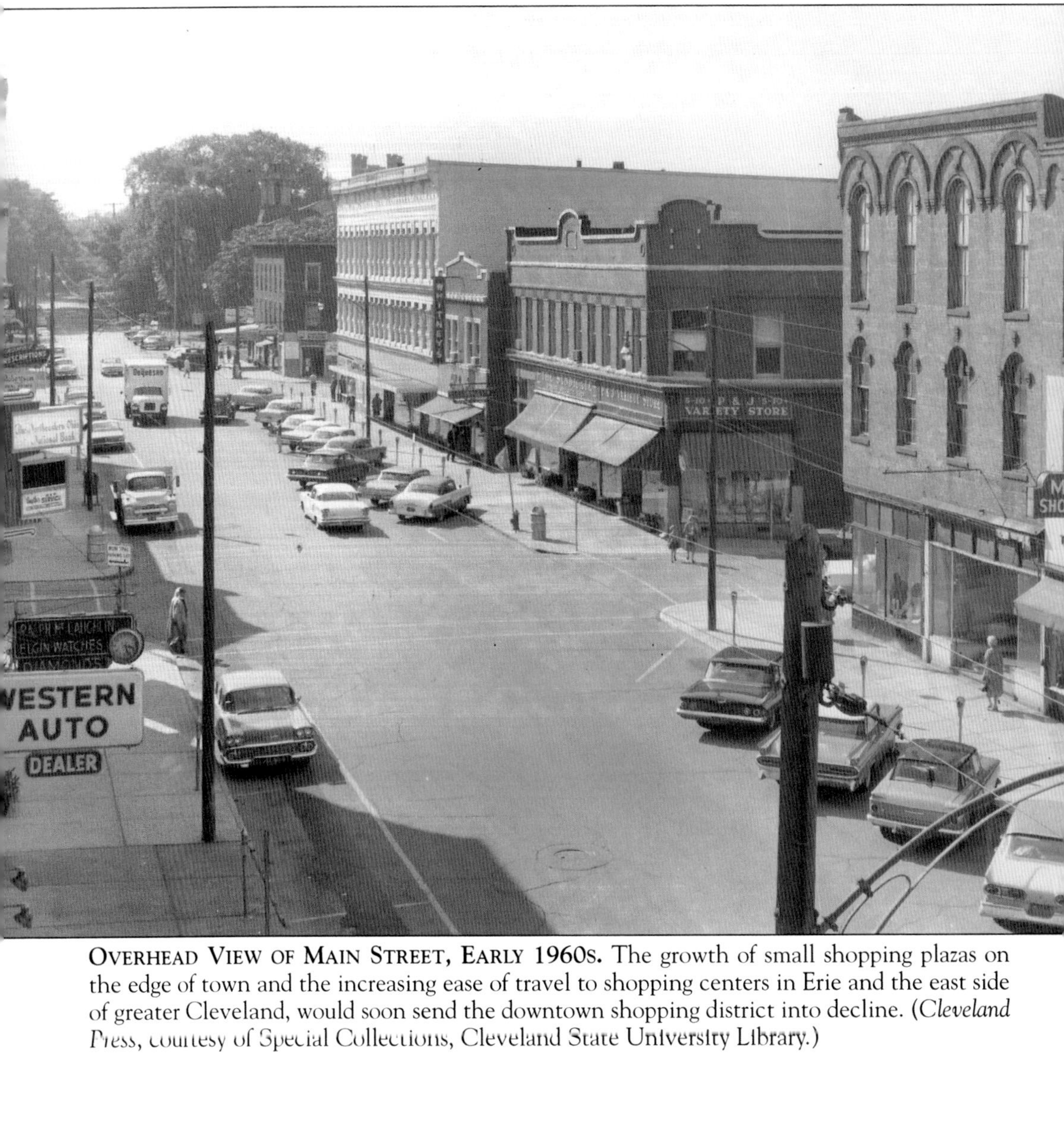

OVERHEAD VIEW OF MAIN STREET, EARLY 1960S. The growth of small shopping plazas on the edge of town and the increasing ease of travel to shopping centers in Erie and the east side of greater Cleveland, would soon send the downtown shopping district into decline. (*Cleveland Press*, courtesy of Special Collections, Cleveland State University Library.)

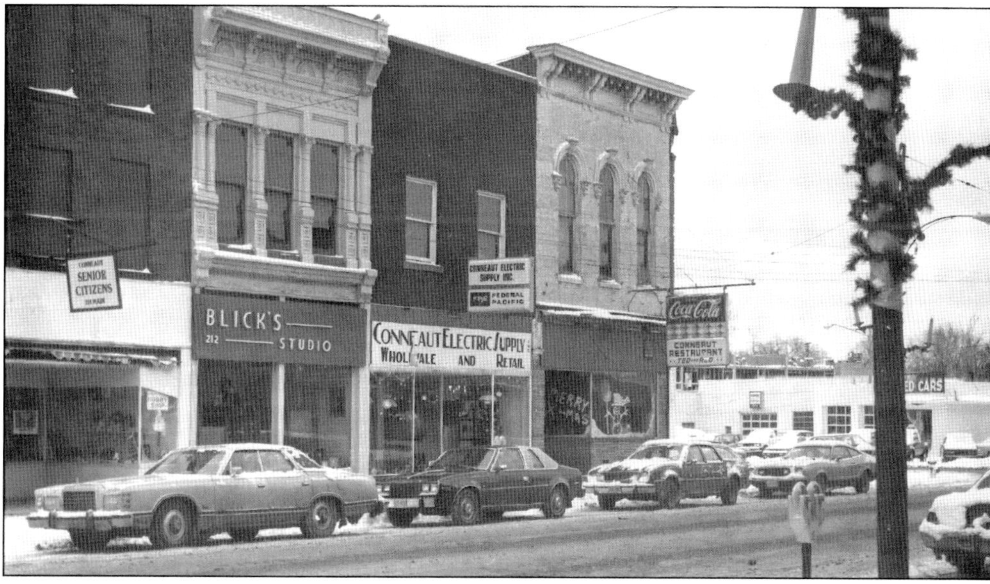

MAIN STREET, 1970S. By this time, I-90 has effectively bypassed downtown, forcing many businesses into closure. (Courtesy of Conneaut Area Historical Society.)

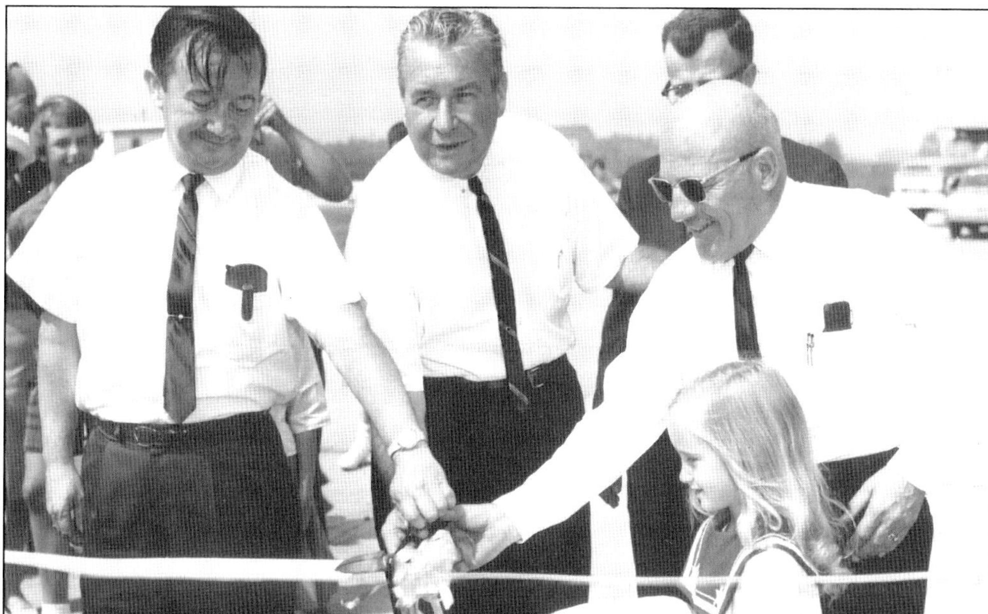

OHIO GOVERNOR JAMES RHODES VISITS CONNEAUT IN THE 1960S. Dignitaries cut a plastic ribbon in ceremonies officially opening Conneaut's new Seaway Industrial Park, a 140-acre industrial subdivision that was expected to bring several hundred new jobs to Northeast Ohio. From left to right are Conneaut Mayor Stanley Robertson, Governor Rhodes, and President H. Fred Campbell of Seaway Industrial Park. Behind Campbell is President John B. Phipps of the Conneaut Chamber of Commerce. The scissors bearer is Sally Ebert, daughter or Mr. and Mrs. Richard Ebert of Conneaut. (*Cleveland Press*, courtesy of Special Collections, Cleveland State University Library.)

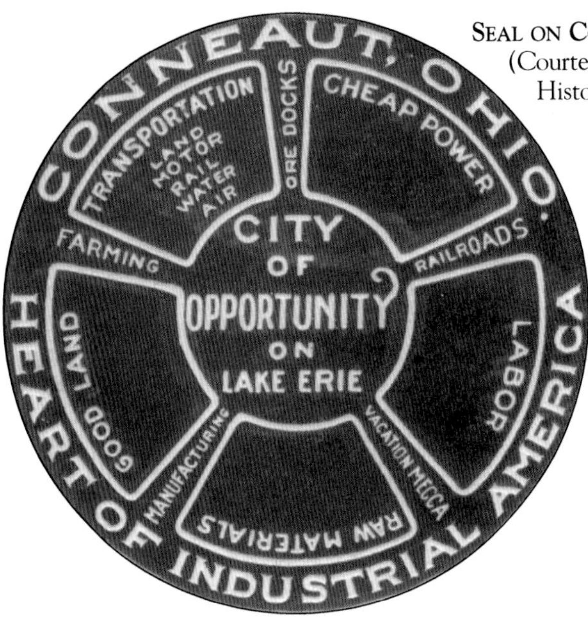

SEAL ON COMMEMORATIVE ENVELOPE. (Courtesy of Conneaut Area Historical Society.)

ACKNOWLEDGMENTS

The Conneaut Historical Railroad Museum, housed in the old New York Central Conneaut depot, is home to the Conneaut Chapter (No. 69) of the National Railway Historical Society, which holds an annual banquet and presents photograph shows with guest speakers. Operating a gift shop and an HO scale layout, the CHRM publishes a newsletter, *Semaphore*, for its members. For information about museum hours and membership, contact the Railroad Museum at P. O. Box 643, Conneaut, OH 44030-0643, (440) 599-7878. Robert K. Leach, President of the Museum, contributed a great deal to the creation of this book. Opening the building for me in the middle of the winter, Bob made available a great many precious photographs and exhibited remarkable recall of his years with the Nickel Plate and of the Conneaut railroad scene in general.

Susan and Arnie Howard were unstintingly generous, welcoming me into their home and sharing the photograph collection of the Conneaut Area Historical Society. Organized in August 1996, the society of over one hundred members is active in the preservation of Conneaut area historical artifacts, memorabilia, documents, and displays. Its meetings are held on the fourth Tuesday of each month with guest speakers, a 50/50 raffle, an auction, and a social hour with refreshments. Membership information is available from Robert Blickensderfer, 235 Fifield Avenue, Conneaut, OH 44030.

Bob, Sue, and Arnie showed tremendous interest in the book, and their review of the manuscript for historical accuracy was crucial; any remaining errors are mine alone. I am grateful also to Bob Blick and Norm Gross for participating in the final proofreading of the book. Elizabeth Seibert and Gail Connors of the Conneaut Public Library were most helpful in making available the library's collection of local photographs. At the Special Collections department of the Cleveland State University Library, I would like to thank Special Collections Librarian William C. Barrow and staff members Joanne Cornelius, Lynn Duchez Bycko, and Bill Becker.

Dale Olin of Ashtabula, Ohio, an electrician who worked with the Huletts in Conneaut, Ashtabula, and Cleveland, had valuable insights and photographs to share. The Ashtabula Marine Museum lent rare photographs from its collection. Thanks are due also to Pamela Lee Gray, Lois Helman, S.M. Timko, Bruce Hearn, and Gary Moser.

BIBLIOGRAPHY

Ashtabula County Genealogical Society. *Ashtabula County History, Then and Now*. Dallas: Taylor Publishing, 1985.

Beaver, Roy. *The Bessemer and Lake Erie Railroad, 1869–1969*. San Marino, California: Golden West Books, 1969.

Dicken, Bruce and James M. Semon. *Nickel Plate Color Photography of Willis A. McCaleb*, Volume 1, "Buffalo to Bellevue." Edison, New Jersey: Morning Sun Books, 1995.

Hampton, Taylor. *The Nickel Plate Road: The History of a Great Railroad*. Cleveland/New York: World Publishing Company, 1947.

Harwood, Herbert Jr. "Summer Frenzy on Lake Erie: Moving Coal and Ore in the 1950s." *Classic Trains*, Summer 2000.

Hilton, George W. *The Great Lakes Car Ferries*. Berkeley: Howell-North, 1962.

Hirsimaki, Eric. "Hulett Iron-Ore Unloaders: Historic Engineering Landmark." *American Society of Mechanical Engineers brochure*, August 1998.

Hirsimaki, Eric. *The Nickel Plate Years*. North Olmsted, Ohio: Mileposts Publishing Company, 1989.

Holland, Kevin J. *Berkshires of the Nickel Plate Road*. Lynchburg, Virginia: TLC Publishing, Inc., 1998.

Klein, Aaron E. *The History of the New York Central*. New York: Smithmark Publishers, Inc., 1995.

Rohrbeck, Benson W. *Conneaut and Erie Traction Co.* West Chester, Pennsylvania: Ben Rohrbeck Traction Publications, 1990.

Williams, William F. *History of Ashtabula County, Ohio*. Philadelphia: Williams Brothers, 1878.

While this book does not contain information from the following websites, they provide information on the history of Conneaut's Railroads:

Nickel Plate: www.nkphts.org

New York Central: www.nycshs.org

Bessemer & Lake Erie: www.gltx.com/bessemer/history.html

Ongoing forums relating to the history of these and many other railroads may be found at: www.railroad.net

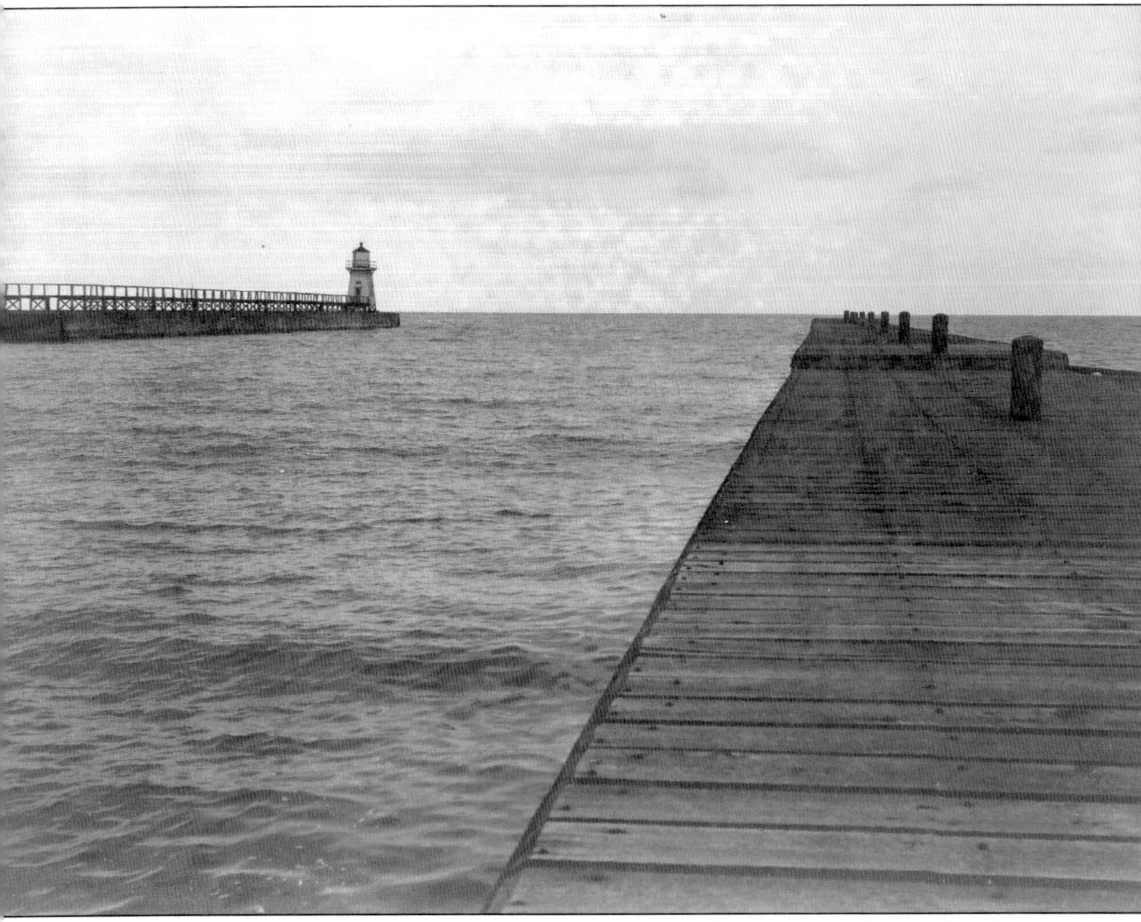

CONNEAUT EAST PIER LIGHTHOUSE, C. 1900. (Naef & Joslin, courtesy of Special Collections, Cleveland State University.)